IN FASHION

IN
FASHION

Dress in the Twentieth Century

by

PRUDENCE GLYNN

Illustrated by Madeleine Ginsburg

London
GEORGE ALLEN & UNWIN LTD
Boston   Sydney

GEORGE ALLEN & UNWIN LTD
40 Museum Street, London WC1A 1LU

© George Allen & Unwin (Publishers) Ltd, 1978

British Library Cataloguing in Publication Data

Glynn, Prudence
   In fashion.
    1. Costume—History—20th century
   I. Title
   391'.009'04   GT596   78–40338

   ISBN 0-04-391003-3

Typeset in 11 on 13 point Bembo
and printed in Great Britain by
Cox & Wyman Ltd, London, Fakenham and Reading

Contents

Illustrations

Prefaces

'Critics are like brushers of noblemen's clothes,' stated Sir Henry Wotton, and while I have loftier aspirations for them in some areas of the design world, when it comes to the raw creative genius of many who are mentioned in this book then I am no more than a brusher, and a happy brusher at that. If this book is dedicated to anyone it is to those designers who have given me so much aesthetic pleasure, so much literary stimulation, so much fun and professional reward. I have tried to place their work in the broad context of their times, and in England especially to calm, if not to lay, the ghost of embarrassment which stalks every corridor of visual talent which does not have a severely practical end-product: the Englishman Swann invented rayon for light bulb filaments, but the Frenchman Chardonnet discovered it simultaneously for ladies' undies.

The book is arranged to an extent in chronological order but that order is broken down into themes. There are certain powerful forces which have run throughout twentieth-century fashion and which never seem to have been explored individually. With my typewriter keyed somewhere between Thorstein Veblen and James Laver I hope that I have included plenty of useful information but also a lot of personal theories and conclusions. Fashion is the most personal and flexible of all the design forms and the best reward for my inspirers must be to spark off a lot of new discussion.

I must thank individually Charles Metcalfe, whose unflagging commitment to our common cause of better design snared him into reading this book in typescript and whose manners and professionalism prevented him from commenting upon anything but the factual inaccuracies which I so badly needed to have picked up. Generous friends include Sir Norman Hartnell, who has let me use one of the sketches of his royal dresses, and the Duke of Devonshire, who suggested the apposite Sargent portrait.

Prudence Glynn

It is more true of fashion than of any other subject that almost any picture helps to tell the story. The sources are vast, varied and widespread, for surely the whole of human life is here, and the task of collection has been facilitated by the resources of the Fashion Research Section of the Victoria and Albert Museum and the holdings of the commercial photograph libraries, whose archive potential is often too little regarded by the serious student. The themes inspiring the selection of illustrations have been, first, to narrate in visual form the fashion and clothing story since the beginning of the twentieth century and, second, to reflect the quintessential in appearance and social attitudes.

I am most grateful to Martin Battersby, Sir Cecil Beaton, John Cavanagh, Celestine Dars, Yvonne Deslandres (Centre de Documentation de Costume, Paris), Erté, Colin Ford (National Portrait Gallery, London), Vere French, Sir Norman Hartnell, Charles James, 'Jon', Elizabeth Lees (British Film Institute, London), the Librarian of the London College of Fashion, Jack Palmer White, Anne Price (*Country Life*), Mr and Mrs A. McCardell, Digby Morton, Julian Robinson, Joe Simms (the Adrian Archive) and Lord Snowdon for their advice and for permission to use their material. Also to all those designers who have so unstintingly placed records and recollections at my disposal. I would like to record my appreciation of my forbearing family, whose reactions helped me to finalise my choice, of Helen Alexander and Carla Tscherny and of my aunt, N R, who has set me a standard of elegance ever since my childhood.

The black and white illustrations are arranged in groups at the end of each chapter. A number in bold type in the text refers to the relevant photograph, which will usually be found at the end of that chapter.

Finally, apologies and thanks are offered to copyright-holders in photographs who despite every effort have proved untraceable.

Madeleine Ginsburg

Introduction

There are two quotations which those whose interest is fashion in dress particularly like to cite in order to prove that they are talking about a serious subject. One is Colley Cibber's remark that 'one had as good be out of the world as out of fashion'. The other is Henry Fielding's more extensive pronouncement: 'Fashion is the great governor of this world. It presides not only in matters of dress and amusement but in law, physic, politics, religion and other things of the gravest kind. Indeed the wisest of men would be puzzled to give any better reason why particular forms in all these have been at certain times universally received and at others universally rejected, than that they were in or out of fashion.'

Although these quotations are used to supply reputable roots for a branch of the arts frequently dismissed as ephemeral, there is really no reason to suppose that Cibber was referring to dress when he used the word fashion. It is indeed likely that he was thinking more of the broader intellectual and social world than of the cut of his coat. Fielding specifically mentions dress fashion as opposed to fashion in anything else. Thus, though champions of sartorial chic may comfort themselves that they have the interest of the great (besides being in many cases themselves great), at the same time their use of the quotations from Cibber and Fielding supports the basic contention of this book: namely, that the automatic assumption that the word 'fashion' implies 'dress' is a modern one. The fashion industry, in the sense of rapidly changing styles of clothing being made available to a hugely increased number of people, is a modern phenomenon which reaches its peak in the twentieth century. It is the child of new leisure and wealth, cheap labour and technical advancement, the adopted daughter of trade, the heir to new spending patterns. What is debatable at this time is whether society is not sated with the extraordinary preoccupation with clothing which has been a mark of the past seventy-five years. If it is, why, and what follows?

Clothing has, of course, always been an informative barometer for those who wish to read between the lines of social history. It remains the unique signalling system by which we make our situation known to others. Why else should anyone have bothered to impose sumptuary laws? Dress is the cheapest, easiest and often, because unconscious, the truest reflection of how man feels. Repression, wealth, power, the victor and the vanquished are all implicit in clothing. In a century which has seen unique advances in communications, it is perhaps only fitting that dress has occupied such a prominent place; since 1900 we have had both Marconi and the mini-skirt.

Tracing the way in which fashion reflects society is in itself a fashionable pursuit now, but it is a course full of pitfalls. It is so tempting to chart the rise and fall of hemlines or décolletages or haircuts in terms of economic or political situations that it can be easily forgotten that dress design, like any other creative art, retains an element which is quite unpredictable—sometimes funny, sometimes whimsical, often baffling—because human creativity defies total prediction. What is sure is that the three fundamental reasons why clothing is worn (decency, warmth and self-adornment) have undergone catatonic changes in this century. No-one is sure now what decency is, the climate is predestined by central heating, self-adornment is beginning to seem less vital than physical and mental self-sufficiency.

On the other hand, as the twentieth century entered its final quarter there were those who saw the hope of mankind's future firmly in terms of a return to the pastoral life with society once more fragmented into manageable communities and not warring states. Coupled with an energy crisis, this could bring back the importance of the second function of clothing—warmth. Small communities with serious objectives tend to be respectable, so perhaps decency will be a factor in future dress. And then, by the very nature of man, self-adornment can never long be absent. What remains to be seen is whether the Age of Aquarius will be celebrated in a St Laurent shift or in cowrie shells and woad.

IN FASHION

Part One

Fashion as an Art

1

Fashion as an Art

The age is father to the need and the need is father to the man. The survival of our species is one long example of resourceful adaptation of everything from anatomy to morals. Tails, teeth, religions, patterns of behaviour, foods and concepts of rule have blossomed or been shed depending on whether they seemed likely to help or hinder in the race of life. Apparent Armageddons have mostly turned out to be another platform for man's amazing imagination.

At the end of the last century there emerged a need for creative artists who were skilled in a new medium, dress. The twentieth century did not invent the fashion designer, who had been around in the capacity of a more or less privileged—usually private—servant ever since there had been employers with the time and money to want to wear something which was a little more than just an arrangement of magnificent fabrics. As his position became more defined, so the criticisms of his trade multiplied. Rose Bertin, one of the earliest 'names', who was dressmaker to Marie-Antoinette, was held as responsible as her mistress for the latter's tactless ostentation.

What the twentieth century did do was to transform the dress designer from a private servant into one who served many—at the peak of couture power, after the Second World War, so-called couturiers had given up even the pretence of dressing known clients and aimed at some mid-Atlantic composite image (the wheel has now come full circle). Charles Frederick Worth, usually cited as the first couturier in the modern sense, began as a modest supplicant to Princess Metternich and died in 1895 still trying to push fashion along a little faster. His sons, Gaston and Jean-Philippe, lived to see la mode a tyrant of discomfort and expense to sections of society who not so long before would have thought themselves fortunate to be adequately clothed.

Although he was shortly to be a new force to be reckoned with, at the turn of the century the dress designer filled his traditional place as a tradesman to the grand and wealthy. The Worth brothers, who in 1900 had opened a London branch, proceeded with such decorum that their young assistant, Paul Poiret, got bored and went off to set up on his own. Even when he was established, Poiret had to contend with the idea that the customer knew best; when he was with Worth, his revolutionary kimono coat, which he called his Confucius model (1), was described by a Russian grandee as reminding her of nothing so much as the shapeless bags used back home for the heads of importunate serfs. After all, the leaders of style were for the most part strong-minded and self-assured women; the time had not yet arrived when the diktat of fashion could be such that all felt obliged to obey it and portly matrons gambolled about in Eton crops and dresses of inappropriate brevity.

Already, though, the publicity generated for the new activity, fashion, was attracting both a new breed of rich customer without the social nous, the taste or the confidence to tell her designer what to do but who nevertheless wanted to be smart, and the traders whose activities are measured in another chapter. Gradually the designer became less servant and more master, and his social stature changed accordingly. As the old world of privilege and established money was knocked for six by the technological revolutions and the First World War, designers had to look elsewhere for their clothes horses. In the most fundamental way they found them in the invention of the professional mannequin, a formerly anonymous figure whom both Poiret and Lucile claim to have raised to individual recognition. As clients, designers found first the inheritors of the old world, the nouveaux riches from every continent, then they found the beautocracy created by the dominant medium, the cinema. Mary Pickford often dressed at Jean Patou, Gloria Swanson at Lucien Lelong. Since Miss Swanson's epic screen personality was accompanied by a frame just over five feet high, dressing her must have called for no little skill on the part of the designer.

The Second World War demolished not only what little remained of the old social ranks but also changed the type of trendsetter the fashion-conscious public wanted to identify with. It became hard to see just who was going to lead style and into this vacuum, which was bad for business, the designer himself stepped. The name of Christian Dior is probably the best known world-wide in any conversation concerning fashion, and it was the house of Dior, backed financially by the textile empire of Marcel Boussac and brilliantly promoted and marketed, which re-established French haute couture after the war. Even those who deplore the intense commercialisation and depersonalisation of dress design admit the debt owed to Dior by the industry.

The pressure to produce newsworthy designs was intense. America had failed during the war years to break the prestige of Paris with home-grown designers, although its vast and sophisticated machinery, coupled to the consumer boom and the most effective promotional campaigns, presented an ever-open maw. The market was enormous, the production geared to numbers, but who was to say what had or had not to be worn? The answer was the designers, who found themselves stars overnight. The slightest details of their lives, their hopes and fears and authoritarian views were avidly consumed and analysed by the industry and mulled over by every level of the public via their favourite media. It was hardly a case of the customer being right. Dior was right, or Balmain, or Balenciaga, or Givenchy, and women from Louisiana, Cologne, Tokyo and Moscow bowed to the new gods and adjusted their hemlines accordingly. Though the English persisted in treating their designers for the most part as tradespeople, in other countries, especially America, they became an integral part of the social scene; the Italians had a useful edge on the party circuit since most of them could claim titles. The French continued to approve their couturiers with a professional eye.

Perhaps the zenith of designer name-power was the creation of complete fabric prints incorporating the appropriate initials, or, in the case of Dior in 1967, the whole word. Earlier, in the 'twenties, Jean Patou had outlined the pockets of a pair of slacks with a J and a P and in the 'fifties Emilio Pucci had signed the noble fist on the corners of his scarf prints. The name game spread and everything from scarves to corsets was licensed out to generate cash (perfume was a long-established revenue booster for the fashion houses). Everything had a name on it, luggage, ties, belts, and women looked like perambulating billboards. It was a far cry from the tactful label sewn under the armpit and visible only to your maid or yourself, and from the jealously guarded anonymity of a 'lady's' wardrobe.

It is regularly one of the more cruel lessons of life that those who because of an exceptional public interest in their profession are elevated out of the true perspective of that profession suffer some sad falls. By the early 1970s fashion designers had become not just arbiters of life and of dress styles but in some cases the pop folk heroes for a certain culture in society. Collections—previously the reasonable preserve of reporters, private customers and store buyers, a few privileged friends and a nob or two to dress the set—became more and more often a sort of ego benefit party for the designers' friends or parasitic entourages. Professional criticism was drowned by the clapping of the committed members of huge, unruly audiences, three-quarters of them irrelevant to the business of fashion or else downright spies. The remaining quarter was harried, shoved or neglected.

Of course, designers have always liked to make a performance out of their collections, and anyone putting together a directory of rudeness could write almost the whole thing from the memoirs of journalists who have had to cover the big shows. Openings at houses where the designer was of particularly uncertain temper were nerve-stretching events; Alix (who became Madame Grès) was usually still shooting her needle through the last vital bit of her famous draperies. There would be hysterics in the cabine as the hairdressers tugged the chignons for day into the beehives for evening and, in the less well endowed establishments, the mannequins snatched the same hats and shoes back and forth. Incidentally, the idea of the fully accessoried show was also a post-war introduction, designed to present a total image (and generate accessory sales) to the new class of fashionable woman. Previously, clothes were shown with beige crêpe pumps, no jewellery and, in the earliest Edwardian days, over high-necked black body-stockings. The implication was that the client knew perfectly well what to wear with what, and in any case dressmakers were not milliners, or shoemakers, or jewellers.

There was also a lot of fun for the fortunate at the shows. Jacques Fath, who died of leukaemia in 1954, used to give memorable parties. His passing left more than a gap on the social calendar, though, for Fath's gift was for really sexy, naughty clothes translated by their exquisite workmanship into an acceptable if daring style. He thus pleased those women who found Dior too bourgeois and Balenciaga too daunting. The Italians continued the tradition of evening gala shows for couture up to the mid-seventies, although by then certain journalists were in revolt about this trespass on their private hours. At least the presentations remained basically professional and to get in one had to be accredited. At the other end of the spectrum, to get into the Kenzo Takada shows in the mid-seventies you needed a strong-arm escort. In the ready-to-wear shows of October 1974 bona fide viewers were being knocked down outside the Bourse as they struggled to get in to see what might well prove the 'hottest' collection of the season.

Britain's pop designer was Ossie Clark (25), a product of Manchester College of Art followed by a stint at the Royal College of Art when it was in its heyday under Professor Janey Ironside. Ossie Clark, friend of David Hockney the painter, mandatory guest at any 'in' party in the late 'sixties, was one of the most talented designers ever produced by this—and perhaps any—country, with a special gift for soft, fluid shapes and a most seductive cut. But after only a few seasons his work became erratic, and, although his name will be remembered as exemplifying a certain pop period in English social history, a certain look in soft frocks after the space-age tailoring of André Courrèges and a certain groupie way of life based around the London district of Chelsea, Ossie Clark never realised his full potential. On the other hand Yves St Laurent, just as much a cult figure but with the inestimable benefit of shrewd management by Pierre Berger and the disciplines of service in French haute couture behind him, never allowed the clique-claque of indiscriminate hangers-on to get in the way of business.

In retrospect, no designer who has run the gamut of mass acceptance has been able to buck the social trend, however he may have appeared to do so at the time. Paul Poiret, whose true genius is usually hidden under the cliché that he 'liberated' women from the corsets of the fin de siècle, began unexceptionally enough as a designer because when he began there was little urgency for change in the air. When he did break away, Poiret was the symptom, not the cause, of a gathering desire for emancipation among women fretful of the suffocating social climate and of the greedy heartlessness of the Edwardian era exemplified by England's fat, tired old king and his middle-aged, monoprowed lady loves. Poiret's radicalism was at best tentative, for he left the ladies hobbled at the feet where previously they had been hobbled at the waist (3).

How much of successful design is calculation is very hard to say. Certainly timing is all important. The world-wide influence of Christian Dior's New Look (15), shown in 1947, is sometimes cited as typical of the couturier's guile, for it did seem to observers still shell-shocked from the experiences of the war that this display of extravagance was no more than a deliberate reversal of every line that had gone before. Psychologically, the New Look was a brilliant coup. But was it radical? Just before the war an American designer, Mainbocher (one of those run-together names like Augustabernard and Louiseboulanger which so confuse posterity), had shown cinched-in waists in Paris. Unfortunately, Mainbocher had only just time to get his idea on the catwalk before the imminent arrival of the Boche caused him to nip back to America. He missed out on the fame of the New Look, but gathered a fat tithe of royalties from Warners, on whose corsets the clothes depended. Warners went on to provide boned, strapless corselets to the last generation of débutantes.

The most practical defence against the theory that fashion design is no more than a business of cunning adjustment of the ins and outs and ups and downs of women's clothes is that so few designers become more than adequately prosperous. The mass copyists, those who picked up the hot-selling dress and got it to market at the right price, made the money out of the fashion phenomenon. The most expensive illustration that the public's readiness for a change of style cannot be computed on the 'long skirts during economic alarm, short skirts during economic confidence' principle is still lodged in the hearts of many who were involved in the midi débâcle of 1969. In late 1968, as the authority of fashion began to waver and its compulsive interest began to wane (both factors bad for business), certain elements in the press and highly interested parties brought pressure to bear on French couture to lengthen skirts again in order to encourage new purchases. The French, well trained to bow to the almighty dollar—the pressure was largely American—let down their hems but, alas, without any conviction that it was the right thing to do. They therefore merely grafted six inches onto their existing, rigid toiles and grafted ten years onto the age of most women who adopted the new styles. In fact, most women did not adopt the new length and in commercial terms the midi was a disaster. Yet at the same time designers such as Ossie Clark and Jean Muir in England were doing longer skirts allied to a totally new, soft, unconstructed cut of fabric, and Laura Ashley was helping to clean up the London pavements by providing those sweeping cotton naïve dresses which have since become her trademark and the uniform of a generation (**31**). The point is that these designers changed style not because it made commercial sense but because it was compulsive in their creative thinking. Their clothes sold, and the young blithely took over fashion leadership from the Establishment.

For many women 1969 was the start of a disillusionment with fashion and fashion pundits, and in opting to go their own ways they rained confusion on the industry which seemed to have them so securely in its grip. Couture panicked. Staid French houses included shorts, the latest fad from London's Mr Freedom boutique, in collections in 1971, and the image of the subject was irreparably damaged.

It is worth noting, by the way, that when fashion became a mass-interest subject it was the skirt which lasted longest as a barometer of chic; in 1969 Mary Quant said we would live to see the length of the skirt no more important than the length of a sleeve, which at the time seemed an impossible heresy—we had only just accepted Ossie Clark's short sleeve over a long under-sleeve, an innovation as startling to the well-bred eye as St Laurent's use of day-length coats over trousers, which were criticised for reminding people of the Blitz when they had jammed on their overcoats over their pyjamas.

The true greatness of a designer lies not so much in his ability to introduce a new and apposite silhouette as in his ability to cut and shape materials, possibly themselves new, in a radical way. After all, there are limits to the dressing of the human figure which you discount at your peril, and the possible permutations of sleeves, bodice and skirt have been tried over and over again. A shrine painting at Knossos shows a woman in a handsome crinoline-skirted gown with short, wide sleeves much like a Victorian fichu in effect; the Greeks spread as comfortably in their chitons as we do now in djellabahs and T-shirts. Mariano Fortuny's crimped pleats (**4**) were high style back in ancient Egypt, and Madame Grès's elaborate drapery might have shrouded both Tutan-khamun and his queen. Bare bosoms, re-introduced by Yves St Laurent, had been seen before, and only a hundred years earlier than Poiret's celebrated liberating chemise beauties were courting pneumonia in Empire-style mus-lins. Even the toga, in its original form of outer cloak, was revived in 1975 as the soaring cost of fabrics and labour and the ambivalence of skirt lengths indicated a return to basic cover-ups.

Paul Poiret's contribution to fashion history is thus less that he was the most percipient designer around when the urge for a wider rôle in society mani-fested itself in women by the demand for greater sartorial freedom, than that when Poiret made those dresses which echoed the way women were feeling he made them with a cut which was quite radical. Although at first glance his most famous chemise was classical in inspiration, it bore no relation to the complicated classical reconstructions of, say, the Regency. Again, the division of textiles into furnishing and clothing types was comparatively recent—as recent as the eighteenth century—and Poiret re-married furnishing materials to high fashion. Realising that style in the true sense covers all sorts of aspects of taste, Poiret hired obscure, subsequently famous, artists to create imposing fabrics which he then threw into apparently artless shapes. In 1911 Poiret established his own interior design studio, Martine, so that aficionados of the style Poiret could round out their surroundings. A year later Martine had a branch in London managed by Marcel Boulestin, a fine illustration of Gallic appreciation of what makes life civilised and elegant, who went on to become a famous restaurant owner. Probably the most famous artist engaged for dress fabrics was Raoul Dufy, and in 1912 Jean Cocteau was writing in his diary that 'Duchesses are ready for Paul Poiret to dress, undress and costume them. All they care about is to be the beloved favourite, the silk and fur pillow covers, the lampshades, and the cushions of the sultan in vogue.' So closely did Poiret align décor and personal adornment.

If Poiret was the first designer to be a personality rather than a servant, he also illustrates the dangers of over-exposure and the ruthless demands on imagination made by this particular branch of the lively arts. In 1973 Diana Vreeland, ex-editor of American *Vogue*, doyenne of glossy transatlantic magazine ladies, and a fine example of the credo that those who report on fashion can stay at the top much longer than those they report on—also that they need to if they are to get a niche in history—staged an exhibition at the Metropolitan Museum in New York of French fashion up to 1940. The most remarkable point made, arguably unintentionally, is that in fashion there is really only room for one talent at a time, however many there may be picking up the right vibes, those who, as the French say, 'fument les bouts'. Thus

25

Poiret's clothes looked muddled and antiquated by the time the next great radical, Gabrielle Chanel, came along with her functional chic and totally untheatrical, clean-cut lines (**5, 6**). Chanel made costume jewellery acceptable in high society—and after the war there was a whole class of nouveaux pauvres who needed just such a brilliant idea to restore their superiority of chic. Again it is problematical whether Chanel deliberately set out to fill a void; given her personality it is more likely that she regarded having the real gems given her by her affluent lovers copied in beads as a witty indication from a poor-class girl that she could not be bought by material presents alone.

Chanel's repetitive discipline and fundamental lack of cutting innovation were rendered obsolete by the ascent of Madeleine Vionnet (**14**). Vionnet must have observed with her artist's eye the deficiencies inherent in clothes which were flat and straight and constructed from material cut in the traditional, on-the-straight-grain way. At any rate, something stimulated her to re-think the way such simple dresses ought to fall over the body to be more flattering. The solution was bias cutting and, though doubtless other minds were engaged on similar lines, it is Vionnet who has gone down in history as the innovator of bias cut. It was revolutionary, and topical too, because the softer fluid lines created by her were possible in the new materials offered by advancing techniques and finishes, and were in tune with the quieter and more settled period of the 'twenties before the great crash.

At the Metropolitan exhibition, Vionnet in turn looks flaccid against the angular exuberance of Elsa Schiaparelli (**10, 11**)—Schiap, whose much-quoted remarks about the sanctity of the human shape did not prevent her from imposing upon it designs as padded out and as artificial as the pre-Poiret styles. She was obsessed by the masculinisation of the female form, building out the shoulders, narrowing and deepening the waist, outlining flat flanks; her favourite mould was the matador, ultimate exponent of virility in dress. Was it because she foresaw the moment when women would have to be men in the Second World War? Schiaparelli shared with Poiret a love of colour and her use of textiles and embroideries has that same sense of freedom; they would have been as suitable for interior décor as for a formal evening dress.

Much has been made of the ten-year cycle of dominance which a top designer can expect, although 'could expect' would be a truer way to express it as the fashion phenomenon winds itself down. At any time the true residence of talent can be hard to spot because there are hosts of lesser fry who are evolving variations on the theme of the master, who himself may well not be recognisable or may be acknowledged only by the most tenacious. These lesser houses often have a profitable and lively clientele who would shy away from the stark radicalism of the innovator, and they add quite a fair degree of personality to what they do; they often attract as much publicity as the innovator and ironically their establishments frequently thrive after the pacemakers have shot their bolts.

In the great commercialised era of couture after the Second World War, Balenciaga, a Spaniard and probably the greatest fashion designer of all time, was overshadowed for many years by the grace and flattery of Christian Dior's work, which was much more easily understood, and which therefore sold better and was better known. Purists always preferred Balenciaga, whose work contained no hint of the retrospective, the calculated or the convenient, and whose uncompromising attitude terrified all but the most confident (**12**).

'What do you need to wear a Balenciaga dress?' Diana Vreeland is supposed to have asked the master.

'Madame,' he replied (she was lucky even to speak to him; he loathed journalists), 'a woman needs nothing to wear a Balenciaga dress. The dress will do everything necessary for her.'

He was truly an architect of dress and the phrase by Sir George Clark in *The Later Stuarts* referring to Christopher Wren is equally applicable to Balenciaga: 'He was capable of lapses of taste in various directions, and he was not a great master of ornamentation but he had in his bones an aversion from the superfluous and the fussy.' Balenciaga cut clothes in a completely new way. His backs were shelled out like a tortoise, he invented the threequarter-length sleeve, he cut away his necklines so that when buyers first saw them they thought they did not fit; in fact they made every woman look as though her head were a precious flower on top of its elegant stem (**13**). Balenciaga invented slit vertical side pockets for skirts and patch pockets which showed below the suit jacket, and he evolved the pencil skirt into the dirndl by taking a soft gather across the front and putting pockets in the two front seams.

Balenciaga clothes were intimidating and hard to wear, essentially sophisticated, inherently grown-up. When the youth cult began it was his pupil, André Courrèges, who modified the idea of the body-skimming or carapace dress so that the mass market loved it; it had the right space-age look for 1964 (**22**). Courrèges' name was much more widely known than was that of Balenciaga, yet such was the pace of fashion change by now that he, who could not do the soft fluid look which came so quickly on the heels of the tailored shift, and who worked on the principle of one dominating garment rather than an assemblage of ideas put together in a new way (the thrift concept, of course), passed his crown in well under ten years to Yves St Laurent.

Despite the diversification of interests which has drawn many women away from fashion, Yves St Laurent is today almost as well known as was Dior at the height of his powers. No-one, it seems, has his antennae better tuned to

27

what the market wants. At precisely the chic moment, in 1971, he kicked his couture colleagues of the Chambre Syndicale in the teeth and announced that he would concentrate all his efforts on his ready-to-wear, Rive Gauche operation. Psychologically it was a brilliant move, as duchesses wanted to look like shopgirls and sections of society were examining the morality of spending a fortune on dressing when half the world was starving. St Laurent allowed himself to be persuaded to continue a tiny section for haute couture, generating the maximum publicity by refusing to let all sorts of reporters in to see it on the grounds that it was not news. Of course it immediately became so. Since a dictatorship of line had been rejected by the young, St Laurent never created demanding new shapes; indeed, it is a moot point whether he could, since to my knowledge he has never devised a single new garment, though what he can do with old ones is incredible (**23**). He styled up a sort of non-fashion which was totally compulsive. A brilliant stylist, he reflected the desire for unostentatious anti-status fashion which is itself a fashion, and he was clever enough to marry this to the incomparable cut and make without which no French woman is ever happy.

A designer who looks set to rival St Laurent is the Japanese, Kenzo Takada (**30**). He was introduced to Britain in *The Times* in 1971, and can be credited with such innovations as the longer, wider skirt (what the Americans called the Big Skirt), the squared-off, deep-shouldered knits based on his national kimono, unstructured coats, shawls and wraps, and a new concept of putting bulk with bulk which changed the silhouette of women everywhere and epitomised the layered look which was such a feature of 'seventies dressing. In 1976 he successfully re-introduced the mini in the form of an elongated sweater or an abbreviated shift which made the wearer look as though she were bound for either Hellenic games or the sacrificial altar. If it seems invidious to pick out Kenzo Takada rather than Karl Lagerfeld or Sonia Rykiel, both effective designers working in Paris at the same time, the influence of Takada was wider than either of the others. He was one of the last names of international significance. In fact, Takada had a rough start, for he had none of St Laurent's couture upbringing or experienced management. His first collections were pirated before he could deliver his own orders, and his production quality was initially low. Paris, however, was still working her old magic, and the authorities closed ranks behind him.

By 1975 haute couture was slipping back to where it had originally come from: in that year the distinguished designer, André Laug, who though French worked in Italy, could say that haute couture was once again a matter between a private client and her dressmaker, and mean it. The ready-to-wear market was where the confirmed trends came from, for it reflected the mass taste, but couture could still provide a superlative service for women who wanted to be both beautifully and correctly dressed. In 1977 the prestigious Bergdorf-Goodman of New York was buying—and selling out of—couture models again. Not only is a couturier expected to be able to make every item of clothing for wear from dawn to dusk, he is also regarded as an oracle on what is appropriate. Designers, as they jet round the world to meetings and parties, keep a weather eye on who is wearing what and where. They are supposed to understand dressing by etiquette, too. In her book *Times to Remember*, Mrs Rose Fitzgerald Kennedy mentions that when she was the wife of the American ambassador to England and was getting ready to be presented at Court, 'the man from Molyneux came over to check details and to pin and secure the three head feathers at the proper angle, as I had no idea about how this should be done. A hairdresser was there to place the tiara on my carefully constructed coiffure.' It seems that, even in the halcyon days of 1938, the gallant Captain Molyneux did not himself make the trek out to ascertain that his clients had everything on the right way round. But, while a surprising number of women still seem to get their hair fixed, if not at home, certainly out of normal hours, it is doubtful whether many couturiers could now be found on hand with the pins at nine o'clock at night, unless of course you have been privileged enough to capture one as a dinner guest.

Mrs Kennedy had in fact selected Molyneux precisely because she had been advised that a British designer would know just what was wanted 'including the dimensions of the train'. She got her money's worth, for in 1961 she wore the same dress for the inaugural ball of her son, President John F. Kennedy. The photographs show it looking no wit diminished in splendour or style, though the ostrich feather fan looks distinctly ratty on the later occasion.

There are pitfalls to dressing public figures. When Marc Bohan put Princess Grace of Monaco into a white cape coat, white muff and white mink hat for the November wedding of Princess Anne of England in 1973, the former film star Grace Kelly got a thorough lambasting from the unchic and chauvinistic English press for seeming to try to compete with the bride.

French haute couture also provides a repository for the astonishing standards to which the art of cutting and sewing has been brought by designers in the twentieth century. Perhaps one day these secrets will be as lost as those of Greek fire, but while enough of the old staff survive they are preserved. In any case, before the appeal of couture became too rarefied, there were plenty of young ready-to-wear designers poised to grab the limelight. For just one moment, in 1971, it looked as though the mystique of Paris would crack. In July of that year, 'nobody' went to the collections. Amazingly, though, 'everybody' turned up at the prêt-à-porter shows in October, which were thus a bunfight of the first order. Emmanuelle Khahn, Dorothée Bis, Michèle Rosier, Daniel Hechter, Jean Cacherel and the rest proved France was still a must on any buyer's schedule.

Very understandably, the success enjoyed by designers in Paris and the preoccupation with their talent which seems to militate against the promotion of native fashion nettles creative artists elsewhere. The lack of patronage and recognition and of financial aid for indigenous designers is legendary now, and over and over again one sees examples of good home-grown designers passed over for someone less good who can give Paris as an address. Allowing for the familiar phenomenon, which is not confined to fashion, of the prophet always being more honoured abroad, it is worth taking a look at the two countries with an industry which might have been expected to support its own products, and which until recently did not. How have designers fared in England and America? How has the art of fashion been rewarded?

Of the two nations, each with an expanding economy and an established clothing industry, America had had a long romance with Paris, garnished from early days with the posies presented to puissant editresses and buyers and with such little comforts as free hotel accommodation. The Edwardian Americans had 'discovered' Europe to the extent of becoming the butt of jokes in *Punch*. In Europe they had discovered Paris, to which, it was prayed, all good Yanks would return when they died. And in Paris they discovered fashion. Thus we find Rose Kennedy as a schoolgirl writing home in 1909 from Germany: 'We really need two suits apiece and one or two light dresses for the boat going home. We cannot get anything satisfactory in Aix La Chapelle. I prefer to wait and get something à la mode in gay Paris.'

It must also be remembered that after the First World War the exchange rate for Americans was incredibly advantageous. Alan Jenkins recalls in *The Twenties* that an average meal, table d'hôte, including wine, at a pavement restaurant in Paris in 1926 could be had for fifteen cents, and doubtless the opportunity to escape from prohibition, to meet and mingle with a new generation of creative people, and with all this to imbibe some culture, must have been a pulling force. After the crash of 1929 French couture suffered a total disappearance of American customers. It is recorded that in the first season after the collapse of Wall Street not one commercial buyer came over. Fortunately, the more efficient houses had taken the lesson of Joseph in Egypt to heart. In the fat years they had stored up for the lean ones, and so they carried on.

The most obvious opportunity for American designers to break through was of course the Second World War, when their country was cut off from Europe with none of the va-et-vient of fashion which had obtained in 1914–18.

The best known before the war, Mainbocher, who had made the Duchess of Windsor's wedding dress and many other items for her, preferred to air his talents in Paris although he went home for the duration. Charles James, a somewhat ambiguous talent in retrospect, was working (**7**); so was Norman Norell, arch-exponent of the French couture tradition; James Galanos, equally dedicated to the complicated construction business though more avant garde in style, was beginning to be known. Bonnie Cashin is recognised world-wide for her revolutionary ideas on layer dressing and applied fullness, which she still does today, but the woman who might well have formed the cornerstone of a whole new way of dressing which could be adapted for any climate, Clare McCardell, is a name reserved for the cognoscenti. McCardell invented the tie-round apron dress, the diaper bathing suit, the bootlace tied-up dress, endless permutations for wearing the same garment (**8, 9**), and in silhouette that tight sweater top and full peasant skirt worn with ballet pumps, the sort of mid-west American look made famous in a hundred movie musicals. In fact it was a fully fledged movie designer, Adrian, who got the most publicity when he moved to New York during the war and imposed his amazing square-shouldered suits on the mass market. Their cut remains unique. Somehow, however, France, always regarded by the less sophisticated American as knowledgeable about things feminine, regained the upper hand after the war.

The English, on the other hand, had made a far more promising start in so far as the patronage of British designers was concerned. It is true that Worth, who was English, had had to go to Paris to find fame, and Redfern, Charles Creed and Lucile found it profitable to have a Paris establishment too. So did Edward Molyneux, who got his start by winning a newspaper competition to design an evening dress. The first prize was a job with Lucile, now somewhat past her best. Lucile was always to say that she launched Molyneux, who became one of the few British designers with an international reputation and opened in Paris in the Rue Royale in 1919. Her later efforts to claim a similar patronage for Sir Norman Hartnell consisted, however, in pirating his sketches and passing them off as her own, and she had to pay damages.

At the turn of the century, though, it was considered among well-bred Englishwomen that to dress in Paris was both vulgar (fairly rightly) and possibly to risk contamination by the demi-monde (very likely). 'No lady should ever dress at Poiret, his clothes are too showy,' decreed Elinor Glyn, a remark which should be read in the knowledge that Mrs Glyn was the sister of Lucile, Lady Duff Gordon, who considered herself more than a match for Poiret or anyone else.

It does not seem to have been fear of contamination by the demi-monde which got the Prime Minister's wife into hot water when in 1909 Mrs Asquith invited Poiret to show his collection at 10 Downing Street. She was censured for insulting British trade, and her husband for 'facilitating the intrusion of foreign merchandise by organising exhibitions in the residence which had been paid for by the nation's trade'—though that trade had been traditionally competitive and free. Poor Mrs Asquith was wrenched from the spangled embrace of Poiret just after she had struck him all of a heap by instructing him, the high priest, in how she was accustomed to dress and by showing him her satin velvet knickers. Mrs John F. Kennedy was likewise plucked later from the salons of French couture and told that as the President's wife she must dress American. She got her own back by picking out Oleg Cassini, who happened to be handy and obliging and who put her into clothes indistinguishable from those she would have been buying in Paris. Mrs Nixon got good headlines when she 'remained loyal to Seventh Avenue' and both French and Italian female nobs are regularly credited for their sartorial support of native designers.

Until the mid-twenties the British upper classes ground dowdily on, with Reville and Rossiter and Redfern bowdlerising from their Paris branches, then Madame Handley Seymour, but by 1931 the situation was artistically and commercially bad enough to warrant the staging of an exhibition to try to revive interest at least in British fashion accessories. Barbara Cartland recalls in *The Isthmus Years* that she was called upon to produce a pageant called 'The Best of Everything', which displayed silks, laces, scarves and gloves—all made in England. 'I also wrote an article in the *Daily Express* in which I said, "Let's drop the French model absurdity and ask for British models—models fit for British beauties."' Mrs Cartland, who was herself spectacularly pretty, patronised British design in the shape of the brilliant and imaginative Norman Hartnell, who had he not been drawn off into the cul-de-sac of royal fashion might have overhauled Molyneux as the best known English designer. In 1927 Barbara Cartland was married in 'the first long tulle dress since the war'. She records that it was made for her by Hartnell, who was a generous friend in hard times, though the caption to the picture of bride and dress in the *Sketch* states that the wearer made it herself. Another example of the way we treat designers?

As in America, after the Second World War national talent gradually gained ground as the concept of individualism in fashion spread. On the whole, designers outside France and Italy remain specialists in one form of clothing, since the demands of couture have never been imposed on them. No-one who has had to sit through the tedious little frocks shown by a smashing tailor, or the dreadful coats done by a man with a flair for draping chiffon, which the traditions of the couture collection demanded, can regret the loss. On the other

32

hand, as fashion merchandising became ever more a game of dominoes built up on the separates theme, and as less efficient buyers lost their nerve in getting the bits and pieces together, the houses which could offer the total look gained an advantage.

By 1975 there was intensive lobbying in both Britain and America to limit the imports of clothing and textiles. For Britain, saddled with an elaborate and free design education programme, the rebuilding of her own image made special sense. There was a fair demand for British students to work abroad, but, if the national industry diminished, where were the rest to go? Perhaps commercial necessity could provide what common sense had so long dictated, a re-appraisal and a maximisation of the talent on one's own doorstep. Ironically, it came at a time when interest in fashion as an art was also in decline.

1. Oriental cut with all its simplicity and in brilliant colours was brought into mainstream fashion by Paul Poiret (1879–1944). It has now been revived most notably by Kenzo Takada. With these full, straight-cut coats from Poiret's 1908 collection (not very different from his famous kimono-based 'Confucius coat'), drawn by the new young fashion artist Paul Iribe, he summoned up the oriental splendour that was to be popularised by the Diaghilev ballet.

2. Denise Poiret was the inspiration of her husband, Paul. Here she wears a dress he designed for her in 1908, 'Sagesse'. The word to him meant a combination of all feminine virtues—modesty, wisdom, discretion. A simple, unlined T-shape tunic in cream and brown, it is the direct ancestor of many dresses on the market today. In its utter simplicity of cut, it was a revolutionary break with the past.

3. Prey or predator? This hobbled huntress, a smart French racegoer of 1911, illustrates the dilemma of the fashionable woman of the belle époque. She is loaded down with furs, all mounted complete with heads, teeth and nails, extravagant and expensive tribute to her status as a prime object of conspicuous expenditure; but she herself, hobbled below the knee, can hardly move.

The photograph was taken by the Seeberger brothers of Paris, who recorded three generations of elegance as it really was.

4. Fortuny of Venice dressed individualists from 1907 to the 1940s and his exquisite pleated gowns have now become a cult. Mariano Fortuny y de Madrazo (1871–1949), Spanish painter and theatrical designer, was inspired by the gowns of classical antiquity and by mediaeval and Islamic patterns. His clothes were dyed, patterned and pleated in his own atelier, following processes that are still secret today. *(Sir Cecil Beaton/Victoria and Albert Museum)*

5 and 6. Gabrielle Chanel (1883–1971) initiated the suit that became the uniform for generations of women. She developed her relaxed sporty style based on jersey fabrics and an insistence on fit and function just before the First World War. Other innovations were costume jewellery with tailored clothes and the bi-coloured shoes. The photographs show Mlle Chanel herself in about 1929, and an outfit she designed in 1970. In both are to be seen the easy fit, the patch pockets, the jewellery and the two-tone shoes. Chanel tweed suits are always lined in silk and a narrow gilt chain stitched round the inside hem of the box jacket helps them to hang well. *(Radio Times Hulton Picture Library and International Wool Fashion Office)*

7. Charles James (1906–), one of the revolutionary creators of fashion, is forever re-defining the relationship between body and fabric. He began as a milliner in Chicago, then worked in Paris, London and New York, always experimenting with new forms and materials. He made splendid, extremely intricate evening dresses, and worked out a new system of ready-to-wear sizing, alas never universally adopted. This quilted jacket of 1938, both fashion garment and an approach to sculpture in silk, was made from white satin stuffed with down and is a starting point for anorak, space man and even fur jacket. *(Charles James)*

8 and 9. Clare McCardell (1906–58) was one of the leading American fashion innovators. Her clothes were easy-fitting, sporty and with an apparent simplicity of line based on ingenious construction. She trained at the Parsons School of Design, New York, and in Paris. Working with Townley frocks from 1932, she produced designs which accorded with her dictum, 'clothes should be useful'. The monastic dress above, created in 1938, is a simple trapeze shape which could be worn free or belted, girdled high on the bust, at the natural waist or at the hips. It swept through the entire American market in 1938 and could still be worn successfully today.

10. Elsa Schiaparelli (1890–1973) brought a hard-edged wit and inspiration to fashion in the 1930s. Italian-born, she was highly cultured and worked well with artists. Christian Bérard, painter, theatre designer and fashion illustrator, first inspired her 'Medusa Cape' (*centre*), brilliant in shocking pink and gold, and then drew it for *Vogue* in 1937—one of his best and most spontaneous evocations of the fashion of the time. (*Vogue*)

11. This shoe hat (1937) was inspired by Schiaparelli's association with Salvador Dali, the surrealist painter. In her hands, the deliberately inappropriate of the surrealists become trim trappings for certain smart women. Daisy Fellowes bought the hat. The tailored suit is typical but there is a witty touch in the lip-shaped pockets. The photograph comes from a series intended to protect couturiers' designs from being copied. *(Victoria and Albert Museum)*

12. A brilliant new talent arrived in Paris when Cristobal Balenciaga left war-torn Spain in 1937. The 'Infanta' dress of 1939, shown here, has a very effective formal, rigid and essentially Spanish quality. It is firm in structure and ultra-fashionable for its time with its tight waist and rounded bust and hips. *(Harper's Bazaar)*

13. The dramatic architectural style of Cristobal Balenciaga (1895–1972) is demonstrated in this stark black dress of 1967, cut, incredibly, with but a single seam. Profoundly versed in his craft, Balenciaga, who trained and worked as a tailor in Spain before going to Paris in 1937, was alive to every challenge and possibility of material, though he preferred the stiff to the supple. His designs have their own rhythm of development and this away-from-the-body line was one he began to exploit in 1946 independently of the rest of the couture.

The photograph was taken by Sir Cecil Beaton (1904–   ), designer and ultimate recorder of fashion and the fashionables in photography, word and sketchbook. Through a long life he has been sensitive in perceiving and showing the line of each age to its best advantage, and his camera style has ranged from De Meyer-like romanticism in his youth through surrealism in the 1930s and now to the dramatic simplicity of this photograph.

14. This classical figure is seductively draped by Madeleine Vionnet (1877–1975). She bias-cut her clothes to cling and then float free from a natural body shape. This photograph from a 1939 *Vogue* emphasises the difference between the feminine curves and flowing lines of 1930s fashion, and the static rectangularity of the previous decade.

15. The New Look was introduced by Christian Dior (1905–57) at his first independent show in Paris in spring, 1947; he called it the calyx line. This suit was one of the most popular and characteristic models on show, with its tightly fitted, cream tussore, moulded jacket, its gentle shoulder-line and its long, very full pleated skirt of black wool, all made over a firmly structured foundation. Its impact was extraordinary and the post-war generation acclaimed it as a style romantic and above all feminine, the antithesis of wartime austerity. It did not go unchallenged and was stigmatised as too decadent and wasteful for a generation which, having won the war, had now to win the peace, but by 1948 it was almost completely accepted. Connoisseurs of the subject might deplore it as retrospective rather than revolutionary, but social historians understood its appeal and in any case, the buyers bought and bought. After wartime recession Paris couture had been re-launched as a national industry of export importance. *(House of Dior)*

16. This 1953 outfit by the wholesale house, Glenny couture, is typical of the suit of the 1950s. Very firmly structured, even in ready-to-wear, it was a much more demanding style than the New Look. Curves were disciplined and restrained and women restricted as they had not been since the 1880s. The sleeve was set low, the waistline was tight and taut, the bust was hoisted high, stomach and hips were flattened and the pencil-slim skirt clamped the knees, though Dior had introduced a special pleat which made walking just possible if it was absolutely essential. This formal and rigid edifice was perched on high stiletto heels. The smart woman reached for her long-handled Italian-type umbrella for balance and support. (*International Wool Secretariat*)

17. The A-line. A Dior design for 1955 marking the final departure from the tight-waisted New Look. It is high-waisted and skims rather than clings to the body though the skirt remains long. The house of Dior and its publicity were very well organised and each season the press got an easily quotable and the world a copiably recognisable new line. No wonder trade and buyer were obsessed with the dictates of Paris. (*John French Photo Library*)

18. Digby Morton (1906–   ), the Irish-born couturier, joined the London tailoring house, Lachasse, in the 1930s. He worked in the United States from 1953 to 1957 and did much to bring a British look to the world market when he started under his own label. *(Associated Press)*

19. Hardy Amies (1909–   ) began his fashion career with the London tailoring house of Lachasse in 1934 and opened his own establishment in 1948. Although as a dressmaker to the Queen he retains his interest in women's fashion, bringing to her formal outfits an easy-moving opulence of style, he is increasingly concerned with men's clothes and has brought considerable flair and finish to multiple tailoring. *(John French Photo Library)*

20. John Cavanagh (1914–) was a typical post-war British couturier. He opened his London establishment in 1952, closing it in 1974. He specialised in unobtrusive, easily elegant clothes very much in the tradition of Edward Molyneux with whom he had trained and worked in the 1930s and whose best-known client, Princess Marina, he continued to dress together with her family. (*John French Photo Library*)

21. South African-born Victor Stiebel (1907–75) was an important addition to the group of young designers who began to work in London in the 1930s and carried on into the post-war period, conscious of fashion as both art and industry. He had an exceptional talent with unexceptional grand clothes and as a member of the Incorporated Society of London Fashion Designers did much to promote the image of British fashion abroad. (*John French Photo Library*)

22. Unmistakably Courrèges style for 1964, this evening outfit for the space age has slinky silver trews and a bareness of bosom only recently acceptable. Courrèges, then a relatively new couturier—he opened in 1961—had concentrated on outdoor and sporty garments, and many considered his evening clothes in questionable taste. Nevertheless, with these striking styles he created the first obviously bifurcated trouser suit which was intended for the most formal occasions. Poiret's pantaloons before the First World War were intended for 'intimate' evenings and Schiaparelli's, smart and daring though they were, looked like long, divided skirts. (*John French Photo Library*)

23 and 24. Yves St Laurent (1936–) opened his own house in 1962 after his departure from Dior. His first independent collections were for young revolutionaries against the suavity of contemporary couture but later he evolved his own style, a brilliant blending of ideas from many sources which tap the conscious and unconscious social and political feelings of the community. He now distributes his designs, for both men and women, through his Rive Gauche boutiques. His success is shown by their staying power—the peasant dress (*right*), made originally in 1973, is now accepted at every level of the fashion market, as is his blazer over patterned dress (*below*), introduced originally in 1970. (*St Laurent/Rive Gauche*)

25. Ossie Clark (1942–) brought an irreverent, sexy new talent to fashion, somewhat in the 1930s idiom, when he began to design for Quorum in 1966. He had already transformed the High Street crêpe frock with his dresses for Radley, which were cheap and overtly seductive. By 1969 his line had softened and the print by Celia Birtwell on the satin trousers and chiffon top of this trouser suit, chosen by Prudence Glynn as Dress of the Year for the Bath Museum of Costume, gives it an important new impact and dimension.

Adèle Rootstein created the display model, an important addition to the mise en scène of modern fashion. South African-born, she was the first to make specially sculptured portrait copies of the modish available for shop display, and to break with the static anonymity of earlier days. (Bath Corporation)

26. In 1971 this high-waisted 'maxi' in brown jersey over a cream blouse provided every girl with the dress she had always wanted. No sooner did the design appear than it was pirated for the popular market. John Bates (1939–), the Newcastle-born designer, began in the classic couture tradition in 1957, but he set up on his own in 1960, later with Jean Varon. (Vogue)

27. Jean Muir (1933–   ) began to create her timeless classic clothes in 1960 when she opened her own house after working as a fashion artist and with Jaeger. She has pioneered a look that is uniquely her own—covered-up and demure, minutely detailed, muted in colour and exploiting the supple qualities of jersey. This outfit, from her 1975 collection, is in wool jersey, a soft gathered blouse with long full sleeves which can be worn either with the culottes, as shown, or with a full, free-moving skirt. *(Jean Muir)*

28. Zandra Rhodes (1942–) is dedicated and obsessionally creative. She came to clothes through her interest in fabric design. Her prints are all her own and this one is signed—as a work of art should be. In exploiting the possibilities of the fabric her clothes set a new style and are very elaborate in construction, with the flowing lines for the 1975–6 season set off by the sharp ripple edges of the knife pleating. In this photograph the dress is worn by the Marchioness of Lansdowne in the specially created setting of Zandra Rhodes' new London shop. *(The Times)*

29. Bill Gibb (1943–), the Scottish-born London designer, devised an entirely new way of treating texture and pattern when he began independently in 1968. He mixes and matches, never letting this distract from his romantic image and essentially straightforward construction. He has now begun to make revolutionary new textured knits. With Zandra Rhodes he is one of the creators of the fantastic evening dress for which Britain today is famous. *(Fashion Weekly)*

30. Kenzo Takada, 1976, a characteristic youth-ful, free, easy-fitting design in the 'put together' layered look of the 1970s, featuring bulky knit-wear. In 1976 he revived the 'mini' in his charac-teristic multi-layered way. He changed the shape of clothes in 1971 with his modern ver-sion of his national kimono armhole, wrap-around skirts and shirts, and quilted cottons. (*The Times*)

31. Laura Ashley (1925–) epitomises the post-Courrèges ecological reaction and has achieved a tremendous success by producing romantic clothes at a low price much appre-ciated by a whole generation of nostalgic, com-fortable young people who share her preference for the natural over the synthetic despite its occasional inconvenience. She designs the prints and produces the cotton fabrics in Wales, where she also has the clothes made up. Her colours are soft yet strong and her prints floral or formal, somewhat Victorian in inspiration. She now has shops in the USA and Europe as well as in several English towns, and produces furnishing textiles and wall coverings as well as clothes. (*Laura Ashley*)

2

War, Need and Social Change

The fearful aspects of war are so familiar that it is sometimes forgotten that the jolt which conflict gives to the machinery of social change can be beneficial. During the first seventy-five years of this century two wars of unprecedented proportions have altered the political and social face of the globe and have catapulted women from a pedestal to the sink.

Most Edwardian women were barely educated and were admired more for their size and complexion than for their intellectual gifts, and also for their sporting qualities in an age when practical jokes at country-house parties—putting butter on the floor to make the others slip up, and pillow rags for example—were considered the height of upper-class fun. The irony is that with so much leisure, with so few responsibilities, with so many servants even at a modest income level, they seem never to have used their time more constructively. Their interests were largely philistine and they themselves were curiously unmaternal, content to commit their children to the total care of nursery staff who were incompetent or vile and to the traumatic cruelties of the English boarding-school system.

Seventy-five years later the situation is totally reversed. The intelligent and conscientious woman, anxious to play a rewarding part in society without sacrificing a home life, finds herself all too often trapped between the demands of children and the failure of the work patterns in many worthwhile jobs to accommodate her schedule. Honours graduates have nervous breakdowns trying to wash nappies with one hand and read or write with the other. At the lower end of the social scale young women find that what was the goal of their own mothers in life, marriage and children (and it is a goal perpetuated by a consumer society which needs a docile and housebound customer for its products), is not a goal but a cul-de-sac. Marriage is not a panacea, it turns out. The cake-mixes do not rise, the children squawl. The rage and frustration which these women feel, especially in countries where there is no religious consolation for motherhood and where the community life-style has broken down, can be measured by the horrific charges of neglect and ill treatment of children brought every year.

In the transition from revered goddess to overworked career mother it is hardly surprising that a great many women have suffered and are suffering a crisis of identity which is reflected clearly in their clothes. As Pearl Binder has pointed out, the wearing of a man-tailored blazer, even if it is made of velvet, over a silky, flower-printed, full-skirted frock (an idea launched by Yves St Laurent in 1972 and enormously successful with all ages) betrays a distinct uncertainty as to just who or what you are. So too do the amazing and loudly condemned platform clog shoes of the same period. By their height they cater to an instinct in women to be taller and thus of more consequence vis-à-vis men. By their construction, which makes walking extremely difficult, they cater to an instinct to remain vulnerable.

The effect of the First World War was to free a great many women from tyranny at home, and the prospect of being consigned to nurse elderly parents, into a situation which, though rough, at least offered more scope. Nice girls were allowed to nurse, their coarser compatriots shovelled explosives into shells, and the middle-class typist was born. From behind the chenille draperies and the stern parental stare came lots and lots of young women who learned, through war, to earn their living and to enjoy a career. This was just as well, since the death toll between 1914 and 1918 was so colossal that many of them would have to earn their own keep without benefit of husband.

By the Second World War the horizons were even wider; pictures of the civilian ambulance drivers in London in 1940 highlight a patrician cast of countenance under the turbans and above the siren suits. This was to be expected, since driving, even with cheap cars about, was for women largely an upper-class accomplishment. (Flying was even grander, the Duchess of Bedford being regularly on the wing.) By the end of the Second World War, women of all classes were shunting lorries and white-knuckled brasshats around.

Apart from the specific factory dress and the adaptation of farmers' clothes (**33**) worn by the girls who replaced the men on the land (and by Vita Sackville-West because she fancied the look), fashion was curiously undisrupted by the First World War. Reports from Paris continued to be available and were much promoted in America. In England, luxurious dress was viewed askance and *Punch* began its series of cartoons aimed at the vulgarities of the nouveaux riches and the war profiteers and their over-decorated women.

Meanwhile, those who worked most ardently to advance the rôle of women in society, the suffragettes and their successors, did so in neat suits and demure toques, anxious not to imperil the image of feminine respectability, even though they preferred an easier skirt-line and a new, masculine convenience, pockets, into which their hustings-chilled hands could be thrust. Although their activities—chaining themselves to railings, in one instance suicide of the most violent and uncertain sort under the hooves of a racehorse in 1913, and enduring the disgusting and barbaric torture of forced feeding—were more physically heroic than those undertaken fifty years later by the Women's Liberation Movement, they specifically eschewed bizarre dress (or lack of it in the case of bras) and the hideous renouncement of elegance associated with the later protest group.

Nor did any revolution in fashion follow the political emollient of bestowing the vote, in 1918, upon married women, women householders and women university graduates aged thirty and over, then finally in 1928 upon all women of twenty-one and over. While married women were distinctly in style, the Prince of Wales' interest in these ladies having taken over where that of his grandfather left off, it was not the fact of having the vote that made them trendsetters. What their clothes reflected was not the opportunity to put a cross on a piece of paper but the aftermath of war.

Now war's effect is usually predictable: too few men being pursued by too many women in a sort of sexual inflation. The most obvious reflection in dress is the accentuation of anatomical differences, for war diminishes the numbers of the species, and a fundamental need of a powerful species is to maintain its numbers. Thus dress reflects the need to make mating a primary consideration. The traditional method had always been to accentuate the obvious erogenous zones, the breasts, the buttocks, the thighs. In more confident times the appeal could be slightly less direct—the sensuality of long, silk-clad legs, the white slope of well-covered shoulders, both leading the eyes towards promised delights rather than explicitly exposing them.

The aftermath-of-war dress of the 1920s was a break with tradition in that it had a go at most of the senses at once. At its most obvious, the brief and shapeless shift can be read as a dismissal of all previous styles which, though far less constricting than those of the turn of the century, were nevertheless only tentative steps along the way to sexual equality and comfort; Poiret's loose-waisted dress which ensnared the knees and ankles makes a good parallel of ambiguity with the St Laurent blazer and pretty frock. Now all constriction was to be shed, save at the head, for the forehead and the hair, both aspects of female mystery and beauty much prized in their periods in history, were extinguished by the most unflattering hats for half a century (**36**).

54

The exposure of so many of the charms of the newly liberated chums poses obvious parallels with the Regency period, although it was not until William IV was on the throne that headgear became so concealing that it was easier to recognise a woman by her breasts than by her face. The faux-naïve muslin chemises, harbingers of so much consumption, one cannot help feeling, or chronic bronchitis at the least, followed a period of dreadful war in which a great many men had been killed, many exhausted, and more rendered blunt in their sensibilities through the horrors of the campaign. The obviously provocative, the sexually stimulating, the almost crude had to appeal if the race was to continue.

Another and decisive factor must be added in assessing the fashion of the 1920s. Along with the liberated feeling of women who had for the first time done men's jobs in the war (no-one ever seems to count working the farm or running the castle during the Crusades as rôle-swapping), went a recognition of something for the first time not totally taboo, male homosexuality: women had to compete for men with men. Men who had been through the most awful experiences had been bound together in adversity by friendships which were not always platonic, and since the dress style of the 'twenties emanated from France one cannot for once blame the English public-school system. These men came back to discover that some women had decided that they too preferred to choose how to dispose of their bodies. Contraception was crude, but it was a topic. The Flapper dress can be read as either the most, or the least, provocative dress, just as argument still rages over the mini; it takes a subtle mind to derive more satisfaction from imagination and guesswork than from what is explicitly revealed.

The real contribution of the First World War was Functional Chic, of which the arch-exponent was Gabrielle Chanel. Taking the same materials, especially jersey, which had been found ergonomic in the fight, moulding everything to her own taste, unable (according to Balenciaga, who greatly admired her) to cut properly, sharp enough to see that the great families were now the poor and that therefore huge genuine jewels were not smart any more, Chanel, like all great designers, interpreted the feeling of an age and realised—consciously or not—the needs of a decade. Interestingly, her clothes which had not changed at all, had a revival in the early 'sixties, after another world war had wrought its desolation. At the time, much was made of the return to couture of Mademoiselle in order to boost the sales of her world-beating perfume (which in 1978 is still outselling most others). A whole musical play, *Coco* (her pet name), which on Broadway starred Katharine Hepburn and was dressed, quite unsuitably, by Cecil Beaton (a fine example of the American passion for the Name is the Game), was based on the

55

rediscovery of Chanel's talent by the American mass-market manufacturer. In England, it was Jeffrey Wallis who made Chanel his own star. The fact remains, however, that so right were her clothes for the second time around, after the cul-de-sac of the New Look and before we were ready for Courrèges, that if she had not already existed we would have needed to invent her.

That same New Look, even if its seeds had been sown by Mainbocher in 1939, should be viewed as the aftermath dress of the Second World War. Presented by Christian Dior in 1947, with the erogenous zone fixed firmly and with a Gallic sophistication at the waist, it can be seen as retrospective, a case argued in the previous chapter. Dior, however, was onto the right idea, even if his erogenous zones were wrong. What the mass market wanted was curves, certainly, but with the accent on the bust; the Sweater Girl had been born as long ago as at the outbreak of war, with Lana Turner as the most prominent example.

Through the long separations and the horrible experiences of the Second World War, the huge, gentle, unsophisticated farmboys of Ohio and the other agricultural states, the GIs, black, white and all shades between, yearned for home and for Mom. Sir Hugh Greene, ex-Director-General of the BBC, recounts in his book *The Third Floor Front* that a suggestion put forward at a SHAEF meeting for a powerful anti-German propaganda campaign was the repetition of just two words, 'pus, Mother, pus, Mother' because the 'vulnerable points in the morale of the enemy could be reduced to two simple concepts, fear of wounds and homesickness'. The idea was, rather sadly I think, never exploited. The cult of the bosom was, much more sadly for those girls who were deficient in this commodity.

What makes the Sweater Girl interesting is the synthetic nature of the shape and consistency of her prized possessions (**41**). This must surely be because while the young soldier dreams of his mother and of her most maternal physical attributes he dreams too of his girl friend, with whom he wants sex, not succour. Since sex with his mother is inadmissible, those female attributes must in his mate be potential, a bank account for his children which he can enjoy fondling but which must for the world be presented as cast-iron brassièred and as impregnable as Fort Knox.

The deprivations of war were felt very much more by fashion the second time around. With the Germans all over France, couture struggled, in the main successfully, to retain some sort of authority. Shortages caused the designers to think up new ideas (**40**). Hats became especially silly, since everything else was drab; shoes were made with cork or wooden soles; buttons of ceramic clay; whole costumes of ribbon, which for some reason was not rationed. In England coupons and price ruled the fashion market and necessity bred gowns of blackout material worthy of Scarlett O'Hara and the drawing-room curtains. There was no attempt, as there had been in 1918, to introduce a standard dress, but when in 1941 the Board of Trade brought out the regulations for 'utility clothes'(**37**), specifications were stark. Between 1 June of that year and 31 May 1942 each man, woman and child was allocated sixty-six coupons, of which twenty could only be used in 1942. The coupons were necessary for knitting wool and dress materials as well as made-up clothing. Different items of clothing demanded more or less of the precious coupons. Manufacturers were allowed to use only a stated amount of material for any garment—$3\frac{1}{2}$ yards, although there does not seem to have been any restriction on the width used—and they were permitted to produce no more than fifty styles in a year. Such is life that in England at any rate the restrictions and controls actually improved quality; it was the last time that native designers were invited by the government to participate in improving national taste, and Hardy Amies's checked suit still looks fine. Some of the best behaved if less innovative manufacturers felt that they had never had it so good. When customer choosiness returned after the war, added to the problems of choosy labour, they resented rather than welcomed the freedoms.

Ironically it was the king of luxury high fashion, Stanley Marcus of Neiman-Marcus, Dallas, Texas, a store famous for its presentation of all that was newest and most extravagant in style, who was picked by the American government to apply the fashion brakes in the interests of conservation of raw materials. The redoubtable Mr Marcus recalls that in 1942, twenty days after Pearl Harbor, he was summoned to Washington and given the job not only of working out the necessary programme but of selling it to the Press, the manufacturers, his own retailing industry, and above all the customer. Somehow Mr Marcus, who was a great merchant, managed to present restrictions on length, sleeve, sweep of skirt, hems and belts as a matter of patriotic chic without the imposition of a statutory maximum yardage. General Limitation Order L85 'effectively froze the fashion silhouette . . . by blocking any extreme development . . . which might have encouraged women to discard their existing clothes'. For so hard a salesman to run counter to his convictions was patriotism indeed. Alas, the opportunity to develop national talent was not taken, though what Clare McCardell could do with two yards French couture needed six to equal. What is more, McCardell's creation could be worn any one of six ways.

As for the changes wrought by the shifts of society, by the drift towards a more permissive climate, by the spending power of the new career girl (as opposed to wife), by the erosion of social barriers which makes it no sin for a patrician to shop alongside a secretary (though it remains a gaffe if they turn up at the same party in the same dress), by the disbanding of an elaborate set of rules of etiquette which affected matching shoes and handbags as much as which corner of the visiting card should be turned down, by anarchical political views, all are reflected in dress. But without any doubt the single most significant factor in fashion as in women's lives in the past seventy-five years has been the development and the mass acceptance—for no style can be credited as successful until the mass accepts it—of the contraceptive pill. Indeed there are those who would rank the effects on society of large-scale birth control with the effects on society of two world wars. The most interesting point about the Pill and fashion is that, although its initial impact on dress was quite crucial, the effect was comparatively short-lived. The unromantic, sexless, aggressively displayed, theoretically immensely chic, extremely flattering, short, straight, brusque clothes of which Courrèges is the finest exponent and Mary Quant the English representative had barely a five-year innings. Perhaps it was because the Pill was linked in many minds with the technocratic imperative of the mid-sixties which was found too dangerous to live with and was rejected by all sorts of groups. Perhaps for the real trendsetters the Pill was only the ultimate and logical flowering of a liberation which had been coming on for a long time. Perhaps the tradition of being the quarry at the most vulnerable spot was too strong—and let us not forget all the safeties, reprieves and delicious homages gained en route, beside all the cruelties bred by the terror and jealousy of the more violent sex towards the other which holds the secret of the survival of the species in its stomach.

Without doubt, the Pill bred the mini (**42**), just as it bred the topless bathing suit by Rudi Gernreich in 1964. Discussing the motivation of both with Dr René König of Cologne University, whose book *The Restless Image* was remarkable for its fresh view of fashion, the conclusion was that neither was intended, by its original wearer at any rate, to be provocative—just the opposite, in fact. They were intended to prove that women were now in control of their destiny, and would choose whom they wished to mate with. If this all sounds too devious, Dr König has pointed out that very little research has been done on the motivation of girls as opposed to young men (because the latter form a larger proportion of the criminal intake) and that it is sensible to assume that the thinking of females is quite different. This would explain the concept that nakedness is in fact a way of cocking a snook at sex, and it would also explain how the mini survives in those pockets of society which are the last to be reached by new ideas, those at the bottom of the social pile.

No chapter about the effect on dress of the century's social changes would be complete without a stab at one of the most universal features of modern

fashion. The blue jeans phenomenon was born out of convenience, not protest. Being quite new on the fashion scene, it had the desired element of
universality, required because of the new mobility of young people and the
consequent levelling of geographical, political and artificial social barriers. It
had democratic and self-sufficient overtones although, as with so much other
dress, those who adopted it from a desire to be in style rather than from a sense
of conviction soon confused the statement implied in the wearing of jeans by
wearing working dress too tight to bend down in, and then by buying
specially faded and patched-up jeans which cost more than a solid new pair
would have done, or buying them made by Yves St Laurent (**45**). That is one
problem of wearing pioneer dress in the richest country in the world, or in a
welfare state.

Why it was blue jeans and not Bulgarian peasant costumes or English
agricultural smocks or Chinese robes or 'bleus de travail' no-one can say.
Perhaps it was because of the emergence of America as the super-power of the
century, a new continent which had a chance to look at Europe. Perhaps it was
because, for the young, America with all its warts was still a country which
seemed able to be forged by new thinking and was not, like Europe, age-old in
its systems and its cynicism.

Probably the harshest change for women in the twentieth century concerned the switch in the community's interest from women to girls. Once,
from her early twenties to her mid-forties, a woman was wooed, courted,
appealed to, dressed and catered for in any rôle she might hold. All of a sudden,
so it seemed, only teenagers were sexy, desirable, worth writing fashion
articles for, worth writing music for, worth listening to. Society demolished
the dignity and reward of age at precisely the time when medical science had
extended the middle period of active life from a likely twenty to forty years.
Not surprisingly, many women felt left out by fashion, and it was not until
they recognised the need to retain mental and physical faculties which
matched up to their increased youth-span that the breach began to heal. As
fashion became ageless, clothes returned to a sort of classic honesty which put
the onus for being flattering onto the wearer and her body.

It has been suggested that when a great nation is in decline its women
experience a flowering of beauty and appeal because, practical as ever and
consciously or not, they await the arrival of the next wave of conquerors. The
strange flowering of styles in Britain in the last quarter of the twentieth
century may yet be read as having political overtones, just as the fragmentation of fashion can be seen to reflect the fragmentation of society in the
face of the alternative of inhuman, or dehumanising, size epitomised by the
world shown in the 1975 film *Rollerball*.

Certainly the pressures of economic need could be read in high fashion at that time. As cotton became the only widely affordable fibre in this decade of wild inflation and consequent escalation of the price of clothes, so cotton became the high fashion fibre to wear; and since it is not in itself sufficient protection against the climate of many countries which had to adopt it, it was adopted in the form of the classic quilted Chinese jacket. Overnight, the product of need became the newest trend. Shoes, too, reflected as always the basic needs of society; clogs and espadrilles, from being a witty whim in the face of a leather and labour shortage, became a year-round style because the cheap materials—wood and rope and canvas—from which they had originally been made from necessity now reflected a need in previously affluent countries. They reflected too the search for old values.

32. Women workers at a coke tip in the First World War. These women doing a man's job are wearing regulation women's overalls which are utilitarian but not entirely desexing. Some found trousers so comfortable that they were unwilling to relinquish them after the war. A good deal of attention was given to the welfare of the working woman at the time since pioneer suffragettes, many of them in supervisory positions, were not going to lose this opportunity of demonstrating their beliefs in action. *(Imperial War Museum)*

33. The Women's Land Army, formed in 1917, was fortunate in its uniform, a waisted overall coat and riding breeches and socks, worn with a dashing felt hat. It was comfortable and functional. In the Second World War the only change was to replace the overall coat with a green pullover. *(Imperial War Museum)*

34. The lady railway guard at Neasden station in 1916 wears her official issue uniform with a certain fashion style and flair. She may do a man's job but she is still very much a woman. The uniform itself is not unpleasant, resembling the coat and skirt worn by many women at the time. Her somewhat soldierly gaiters are the precursors of the 1977 leg-warmers. Contemporary observers were always astonished and usually delighted at the care the wartime working woman gave to her appearance with new clothes, make-up and scent. There is no morale-booster like an adequate pay packet and a sense of personal worth. *(Imperial War Museum)*

35. Woman dressed as man is an old joke, but had new poignance in the 1920s when there were so few young men left. This smartly tailored young woman in 1926 has her dinner jacket as her husband has his, and there were Paris couturiers who produced quite creditable masculine dinner jacket suits. Daisy Fellowes, acme of elegance, gave it the ultimate chic in the 1920s when she wore one of scintillating sequins with a green carnation in her button-hole. (Punch)

36. These conventionally elaborate racegoers in 1928 are elegantly tubular of figure, flat of bust and neat of ankle. Skirts had reached their shortest level in 1925 and were now on the way down again, reaching mid-calf by 1930. The skirt is no longer so straight and godets provide a feminine flair. The materials are soft and floaty and the printed pattern fashion is art deco. The hats bury everything to brow level. Stockings have patterned clocks and the wrinkle almost inseparable from real silk is clearly visible at the ankle. (Syndication International)

37. The Utility scheme was promoted with considerable élan by *Vogue* in 1942. It showed the prototype clothes which had been designed anonymously by members of the Incorporated Society of London Fashion Designers—Hardy Amies, Digby Morton, Victor Stiebel et al, and which were all available in the shops (if you had the coupons) at moderate and regulated prices and in materials of reasonable quality. Cecil Beaton took the photograph, adding impeccable wartime touches such as the string bag, the shopping basket, the bicycle and a feeling of backs-to-the-wall. The Board of Trade were concerned to husband valuable resources, to regulate price and quality, to prevent profiteering and to encourage fashion as a morale-booster. With considerable foresight they encouraged high-style design as a shop window for British cloth exports. What it did for a smug British fashion and textile industry is still implicit in outdated machinery and attitudes. *(Vogue)*

38. Churchill's 'siren suit' became a symbol of a Britain vigilant and adaptable in time of national peril. Similar all-in-one coveralls considerably antedate the Blitz for they appeared in Paris collections of autumn 1939. Genuine shelter dwellers tended to wear more miscellaneous garments. Churchill, one of the few men who adopted siren suits, gave their pockets a military touch and found them useful for the round-the-clock conferences and emergencies which were part of his rôle of war leader. Also, the suits were similar to the overalls worn by many civilian war workers. Churchill is shown here wearing the suit during his wartime visit to America in 1942. *(Imperial War Museum)*

39. 'Make Do and Mend' was a slogan coined by the wartime Ministry of Information to save valuable war materials. One of the first effects of any modern war is pressure on the textile industries—wool, cotton, silk and synthetics have valuable military uses, imports are cut and labour is short. In 1940 it was estimated that a programme of improvisation of this kind could save 25 per cent of national production. One of the results was a boom in hand knitting and home dressmaking, though the coupon allocation applied to both yarns and fabrics. *(Imperial War Museum)*

40. Paris couture flourished during the occupation after Lucien Lelong, who designed the dress in this 1943 French fashion photograph, had persuaded the Germans not to remove its centre to Berlin. There were severe shortages of material but no lack of inventiveness in making use of what there was, surely the true test of the creative designer, though the best and most ingenious clothes were to be found in the street rather than in the atelier. Hats were made from wood shavings or paper and shoes were soled with wood or mounted on cork. The patrons, mainly Germans or French black marketeers, seem to have had a stimulating effect on French couture and it is interesting to compare this bizarre lady (and she is by no means the most extreme) with the understated restraint of British and United States fashion at this time. *(Frères Seeberger)*

41. Mamie van Doren, the pin-up par excellence, and one of many Hollywood starlets known more for vital statistics than for her acting ability. Once the wire-framed canti-levered bra was invented in 1946 there was no limit on size, and the possessors of the best-known breasts of the time won international renown—in the US Jane Russell in *The Outlaw*, in Britain Diana Dors and in France Brigitte Bardot. *(British Film Institute)*

42. The 'nude look' was not an easy one to wear and the 'mini', a style that appealed to the young, needed more attention to detail than it usually got. Originally it was a strident expression of sexual emancipation and equality but in its more popular versions at least it does not look desexed. Comfortingly, there are those who see short skirts as a sign of economic optimism and sheer joie de vivre. Is it significant that they are still worn, accompanied by huge platform-soled shoes, by the socially less privileged class, and revived as high fashion for the top end of the market by Kenzo Takada? (Keystone Press)

43. Odile Rodin wears an elegant version of the nude look in Paris in 1967. It was a style too easily vulgarised to retain its popularity, and bare-breasted barmaids in drive-in restaurants soon robbed it of chic. But, confused with the women's lib 'burn the bra' movement, it left many willing to do without the brassière for the first time for forty years. Saggy or baggy the bust-line may be, but now the nipple has become an unremarkable element in the fashion scene. (Camera Press)

44. Unisex at Harrods' Way In in 1968: His and Hers matching trouser suits. The fashion was launched by Cerruti, but the idea probably came first from those supremely elegant pictures of Marlene Dietrich 'en travestie' in Paris in 1932. Harrods was among the first of the big stores to recognise the trend which had started in the boutiques of Carnaby Street. (Harrods)

45. This advertisement for jeans, 1975, illustrates the contemporary contradictions: workmen's denim with ballroom block-soled shoes. The erogenous zone is the bottom—all the more noticeable with the complications and contradictions above and below. The young man is plainly dressed but oddly hermaphrodite with long, rather pretty hair, jewellery and slim-fit shirt emphasising breast and waist. Yet below the waist there are those very tight, crotch-moulding jeans. It is the same confusion of thought which makes a girl wear a blazer over a chiffon frock, as well as a basic confusion of sexual identity. (Jet Jeans)

3

The Performing Arts as Catalyst

Many of those who review with dismay the social carnage of the 1960s have concluded that the drugs epidemic which preyed on the children of labourer and nobleman alike was ineluctably linked with the pop music scene. It may be some consolation to them to reflect that, just as fashion designers appear to have a limited lifespan of real influence, so too it seems that the public taste—and in these days of mass media it is very public—is preoccupied with a procession of stimuli with a similar lifespan. It is therefore reasonable to expect that public interest should now swing away from pop music and focus elsewhere. The ear has been so assaulted, and the eye so ravaged by the clothes which illustrate pop, that one might guess, even pray, that it is the turn of another sense to be exercised.

Of those stimuli which prick the public interest it is, naturally, the performed arts which most affect fashion. Since dress is an integral part of the impression which the individual creates, it stands to reason that if that individual's living is conducted largely in public his clothes will play a proportionately large part in his public image. Dress, like a given talent, is a classic element and a potent weapon in the individual's struggle to raise himself (perhaps in these egalitarian days identify himself would be a better phrase) in a society which for convenience prefers the status quo. Dress is less important in the wider context because it can be, and often is, entirely an acquired facility, while a talent presupposes some original creative gift or inspiration; but in the immediate context of the live performer it is hard to be sure how to separate the appeal of the appearance, generated by dress, from the appeal of the talent, so mutually can they be identified in the public mind. How many, for example, remember Liberace more for his piano playing than for his sequinned jacket and his candelabra? Gaby Deslys has come down to us famous not so much for her 'canary voice' as for her diamond-studded heel

which so entranced the young Norman Hartnell, not for her moderate dancing but for the $320,000 worth of jewels, many from a royal lover, with which
she startled New York, for her bizarre and extravagant clothes by Reggie de
Veulle, for her hats which would have caused a conservationist to have a fit,
and for the costume of black satin lined with cerise velvet, trimmed with
chinchilla and garnished with enough pearls to pay for a Second Front, in
which she elected to entertain the brave troops during the First World War.
What everyone is agreed on is that she had star quality and sensational allure.
Her clothes rendered her immortal even if her talent was minimal (**47**).

Another good example of the theory that any performer's interest in and
success with dress is in inverse proportion to his or her talent would be the
Polish opera singer, Ganna Walska. In 1920 the famous stage designer Erté was
invited by Madame Walska to provide costumes for an amazing repertoire
which she planned to sing at Chicago. It was in the days when stars bought
their own wardrobes. The repertoire was too amazing for Madame, who
seems never to have got further than a few dreadful screeches before being
carried off paralysed with stage fright (she was in any case a very awkward
mover on the stage) and thus seems to merit no description more just than that
given to the peacock: 'the dress of an angel, the step of the thief, and the voice
of the devil'. Madame Walska had a certain success, however, after her
combine-harvester-inventing husband bought her her own opera house.

It would be more constructive to recall which performing arts held sway in
the popular imagination at particular times and to assess the effect which the
clothes they inspired had on fashionable taste. In some instances the effect was
minimal, because the clothes were too grotesque and individual and were a
part of one special personality or were perhaps reflections of styles already
accepted. Thus Camille Clifford was famous as the Gibson Girl in the early
years of the century, but the Gibson Girl had been drawn by 1890 by the
American artist Charles Dana Gibson and was modelled on his wife Irene
Langhorne, the sister of the future Lady Astor, MP. Mr Gibson had already
put the world into blouses and petersham belts; Miss Clifford confirmed their
fame (**46**). Likewise Lily Elsie, dressed by the fashionable Lucile for her star-
ring role in *The Merry Widow*, in fact merely wore an idealised and extravagant
form of current fashion. Dressed for *L'Aiglon* in 1900 in knee breeches and
cutaway coat by Poiret, the portly Sarah Bernhardt, however divine, hardly
set a style for trouser suits, but then one could not say that she represented
current fashion either. What she illustrates is an early implication of the new
wave of fashion designers in theatre costume, a tradition pursued by Poiret
and still kept alive by Yves St Laurent in his costumes for Zizi Jeanmaire.

Indeed, the most important effect of the fashions inspired by the performing

68

arts in the earlier years of this century was on the designers because, with style still dictated by the few and descending from the top, the designers were the logical lightning conductors of any new flash of trend. For the purposes of this book the designers considered are those who worked for the fashion market principally, not painters such as Léon Bakst, who also worked in theatre design, or Sonia Delaunay, whose fabrics incorporating the principles of abstract painting with the potential of textile machinery and the needs of dressmaking caused a sensation at the 1925 Exposition Décoratif in Paris, or Romain de Tirtoff, whose initials R T were translated to Erté when the artist began to work in Paris in 1912. Erté did in fact work for Poiret but a study of his style makes it quite clear that, though a supreme illustrator, he never had Poiret's inherent understanding of the human body, without which real-life clothes can never be successful. His 'effect' costumes and his décors were ravishing, but his clothes, even for costume films, look most peculiar when actually worn. He was frustrated by Hollywood, which must have seemed so fine a métier, and the actresses photographed in his costumes look most uncomfortable, poor dears.

It is through the fashion designers while their influence was paramount and then through its effect on the audiences which were creating fashion from the street that the catalytic pressure of the performing arts was felt on the everyday wear of millions. There is some argument for including all arts, not just those performed, in a survey of fashion trends, for had not Gibson invented his Girl? Further, in the last quarter of the nineteenth century the Pre-Raphaelite painters had been supporting aesthetic dress from the sympathetic Liberty store, and however much of a shock Art Nouveau was to the masses who saw it for the first time in Paris in 1900, to those faithful followers of Hunt and Millais its fashionable corollaries can hardly have been that surprising. The wonderful jewellery of Lalique, Fabergé, Fouquet, Paul and Henri Vever and Eugène Feuillatre seems in retrospect to be the natural adornment of the customers of Morris and Rossetti. But, however ravishing his posters seem today, women did not run out and dress after the style of Alphonse Mucha, the great Czech illustrator, nor even ride their bicycles in costumes more than approximating to those with which he enhanced the products of his commercial clients. Like Erté, Mucha was an illustrator of a way of feeling, a supreme fantasist. It was his luck that his major working period overlapped with a popular interest in musical comedy and operetta (and indeed in posters themselves), not in spectacular revue, cabaret or films. Was it bad luck? Untranslated into the wilful cloth, untrammelled with seams and sags and the limitations of the human dimension, Mucha's exquisite image of woman survives intact.

It is traditional to see the arrival of the Ballets Russes in Paris in 1909, or the exhibition in 1906 of Russian Art at the Salon d'Automne organised by Serge Diaghilev, as the seminal influences of the performing arts on mass fashion. It is also technically correct to date from this point the re-colouring of the vapid gowns which women had been wearing, the new freedom of movement which the dance and ethnic costumes provoked, and the new ideas in make-up and hats, notably turbans, inspired by the vivid semi-oriental costumes. On the other hand, the market was ripe for emancipation, and Poiret had been infected by orientalism some while before the Ballets had provided an ebullient peg on which to hang his new styles.

The interest in far-eastern colouring and prints and simple constructions was nursed in England by Arthur Lasenby Liberty while he was still working for Farmer and Rogers and it sprang from his enthusiasm for the Japanese section of the Exhibition of 1862. Liberty was not the only English merchant to pursue the primrose-yellow path (chrome yellow was right out, along with crude aniline dyes): Whiteley's of Bayswater also had an oriental department in 1874. Liberty, however, established a following on the Continent, so much so indeed that his designs were disgracefully plagiarised, and by the turn of the century interest in oriental décor and dress had a footing in smart society. With typical panache Liberty had placed the overall control of the gown department, set up in 1884, in the hands of a distinguished architect, E. W. Godwin. Poiret had tried out a kimono coat in 1903, without much success, and we are not told even whether it was constructed on the classic Japanese principle of having very few, very large stitches so that the garment could be taken apart each time for washing. (When the Singer sewing machine company attacked the lucrative Tokyo market they had little success until they made a machine which did enormous stitches.)

Orientalism was a delicate affair of soft colours and limpid gestures, but the Russian ballet, with its barbaric undertones and its overwhelming personalities, swept aside any connotation of the effete and centred popular interest on dance, the second mass preoccupation of this century. While Poiret and his many imitators launched into the lampshade silhouette made up in fabrics of a new lustre and texture, another dancer, Isadora Duncan, was inspiring the most unpromisingly shaped women to 'translate emotion into motion' and to take up aesthetic dancing in a garment which was a cross between a gymslip and a nightdress. By 1913 the craze for classical aesthetic dance was sweeping America. No concert stage or sylvan dell was immune from the hordes of determined nymphs ecstatically carrying out the Duncan theory, according to Mrs Woolman Chase of *Vogue*.

Not only classical dance was sweeping the country. Again according to

Vogue, 'Take up the rugs and let's trot' was the after-dinner slogan of America. What they trotted was not Miss Duncan's improving style but the sharp new choreography of Vernon and Irene Castle (**48**). The Castles are usually associated with the 'twenties and the shingle-haired flapper era but in fact they were at the height of their popularity before the First World War, and Mr Castle, who looked after his wife's hair as well as her footsteps, had performed his celebrated topiary work on her head and set a new world fashion by 1914. The Charleston, equally connected in the popular imagination with the 'twenties, had been born the same year.

This obsession with the goddess Terpsichore was in no way matched by a loosening of men's clothes. Not for the night-clubber or the ball-goer or even the exhibition dancer the aesthetic robes of Isadora or the ergonomic liberties of Nijinski. For foxtrot, Charleston, black bottom, rag, the properly dressed gentleman can be seen in white tie and tails. No-one has ever thought it anything but quite natural that when Fred Astaire was getting dressed up for a stint of gymnastic prancing, white tie and tails should have been the outfit he immortalised. One can only suppose that laundering was more efficient then. People must also have had appetites, for they danced at tea and between the soup and fish, the entrée and the pudding, the pudding and the savoury, the savoury and the coffee, and then they went on to one of the new night-clubs and danced between drinks.

What did happen in the 'twenties was that Terpsichore was joined in popular worship by whichever muse it is that looks after rhythm and melody. Jazz, strident and subtle, performed by solos, duos, quartets, quintets and big bands, ushered in a new era of spectator enjoyment. In fashion, it brought with it a taste for African decoration best illustrated by Nancy Cunard's superb but chattering ivory pieces which led her to be described as sounding, when she moved, 'like a skeleton doing the cakewalk'. Socially, it brought a new permissiveness in black–white relationships.

But already the cinema was a formidable rival for the public's attention in entertainment. Maybe people were worn out from dancing, maybe their feet were killing them, maybe it was just time for the stimulation of some other sense. Perhaps it was its awe-inspiring technical novelty, or the amazing range of geography and social behaviour which it was able to portray that made the cinema such a powerful force. Certainly its rock-bottom cheapness enabled it to reach a vast, new, unsophisticated audience. As far as fashion went, the silent films were even more potent since the clothes were necessarily as typecast and exaggerated as the actors. To go to the movies became a part of a way of life after the Depression had knocked the roaring real-life 'twenties on the head. The element of escapism was all-important.

Assessing the fashion impact of the cinema must begin with a re-iteration of the theatrical belief that the theatre is but a reflector of life, not its moulder. Most actors, especially when their art is under fire for promoting violence or obscenity, or for being socially destructive in one way or another, will fall back on this excuse. Up to a point it is valid, if the actor sees himself solely as the vehicle between author and audience. The rôle of the director is more questionable, but that is another story. In terms of clothing, films can indeed be seen as a reflection of existing life although, perhaps because the medium of film is both depersonalising and super-personality-oriented, the clothes are always exaggerated. Just as the old presentations of the great designers were often concentrated excessively on one line because the designer well knew that unless he began full strength his final offering would, after the inevitable watering-down for the mass market, be a weak drink indeed, so film clothes of the early years are always just that bit larger than life, like the heroes or heroines they dressed. The public likes something larger than life when life is harsh, as all sorts of popular interests from Christianity to the drug cults have shown. When life became more pleasant, film clothes lost their dream quality and a cabaret star such as Juliette Greco could appear in a plain black jersey and rely on talent.

The history of film clothes has come full circle. In the earliest days actors and actresses bought their own, and might even be hired on the strength of their garments or have their garments hired instead of themselves. There is the famous quote from the wife of D. W. Griffith (*Birth of a Nation*, *Intolerance*, etc.) about her husband's hiring of performers: '"I have no part for you, Miss Hart, but I can use your hat. I'll give you five dollars if you will let Miss Pickford wear your hat for this picture." Clothes got five dollars always, laughter and merrymaking upstage went for three.'

In 1974 the indefatigable Diana Vreeland staged an exhibition of film costumes at New York's Metropolitan Museum, entitled 'Romantic and Glamorous Hollywood Design'. Reviewing it in the London *Times*, David Robinson recalled that the MGM motto was 'Do it Big, Do it Right, Give it Class', and that such a motto was well in keeping with a new industry created by immigrants who knew only too well how much people needed dreams and spectacle at that time. Strangely, many of the greatest producers had been in fashion. Perhaps it is not so strange. Fashion, too, is a thing of dreams and inspiration and a seat-of-the-pants business, in which the public taste is notoriously hard to predict and ineffably fickle. Sam Goldwyn had manufactured gloves, Marcus Loew and Adolph Zukor had been in furs; while Zukor was at Paramount furs had to be used on everything possible.

Film clothes moved very fast from hiring hats from aspirants to the discovery that designing for the cinema, like the cinema itself, was a new art. Henri Bendel's immaculate store provided from its custom workrooms the lace négligé with the gold and rose brocade hem which Lilian Gish wore for *Way Down East* in 1920, but for *Romola* (1924) Miss Gish told David Robinson that the studio had gone to Florence, to the costumier of the Milan Opera, 'to get it absolutely right'. The Metropolitan Museum did not include what is described by Jacques Manuel as the first specially created film costume. This was designed by a Frenchman, Louis Gasnier, and consisted of a black suit with a white blouse and loose tie, worn with a velour beret. It was the 1916 ensemble of Pearl White (she of the weekly cliff-hanging series). Interestingly, it became almost a uniform dress for New York typists, whose mechanised life presumably made them identify with the perils of the intrepid Miss White even as they pounded their unexceptionably respectable keys (**49**).

The movement into professionalism was not fast enough to prevent some painful experiences. Just as many notable writers were hired in the early exuberance of Hollywood and found themselves in an alien and baffling world, so too were distinguished designers taken on, only to wilt under the arc-lights of the studio. The most famous failure is Erté, whose exquisite illustrative talents must have seemed to Hollywood the answer to any producer seeking the spectacular. Charles Spencer, Erté's biographer, says that it was Cecil B. De Mille who first approached Erté. At about this time two other protégés of Paul Poiret's, the artists Paul Iribe and Georges Lepape, were summoned to the cinema and shortly afterwards Georges Barbier, another famous illustrator, received the call. In 1918 Lepape did the costumes for the French film *Phantasmes*, and in 1919 De Mille's *Male and Female* with costumes by Iribe was released. Students of J. M. Barrie might care to recall that *Male and Female* was Hollywood's version of *The Admirable Crichton* and included, Heaven preserve us, a Babylonian flashback with young Martha Graham doing a 'lascivious' dance. Barbier dressed the Rudolph Valentino film of *Monsieur Beaucaire*.

William Randolph Hearst, who in 1913 had bought *Harper's* (now *Harper's Bazaar*) and to whom Erté was under contract, was himself in the film industry. He had produced in 1917 a film called *Patria*. Irene Castle starred in it and her costume was in the Metropolitan Museum's exhibition; 1917 was the year Hearst met Marion Davies, the girl he loved devotedly and must have made miserable with his Pygmalion-like determination to prove her small talent something it was not. It makes one think of Goldwyn's similar determination to prove with Jane Russell that the director is greater than the talents of the parts. The pathetic aspect of such a misdirected domination has been

73

preserved for ever in Orson Welles's film *Citizen Kane*; it should be a warning to all dress designers who want to make a silk purse out of a sow's ear.

Hearst's paranoia towards his staff and his insistence that Marion Davies should be surrounded by the best that money could buy—and this included revamping the cinemas in which the premières of her pictures were held—made it natural that when De Mille wanted Erté, so too did Hearst. The first film on which Erté worked, *Bal des Arts*, is regarded by Charles Spencer as 'one of his finest achievements'. This success was not repeated. In 1924 Louis B. Mayer announced that he would make a film about a French couturier, to be called *Paris*. Since Mayer was a friend of Hearst's and Erté was a famous illustrator and costume designer for revues and spectaculars (not at all the same thing as a good couturier, as it was to be proved), Erté was plucked across the Atlantic with a typical movie fanfare.

The script for *Paris* was a long time a-coming, but in the meantime Erté did speciality costumes for films such as *Ben Hur*, and spectacular décors and curtains and bits and bobs around Hollywood. He also did costumes for King Vidor's *La Bohème*, which led eventually to a row with the star, Lilian Gish, which lost nothing in the telling when Erté finally left Hollywood. He left, in short, because when the details for *Paris* were finally shown to him he discovered that the locations, styles, text and facts of the film were totally inaccurate. The press, which insisted on calling him Romain de Tirtoff-Erté, quoted him as saying that he 'found the scenario dealing with Paris life simply impossible, ghastly in fact. Neither the director, nor the scenario writer, nor the stars, knew the least bit about life in Paris. It was a huge joke. They were writing about Paris, Texas, and did not know it.' Erté refused to allow his work to be used.

The Gish row is a perfect vignette of the internecine warfare between artists. She wrote in her autobiography that Erté had been got over specially to do her costumes for *La Bohème* (he had not; he was over anyway to do *Paris*). She did not like his common calico for her gowns and thought the dresses would look 'too new'. Erté's recollection is that the great star thought her skin too delicate for anything but silk. She did her best to persuade her co-star, Renée Adorée, to chuck Erté's costumes for Musette too, but Miss Adorée stuck by him.

Without doubt the most influential film clothes have been produced by designers aware of the arts of couture, of balance and proportion, and at the same time wise to the needs of the new medium. The movement was not all one way, from couture to films, since the great Norman Norell started his career in Hollywood, and Gilbert Adrian went on to a second and even more publicised market when he began to produce for the wholesale trade in the war years. But Hollywood certainly developed its own genre of creative

74

dressmaker. One of the early successful women was Natacha Rambova who, as if being married to Rudolph Valentino was not enough, scored personal triumphs for her clothes for that hoary old box-office horse, *Salome*, in 1922. History does not relate whether Madame Rambova subscribed to the theory of an American scholar, which Erté mentions apropos of his own designs for the opera of the same name, which was that Salome was really a boy.

Gilbert Adrian (**52**), who had trained in Paris, is most associated with Greta Garbo, for whom he designed the most ravishing clothes on an extraordinarily broad palette. Adrian was as much at home flouncing up crinolines for Camille as he was draping vamp dresses and jewelled exotica for Mata Hari, but his most copied dress was for Joan Crawford. In *Letty Lynton* those famous square shoulders immortalised later by Adrian were covered in organdie ruffles (**53**). The dress was a major fashion hit, and in 1932 Macy's of New York alone sold 500,000 copies. Adrian died in 1960, having designed the clothes for the stage production of *Camelot* on Broadway.

Howard Greer was an early name who had worked for Lucile (Lady Duff Gordon) in her couture salon, and had also worked with Poiret and Molyneux. Travis Banton worked initially for a couture house named Madame Frances in New York, and the most famous film personality for whom he designed was Marlene Dietrich. His 'look' was much softer than that of Adrian, equally seductive but in a less stylised way. Walter Plunkett had wanted to be an actor so perhaps it is appropriate that his lasting memorial remains the costumes for that most famous film epic of all, *Gone with the Wind*. That he was also able to dress *Singing in the Rain* and *Seven Brides for Seven Brothers* shows his intellectual capacity to interpret with freshness and vigour what are basically traditional ideas.

Jean Louis was French, and on arrival in New York in 1935 was hired by Hattie Carnegie as a designer. His most famous dress is always said to be the black strapless number worn by Rita Hayworth in *Gilda*. The actress maintained that the dress stayed in place 'for two good reasons', namely her breasts, but examination of the interior of the gown suggests that it stayed in place because Jean Louis was a superb craftsman (**54**). During his career the whole concept of dressing stars changed. 'We moved,' he said, 'from the era of camouflage to the era of honesty in clothes. Originally we used to dress an actress as a perfect package, ironing out her figure faults, squeezing her, padding her, making her look taller or smaller and dressing her according to rules for the character she was playing. Now they all just want to look like themselves.' The total success of Jean Louis in dressing one famous star is nicely illustrated by the reaction of a Hollywood window-cleaner who, knowing Jean Louis to be responsible for the film wardrobe of a certain homely comedienne, called round to congratulate the designer after he had got a peek at the lady unadorned through her newly washed windows.

Helen Rose made not only the costumes for Grace Kelly in *The Swan* and *High Society*, but also the wedding dress in which the Irish-American actress became Her Serene Highness Princess Grace of Monaco. She thoroughly grasped the theory of camouflage, enhancing for example the ravishing Kelly face and minimising the less ravishing Kelly hips and legs. Edith Head was another woman to come to prominence in the 'forties, when her designs for the Paramount star, Barbara Stanwyck, brought out a new dimension in the actress's personality. Irene Sharaff specialised in the lavish, most spectacularly in her costumes for Elizabeth Taylor in *Cleopatra*. Aesthetically these could be criticised since they certainly did not improve the figure of the expanding Miss Taylor, but to be fair one would have to know the amount of freedom allowed to the designer.

Already many of the stars were being dressed by their favourite couturiers anyway. Audrey Hepburn exemplified the chic Givenchy look, Romy Schneider that of Chanel, Elizabeth Taylor wore Valentino. The dream quality was fading. Real-life situations became the rage, heroes became anti-heroes. The physical attributes of the star became as important as her clothes; one generation grew Veronica Lake curtains of hair which had to be bound up in turbans to be kept out of the munitions machinery, and another generation puffed out its chest in vain imitation of the voluptuous Gina Lollobrigida.

With neat timing, at the moment that the cinema became visually pedestrian the public removed its desire for spectacle to pop music, which in sight and sound provided a stimulus in keeping with the new world. In the pop scene dress was an essential part of the appeal. A whole cult of Teddy (short for Edwardian) boys dressed in broad-shouldered, long, draped jackets, bootlace ties, suède shoes and narrow-ankled trousers, and dressed their hair into a greasy quiff in emulation of the one and only Elvis Presley (**56**). Elvis, who died in 1977, was still ostensibly heterosexual, virile, and dressed to get the girls screaming. The time had not yet come for the unisex costumes which were needed to turn on an audience in the 'seventies.

In October 1962 four boys who called themselves the Beatles and hailed from the Liverpool area made a record called 'Love, love me do'. It sounded different, it sounded right, whatever that was, and within a week it was in the hit parade. The record sleeve of the first long-player on which this seminal song appeared makes piquant reading now, since it expresses no more than a cautious hope that the Beatles may prove a mainstream success; the writer obviously did not believe the theory of rotating public taste, since he pointed out with relief that the group had enough home-produced songs written to see them through to 1975. By 1975 the Beatles had long since disintegrated as a group and the American authorities were doing their utmost to boot the quixotic songsmith John Lennon out of their shores.

What sort of man were the Beatles inviting us to love all those years ago? Well, presumably he looked something like themselves, and their contemporary pictures show them as a group of crop-haired country-looking boys who might have fought in the Protector's army, straight and smiling, with a veneer of sophistication as deep as the velvet on their collars. They are quite, quite different from Elvis Presley. They look young, they look vulnerable, they look pensive, and even George Harrison, whom most people would consider the most conventionally virile-looking, has none of the agressive, suggestive panache of the rock 'n' rollers (**58**).

If the Beatles had a neuter quality, the Rolling Stones, who had to follow them and somehow top their style, have seemed to many people the epitome of evil. Is there nothing too outrageous for Mick Jagger to wear? The Rolling Stones proved that sex had nothing to do with dress, and expressed the new freedoms of homosexual relationship which their audience had found and which legislation and society had smiled on (**59**).

But the musical scene was struck, as was fashion, by the explosion of the do-your-own-thing idea, and by the 'seventies there were as many different styles of popular music around as there were skirt lengths. It has been argued that music sets fashion, and that fashion precedes musical trends. Which came first, Donny Osmond, pop star at sixteen, or the craze for baby blue or pink fluffy bedjackets in 1973? However it may be, the girls serving in the record shops calculated that they could tell what the customers would buy by what they were wearing, so entwined were tastes in dress and entertainment. The gap between what was worn on stage and off narrowed; stars dined and partied with their designers and the press recorded who dressed whom, so the impact through the market, especially for menswear, has been extensive. On women's clothes, since most of the popular performers are male, the influence has been more diffuse, the girls dressing to suit a frame of mind exemplified by their idols. Many fan clubs had their own uniform and in 1975 a group called the Bay City Rollers from Scotland were responsible for a wave of tartan as virulent as that which Queen Victoria initiated (**57**).

What of the Cyclops of the living-room, that most pervasive and novel entertainer, television? What effect has that had on clothes? The easy answer would be 'none', since television came into popularity at a time when the theatre and films were at their most prosaic in dress and in their most adamantly reflector-not-moulder-of-life-style periods. Actual coverage of fashion events has been deplorable, veering from the reverential and plonking to the determination to liven things up by presenting fashion in a spectacular revue setting quite out of context for the real purpose of the garments. Television is at its best showing a subject as news, history, entertainment or spectacle, so the opportunities for showing fashion are limited. Serious fashion is best presented as a service, something which loses from the speed of the screen. It is also extremely personal, requires great knowledge and authority to put across convincingly, and really needs the sort of loyalty and market specialisation which a magazine attracts.

Where television has been influential is in the creation of personalities whose talents or appeal can be translated into clothes which, if not designed by them or even actually worn by them, carry their name and advocacy. These clothes inspire the huge army of spectator sportsmen, for example, with the vicarious prestige of playing with Jack Nicklaus golf clubs, or kicking with a George Best boot, or wearing a Tom and Jerry T-shirt. Television has brought the name-licensing system within reach of all sorts of performers and an enormous potential market.

Where television has been much criticised recently is in its rôle of purveyor of nostalgia, the curse of modern dress in the eyes of many professionals. It is true that for all sorts of reasons television did show the new, young, impressionable audience, who are now designing, a surfeit of old movies and documentaries, but the criticism is too facile. Nostalgia is indeed deplorable in any creative art unless, as the Pre-Raphaelites did, you inject some totally new dimension into the picture, but the fact is that the fashion phenomenon has proved inexorably voracious and in seventy-five years it has exploited virtually every silhouette known to history and lots more besides. It is not simply dissatisfaction with present-day society which makes for backward-looking trends. Just as it seems that the world's ecological and economic problems will require a solution of genius, so too will genius now be required to invent a garment no-one has ever seen before.

46. The Gibson Girl was the turn of the century's ideal woman. Created by the American artist, Charles Dana Gibson, she was elegantly triumphant over all her menfolk whether in the ballroom or on a board walk. She was tall and athletic, well developed but not exaggeratedly so, her figure shaped but not distorted by her S-bend corset. She looked well in ball gowns but superb in the blouses and skirts which were conventional day wear for women of all classes.

47. Gaby Deslys in 1910, the prototype showgirl, all feathers and glitter. Born Gabriella Caire, in Marseilles, she gave the statuesque beauty of the Edwardian era a more exotic, restless image. The heroine of dozens of well-dressed musical plays and reviews, she died aged only forty in 1929, leaving her fabulous jewels to the town of Marseilles.

48. Irene Castle became a leader of high-society style as well as a hard-working dancer. For most of the flowing, lightweight frocks that she wore she went to Lucile but others she is said to have designed herself. She brought a lithe and active grace to fashion and the clothes she popularised were much less elaborate than the current vogue. The simplicity coincided with the style which Paul Poiret was introducing in Paris. The photograph is typical of the work of De Meyer, 1918, one of the first to use the flattering technique of back lighting. *(Victoria and Albert Museum)*

49. Pearl White in *Plunder*, 1922–3. Arguably the first film trendsetter, she is wearing a costume designed by Louis Gasnier. Any young woman of the time would have been proud to own her coat and skirt of black velvet bound with silk, and indeed many of them did, for it was copied by the thousand for the new mass market, the working girl. *(British Film Institute)*

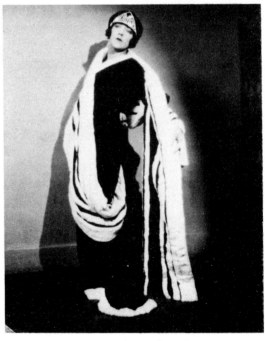

50 and 51. Sketch and realisation. Erté, Romain de Tirtoff, (1892–) made this design for Aileen Pringle in *The Mystic*, 1925. Black velvet with white ermine trim, it almost makes one wonder whether Erté's troubles with the studio were all one-sided. But it is important to remember that this was a 'movie' costume, and that the furry bundle might have looked better trailing down miles of marble vista.

52. Gilbert Adrian (1903–59) designed clothes which were among the most exciting things on the American fashion scene before and during the Second World War. During his twenty years with MGM he became well known for the broad-shouldered outfits that he designed, in particular for Joan Crawford, and these he launched on the United States fashion market in 1942. Their architectural qualities and superb construction brought them success far beyond Hollywood. *(Adrian Archive, USA)*

53. The 'Letty Lynton' dress worn by Joan Crawford was designed by Gilbert Adrian in 1932 for the film of that name. Launched on the popular market, it was an immediate success and Macy's of New York alone sold 500,000 copies. *(British Film Institute)*

54. Rita Hayworth was glamour personified in the svelte black satin dress she wore in *Gilda* in 1946, and long hair and cleavage have remained the staples of sex appeal. Jean Louis, the designer, ingeniously solved the problems posed by Miss Hayworth's energetic dance routine; the strapless bodice was supported on pre-formed plastic bars, and the draped bow moulded her hips and stomach without the need for a corset. *(British Film Institute)*

55. Gary Glitter's stage clothes are an indispensable part of the soft-rock pop star styles of the 1970s. The gleam and shimmer skilfully exploit stage and TV light effects, and under all the iridescence there is an image which, with its DA hair-do, low-cut shirt, cowboy waistcoat and boots and slim-fit jeans, is remarkably close to that of the Elvis Presley of the 1950s. *(Gary Glitter)*

56. 'Teddy boys' were so called after the Edwardian-style clothes that they adopted in the early 1950s—almost a masculine 'New Look'. The long jacket, the velvet-faced collar and the tapered trouser were a development of the upper-class Guards 'mufti', but drew even more on the Hollywood riverboat gambler image. The cult, essentially working-class, coincided with the rock 'n' roll craze, and dance halls became the scene of a competitive masculine elegance. The clothes were expensive and this dandyism reflected the high wages that youth began to attract during the post-war boom. These lads are dressed with an exact fidelity of detail (they even used the same tailors) for a revival Rock festival in 1972. *(Keystone Press)*

57. Today's Bay City Rollers fans have done wonders for the tartan market by wearing the colours of their Scottish-origin pop group. Under the tartan trim are those teeny-bopper 'steals' from the 1940s collegiate market, T-shirts and pedal-pusher trousers. The clothes provide an easily purchasable emotional security through association with a group identity. *(Press Assoc.)*

58. The Beatles made their appearance in effigy at Madame Tussauds in 1964. They are wearing the slick soft tailoring of the new Carnaby Street image, somewhat Italian in its preference for shiny lightweight materials, Cardin-inspired, short, collarless jackets and tight, tapered trousers. The waxworks wear the stage suits which approximate to outfits of the more formal type, while the real Beatles wear what most young men were wearing. The 'shortie' overcoat was a relatively new style which was more comfortable for wear in cars. The Beatles' image of 1964, in part the creation of their then manager, Brian Epstein, was quite different from the tough student look of their earliest 'beat' days or the hairy ethnic of their later style. *(Syndication International)*

59. Mick Jagger and Keith Richard of the Rolling Stones. The group set an image like their song style: international, iconoclastic and anarchic, with overtones of a mystic India. On stage the clothes were skintight and revealing, the appeal overtly sexual. *(Warner Records)*

4

Mainstreamers and Breakaways

'We must remember that society and the individual are constantly at war with each other. Society desires the individual to stay put in his allotted place, whereas the individual desires to elevate himself from his allotted place into a higher social place. . . . Dress is the most powerful single aid in this historic game of snakes and ladders.' So states Pearl Binder in *The Peacock's Tail*.

'It is true that being poor is much more difficult for a man than for a woman. So long as my sex can afford a decent dress one can go anywhere and everywhere and it can cost one nothing,' remarks Barbara Cartland in *The Isthmus Years*.

'The effect of singularity in attire is to incur a social martyrdom out of all proportion to the relief obtained. It is vain to be comfortably and modestly attired if one is made an object of observation or ridicule,' regretted a correspondent in the Rational Dress Society's *Gazette* in 1888.

To be wrongly dressed for some occasion is a familiar part of bad dreams because dress can open—or close—so many doors, professional and social. One of the prime reasons why people regret the disappearance of strict guidelines on what to wear for what is that their appearance is so important to themselves, because of what they feel it tells others about them, that they live in an unconfident tizzy that they will commit a dress gaffe. One of the prime reasons why people rail against the 'anarchy' of dress today and call it disgraceful that a navvy should dress like a nobleman is that they are terrified by the changes in society—political, economic, total—which this reflects. Whether they are right to be frightened or resentful is of course their own business, though in so far as many of the critical voices have a middle-class accent they are certainly right to read with acute attention the signs of change implicit in the change of dress. In January 1975 the London *Times* carried an article by Ian Bradley which mapped the rise of the middle class in England and concluded that its fall was imminent. It is in the areas where the middle class congregates that the telephone wires are jammed before every party with calls beginning 'What are you going to wear to . . .?'

Originally, the groups of people who had any choice in what to wear—those who were not bound by poverty, traditions of profession, practicalities of their trade or sumptuary laws—were very small, very close-knit and automatically knew what was correct gear. Just as introducing people to one another is a comparatively modern and essentially middle-class habit (when society was based on the Court and so few were receivable, it was taken for granted that you knew everyone it was suitable for you to know), so is the anxiety about what to wear. Advice in the form of ladies' magazines was not slow in being proffered, but it was not until fashion was married to trade at the beginning of the twentieth century that it became obvious that some sort of authoritarian régime and some suitably grand figureheads must be promoted to boost this new mass-market interest.

Already by the mid-1850s the scrum of those wishing to be presented at Court (as opposed to just appearing there by right of birth) promoted the magazine *Punch* to suggest a preparatory assault-course training for participants and to print a cartoon showing these social climbers, dressed to the nines, sprinting over and around the discomforts they might expect to encounter amid a shower of fans, feathers, gloves, bouquets and entangled crinolines. The idea of formal presentation occasions was engendered by the greatly increased number of persons who, in the reigns of Victoria and Edward VII, had advanced themselves sufficiently by trade, marriage or the new professions to expect an opportunity 'to show loyalty to the Sovereign', and by a newly created desire to secure a passport to 'Society'. Certificates of Presentation were first granted in 1854.

Before that time, it must be remembered, the English aristocracy was really a very small and tightly knit community, each member of which knew or knew of all the others. Those who had the right to attend Drawing Rooms were therefore known automatically to the Sovereign, who had a vested interest in allowing the traditional rights of his subjects to meet him, and in seeking to attach the peerage and other notables to his person for political reasons; in times of variance with the Prince of Wales, a not uncommon occurrence in the Hanoverian period, alas, the King needed to know what degree of support he could count on against his son. Even until the end of Queen Victoria's reign the privileged could leave cards at the Lord Chamberlain's office when they intended to come to Court and were automatically included. King Edward VII changed the afternoon Drawing Room

86

presentations to evening affairs. George V and George VI continued this custom until 1939, when it lapsed at the outbreak of war. Levées, presentations for men which had been instituted in 1737, also ended in that fateful year and were never revived.

Presentations for women were revived in 1947, by which time it was estimated that there was a backlog of 20,000 waiting to apply. As this horde could not possibly be fitted in to the traditional evening court pattern, presentations, which now were for débutantes only (formerly married women had also been admitted), took the form of mammoth garden parties. They must have been unlucky with the weather in 1947, because in 1948 the parties were transferred indoors. The King and Queen circulated among the guests picking out the fortunate few, though all were officially recorded as having been presented. By 1949 the Diplomatic Corps was flexing its muscles and wanted individual presentations for its ladies, who duly curtsied one by one in the ballroom. By 1951, King George VI, not perhaps the father of two girls for nothing, re-instated individual presentations complete with curtsy for every unmarried débutante. But 1958, with one of those daughters on the throne, saw the last Vacani-trained deb make her bob.

The English Court, in the guise of the Lord Chamberlain, was early on the fashion advisory scene, guiding the parvenus and infiltrators of the old order in what it was seemly to wear. Today, royal functions must be one of the last preserves of the authority once exercised by fashion editors and designers and by convention. For gentlemen they are specific as to dark lounge suit, morning dress, decorations (which means white tie, since decorations are never worn with black) or perhaps uniform. When the regulations for dress in the Royal Enclosure at Ascot were relaxed to allow lounge suits in 1968, so few men availed themselves of the chance to change that in 1969 the rule of morning dress was re-introduced. It is a nice point to ponder whether the curious lack of change in menswear is as much their own doing as anyone else's, but by giving the test relaxation a run of only one year, the authorities, however well intentioned, could be accused of making a bow to modernity and of retracting it with an unseemly haste which smacks of relief.

The Lord Chamberlain was equally at home in advising the ladies. In 1900, to be presented at Court you required a white dress, white gloves, a veil and two feathers pinned to the head, or three if married (**64**). Furthermore, the dress had to be décolleté unless you could convince Queen Victoria that your health would not stand it. By 1908, King Edward VII, feeling perhaps that the subject of ladies' necklines, while of abiding interest to him personally, was not a suitable one to concern a monarch, had decreed that a high-necked dress was all right for anyone who could persuade the Lord Chamberlain that they were old, ill or infirm, and it was he who now had to assess whether the appeals for cover were prompted by health or vanity.

In 1937, instructions for Courts stated that dresses must be long (they had hitherto been of the prevailing fashionable length), with a train not more than two yards in length and extending not more than eighteen inches from the heel of the wearer when she was standing with the train attached to her shoulders. Forty-five inches was the maximum length for the veil. Married or not, a woman wore three feathers, always white unless she was in mourning, when they could be black. There was no restriction on the colour of either the dress or gloves of anyone presented.

The royal enclosure at Ascot still demands the wearing of a hat and until 1970 trousers were barred for women, though at royal garden parties the Court rose above publicity seekers with supreme disregard. Even now Ascot would ban 'untidy' trousers.

If the Court was a great regulator of dress, so too was convention. Lady Ashton, known to the fashion world as Madge Garland, fashion editor of British *Vogue* until she took over as the first head of the fashion department of the Royal College of Art in 1948, recalls that in her youth make-up, mink and diamonds were rigorously eschewed by the well-bred unmarried young woman. All the nicest perks were thus reserved for the chic matrons, which may be why they were so much more dashing than the debs. It certainly gave the matrons an advantage. Make-up and extravagant clothes are after all a handy prop to those lacking confidence. Lady Ashton herself remembers that she never dared to make a speech in public until lipstick, that great morale-booster, was acceptable in society in the middle of the 'twenties.

Other conventions covered the wearing of gloves, a tangle which continued right up until 1970 because, even when convention had relegated their necessity to occasions on which one might have to take the royal or noble hand in one's own sticky paw, Jackie Kennedy had made little white gloves a high fashion item (**73**). In more remote parts conventions were slower to die out. Though the memsahib in India in the 'twenties and 'thirties tried to keep up with British fashion as far as the climate allowed, slacks, jodhpurs and breeches were worn regularly by women, with shirts, sweaters and tweed coats, an innovation which old-style Indian servants greeted with horror. But on more formal occasions gloves, preferably long and of white kid, were thought appropriate despite their discomfort and expense and the problems of cleaning (the dhobi presumably not being able to bang such items on the stones with the rest of the wash). It was not, however, done to wear gloves in the jungle. 'After the first time I did this,' Iris Portal is recorded as saying in *Plain Tales from the Raj*, 'my husband said to me, "If you wear gloves in the jungle again I will divorce you.'" The Empire also kept up the tradition of hat-wearing. Usually it was the topee (by 1975 a high fashion shape for both young men and women, the latter charmingly veiled) or, for more casual affairs, something called the double-terais, which was two felt hats, one on top of the other. Of course in this instance convention was dictated as much by the climate as by social niceties.

Elsewhere hats gradually lost out to hairstyles. Before the Second World War it was considered almost improper for a woman to be seen in public by day with her head uncovered. Some women, such as the incredibly beautiful Comtesse Henri Greffhule, a friend of Marcel Proust, went so far as to wear their belle époque platters indoors at home, too. Lady Chatterley, fresh from twining forget-me-nots into the pubic hair of her gamekeeper lover, is always taking off her hats when she gets home, and this in the late 'twenties. Conventions differed from country to country. In Paris one dined in a hat but in England restaurants had strange rules against this, which, in view of who pays the bill, seem as impertinent as the banning of women in trousers from certain public eating places, which remained in New York and London until 1974. By 1974 hats were a fashion fad for a whole new generation.

It is hard to decide whether the social need to cover the head was bound up with the traditional, ancient and indeed mysterious properties attributed to hair, or whether, since hair is one of the erogenous zones which rotate into fashion from time to time, low-cut belle époque dresses, short-cut 'twenties shapes and tight-cut 'thirties designs had simply kept the eye occupied elsewhere. It must also be remembered that before modern hairdressing few except young women had retained hair of sufficient beauty and elegance not to benefit from a charming hat.

Not everyone welcomed the new freedoms in dress, anyway, but for them there was a delicious compromise in the form of the tea-gown, which lingered on far after its value as a release from whalebone was gone. The tea-gown was described in 1915 by the copywriter of Debenham and Freebody's advertisements with a certain equivocality as the 'Tea and Rest Frock'. He (or she) had presumably never heard of the French notion of le cinq-à-sept, and it reflected the nostalgia with which some women looked back at a past more leisured and elegant and felt nervous of the brisk future. The tea-gown was the sartorial bridge between the corset and the gasper.

Something else which lingered on was snobbishness in dress. The prominent socialist, Beatrice Webb, who, when her husband succumbed to a peerage in 1929, refused to be addressed as Lady Passfield on the grounds that by her refusal she would be undermining the foundations of British snobbishness, was very sharp about the sartorial pretensions of the wives of Labour fellow-ministers. Of a Buckingham Palace dinner in 1930 she comments tartly: 'Mrs Lunn, the Under-Secretary's wife, had donned a conventional black satin, obviously bought for the occasion from the local Co-op. Ethel Snowden, with a paste tiara and a cheap, fashionable frock, was the intermediate link between us humble folk and the Court circle.'

The decencies of mourning were not widely discounted until after the First World War had made mourning appropriate for too many (**66**). Ascot and the Derby were blacked, dress-wise, in 1910 because of the death of Edward VII. Sir Henry Channon, an invaluable source of sartorial gossip, records in 1936 that though the King, Edward VIII, had stated it should be white tie for private dinner, the men were still in black waistcoats because of the death of George V. In the past, the length and extent of mourning had led tradesmen to lobby the throne because it was so bad for sales. By 1900, the directions for mourning (family as opposed to State) were: widows all in black; skirt entirely of crape or of crape from hips down; crape yoke and collar; crape worn for a year and a day, then plain black for another year. By 1940, full mourning, with veils, was practised only by the Royal Family or by individuals who felt so inclined (**84**). Not surprisingly, the number of those individuals is much higher in Catholic countries and among the less sophisticated communities.

On a lighter note, wedding dresses have had a remarkably long run. These too were an invention of the affluent fashion society, which changed the idea of merely wearing your best dress in a pale colour to be married in and to wear to balls afterwards, into the idea of appearing in what was frequently fancy dress. By 1930 the wedding dress had been taken out of the fashion scene proper. Although it is still the culmination of every official couture showing, the point was made when Yves St Laurent started presenting 'joke' wedding dresses of see-through tulle, or girls dressed as a flower, or some such psychedelic thrill. Strangely, in these days of quick marriage and quicker divorce the white wedding dress remains the goal for the majority of girls, though what it looks like is entirely up to them. Tudor, Stuart, Space age, Romantic, it can be any wild exuberance they feel. It is impossible to imagine what they wear them for afterwards, which may account for the rising trade in hiring wedding dresses. In 1911, however, it was taken for granted that 'for the ordinary middle-class girl of average means the bridal dress is worn as a best evening gown afterwards', and similarly in 1931 the *Essex County Standard* was extolling the virtues of a wedding gown in which 'after you take off your veil you slip into a little bolero jacket with elbow sleeves banded in white fox or ermine which will make a perfect evening ensemble'. Of course, in 1931 marriage was still the destination and the hope of most women. Perhaps one should see the strange concoctions worn to the altar now as an indication that the bride wants one marvellous, escapist, romantic moment in an otherwise drab life, or that by wearing archaic dress she is stating her unconscious belief that the ceremony itself is archaic.

All the rules of Court, of mourning and of wedding applied to very definite sets of circumstances. Not everyone was going to Court or being bereaved or getting married, so what was needed for the new mass market were authorities, the grander the better. Since—as Pearl Binder so rightly says —dress is a key to social advancement, it followed that those who patronised dress should be at the top end of the social scale. Typically, it was America which first coerced high society into public patronage of fashion and thence eventually into sharing their wardrobe secrets with millions of women. America constructed the super fashion consumer, epitomised by Jackie Kennedy and aped by a whole continent, and when the real aristocrats proved too poor or too recalcitrant to fill the rôle of patrons a whole galère called the Beautiful People was invented to lead where their creators would have them go. In 1914 Edna Woolman Chase was timorously tackling Mrs Stuyvesant Fish for the very first of those fashion charity shows which are an intrinsic part of life in the USA now, and getting snubbed for her pains. By 1970, *Women's Wear Daily* could reduce a rich and happy woman to tears by its neglect, or, worse, its critical attention.

The Woolman Chase story deserves repeating because it can be seen as the very start of the undermining of social confidence by uncertainty about the right dress which was to be so beneficial for trade. Mrs Woolman Chase, bright, effective and even then knowledgeable, was confronted in 1914 with the problem of how to promote fashion (which came from Paris) in *Vogue* when it appeared that couture would shortly be swept under the boots of the German army. On the top of a bus, she tells us, she conceived the idea of a presentation of model dresses made by the top New York houses, led by Bendel's, before an audience of the social register élite, to benefit a French charity. (Here you have in one clause the requisites for a fashion success in America, snobbery, charity, France.) Her boss, Condé Nast, was dubious about her chances of gaining the patronage of those she wanted, saying that she would never get 'really smart women interested in this. They wouldn't dream of it; it has too much to do with trade.' Mrs Chase thought he had a point. 'At that time,' she relates, 'society women were not in the habit of endorsing commercial enterprises, and although the show would be for charity commerce was certainly involved. Well-bred ladies lived practically in purdah. The cold cream they rubbed into their skins was their secret as were the cigarettes they smoked, if any.' Yet the early 'twenties saw the first ex-débutante mannequin, Paula Gellibrand, and by 1932 Ponds cold cream had garnered the advocacy of the chic and titled for its bland charms, paying married aristocrats £150 a plug and the unmarried (who were less important socially) £100. By 1935 the Countess of Warwick was advertising a Paris hotel while the Countess Howe was prepared for a fee to tell the world that the secret of a good cocktail was Gordon's gin. O tempora! O mores!

Mrs Stuyvesant Fish, though, proved less receptive to the blandishments of publicity, but in the end she gave in and assembled a list of patrons for *Vogue's* first show which included Mrs Vincent Astor, Mrs J. Borden Harriman, Mrs Arthur Curtiss James, Mrs August Belmont, Mrs Bradley Martin and Mrs Amos Pinchot, in other words the cream of New York society. The designs they saw were made by Henri Bendel, Mollie O'Hara, Bergdorff-Goodman, Gunther, Tappe, Maison Jacqueline, Kurzman 'and all the other first-class houses'.

Although these grandes dames might lend their gracious presence to fashion for charity, it was a far cry from getting them to wear what the promoters wanted. The underpinnings and the creations of their gowns remained information which was their private property and it was not until the Second World War had demolished another set of social barriers that those who wished to open the doors of Mrs Stuyvesant Fish's successors' drawing-rooms found it convenient to know from the press who was the lady's dressmaker and to use his talent as the entrée. In the 1960s when the promotion of the most extraordinary and often ephemeral people as pop fashion leaders was booming, the really grand, and those who had themselves moved upwards in society, had to be wooed by the inspired concept of persuading them that they were really performing a useful community service or advancing the cause of the arts, not just acting as clothes horses for a multi-billion-dollar industry which was generating occasions to show off its products. In her perceptive and informed book, *The Beautiful People*, Marylin Bender states: 'She would never admit that was her purpose, showing off clothes. What she told everyone she was doing was opening art exhibitions and listening to symphonies, reading Urdu fairy stories to her children and standing decoratively about when her husband came home from a hard day. . . . These superconsumers of fashion, these negative heroines, serve a double purpose. Not only do they set an example of product use, but they give the fashion industry what it has never had and always yearned for, social acceptability. Hand in hand, the woman who wears the dress and the man who designs it have become fashion celebrities and leaders of the new pop society.'

The ultimate aim of respectability was gained for fashion when Senator J. K. Javits 'stage-managed the plot' (Miss Bender's words) to have fashion included in the list of arts entitled to federal subsidy. Not bad going, for a seat-of-the-pants business which many consider not just a minor but a minimal art, but then Mrs Javits had been sucked into the pop fashion pages of the propaganda makers. 'Congress supported the proposition that fashion was art,' writes the trenchant Miss Bender, 'just as the critics who dissented from pop art were lamenting "the transformation of art into fashion".'

Thus was dress built into a prime necessity for social climbing in America. The wardrobes of public figures were dissected with extraordinary ease because so many of the suppliers, if not the customers, were in on the game and did not dare to be left out. In 1969 the *New York Times* could report with authority that Mrs Richard Nixon had spent $19,000 on American designers' clothes, which included twelve dresses from Adele Simpson, two from Geoffrey Beene at about $800, five from David Kidd of Marquise, ten from Harvey Berlin, ten from Malcolm Starr for $2,000 and twelve from Countess Alexander. There is also mention of forty-five dresses for the Nixon daughters from Mignon, and so far as anyone knew (went on the report) the President's wife had made no European purchase. She gets her reward further down the column: 'She's slimmer than Mrs Kennedy,' enthused one Larry Croen of Marquise, who perhaps had not had the pleasure of the patronage of the First Lady who had been the fashion goddess of America until she fell from popularity, carrying short white gloves, black patent pumps and pillbox hats with her. It is hardly surprising that with your intimate fitter ready to betray your size most women should prefer to co-operate, but real trendsetters they could never be called, because they wore the digested styles of others. Even when fashion began to come from the streets, and they wore that too, it was not the American streets.

Europe, of course, had less need to create a fashion aristocracy for other people to try to emulate because it already had a much more distinctive class system. From the turn of the century, Paris had been accustomed to dress, discreetly, very grand ladies with ancient and aristocratic names and, much more extravagantly, very grand demi-mondaines such as Gaby Deslys and Ida Rubinstein. Cecil Beaton's descriptions of these ravishing creatures arriving, with matching borzois, in the Bois de Boulogne in full afternoon toilette are unsurpassed. After the First World War international society flocked into Paris and one has only to pick up any book of memoirs or any novel, or indeed read almost any reference, to realise how obsessive was the interest in clothes. We have Lady Diana Manners, too poor for the real thing, sticking a pin into her splitting home-made copy of a Lucile model. We have Barbara Cartland recalling how useful were the second-hand shops which sold famous-label clothes to those with pretensions but no cash. We have Mrs Reginald Fellows wearing Schiaparelli's silly hats and we have Emerald Cunard looking 'like

Pavlova in white . . . and Honour in cyclamen with her rubies' (Sir Henry Channon).

When two wars had decimated European society and the Americans were creating their fashion aristocracy, both Paris and London produced a new jeunesse dorée whose members, if not exactly trendsetters, because they were intimately connected with the fashion world were certainly the prototypes for trends with a world-wide following. Marisa Berenson and Louise de la Falaise (an extremely grand French name) were indispensable for any smart party in their latest St Laurent outfits. Twiggy, Bianca Jagger, Penelope Tree and a host of designers, photographers and hairdressers were international fashion figures, all involved in what had become a commercial explosion. The fashion phenomenon was at its height. Even the Roman Catholic Church was infected by the need to look trendy, to acquire the key to the kingdom of style, and nuns in the 'sixties were dressed by Christian Dior, Sybil Connolly of Dublin and, in New York, by Bergdorf-Goodman.

With hindsight, however strange it may have appeared at the time, this was mainstream fashion. With hindsight, too, it can be seen how few designers produced work which was seminal and how few out of the close-packed ranks of the fashion industry were true innovators. Of most it can be said that 'ils fumaient les bouts' of the great.

Despite the apprehension of the correspondent in the Rational Dress Society's *Gazette* quoted at the beginning of the chapter, ever since fashion began to wear the mask of a tyrant there have been groups who have been determined to deny its authority. Their initial motivation was that of health and hygiene—even the promotion of trousers for ladies, begun by Mrs Bloomer in 1851, had these in mind as well as common sense and comfort. Madame Dieulafoy had been clad in something called a 'masher suit' for her mission to Persian women, and the ergonomic and practical aspects of her dress persuaded the Shah to receive her against his original feeling that she was in masculine clothes. In 1889 the publication *Woman's World* had run an article on Women Wearers of Men's Clothes, records Stella Mary Newton in her book *Health, Art and Reason*, adding that Joan of Arc was the most famous example. I would be less certain about that. Joan of Arc's dress was unique in her time and was the product not of fashionable motivation but of dire necessity. George Sand, on the other hand, dressed as a man because she wanted to. There is also the problem of just what is man's dress and not woman's? Trousers are not the deciding feature, after all, since they are worn by women all over the world as part of their traditional costume, and the trousers worn by the leader of the dress reform group in England, Viscountess Harberton, are described on one occasion as being of black satin, cut to the

94

Turkish pattern, and worn with a black velvet jacket and white satin topcoat. This formidable lady's outfit was completed with a riding whip, which may have given her views more point.

As far as one can tell, the adoption of male dress in whatever proportion did not at this time carry connotations of lesbianism. The publication of *The Well of Loneliness* by Radclyffe Hall (a book which caused infinite scandal at the time and whose greatest impact on a modern reader must be one of wonder that any parents could be stupid enough to bring up their child in such a way without expecting frantic consequences) was fifty years away (1928) and the relationship described by Nigel Nicolson in *Portrait of a Marriage* was still forty years in the future, and in any case was to be known in detail to very few people.

In 1881 the Rational Dress Society was formed (there was already a Dress Reform Society) and in 1884 the International Health Exhibition in London included among its drains and its 'illustrations of all that must affect the welfare of the people, not forgetting the poorer classes', a very popular section on dress. The poorer classes flocked in to see Lady Harberton's Dual Garmenture, which was a divided skirt worn under an ordinary skirt of almost the same length. By far the greatest interest in dress reform, though, was concentrated on what went on underneath the dresses—on underwear and on corsets. Mainly the interest was in hygiene, though the aesthetic aspects were recognised by E. W. Godwin at the Health Exhibition when he said that 'without a warm and reasonably tight-fitting bifurcated garment such as that known as combinations the characteristic beauties of classic dress cannot be realised' in cold, dirty England, even though all agreed that classic dress was far to be preferred to the ostentatious and unhealthy extravagances then in fashion.

Curiously, in spite of the very obvious damage done to the physique by corsets, which were far too tight and which imposed a distortion on the body, they were not totally condemned. Moderately tight lacing which released the blood from an inactive locality and left it free to be used in the brain and elsewhere had its champions as late as 1888, but the exposure of this advocacy by distinguished members of the medical profession caused a frisson among those whose blood was already circulating to their brains and elsewhere very nicely, thank you.

The most famous name associated with dress reform is that of Dr Gustave Jaeger, whose theories on the wearing of wool had been printed in 1870 (**60**). To adhere to the total Jaeger concept meant real dedication and a real breakaway from fashion, since clad in wool alone you could not go to Court or to many other festivities. Nor could you have looked very lovely in undyed stockinette, complete with digital socks (though those same socks, gaily coloured, were to form part of the ethnic dress revival of the mid-seventies, when they were hailed as coming from South America and not Dr Jaeger at all).

Since these reforms were implemented by high-minded and humanitarian people, it is perhaps not surprising that the first ideals of humanity and species conservation in regard to fashion made their appearance at this time. At the turn of the century, it is estimated, upwards of 200 million birds were being killed each year for their feathers, often by methods of the greatest stupidity and brutality. For example, the wretched white heron, or egret, was regularly slaughtered on the nest or in the breeding season, leaving chicks to starve and die out, because it was the bird's marriage-dress plumes that fashionable ladies demanded.

America was ahead of Britain in the execution of protective legislation, perhaps because America was herself a supplier of plumage and thus a loser from the depletion of species, while Britain was merely an avid receiver of the plunder. Queen Victoria, it is true, was quick to see the scandal of wholesale destruction for no other purpose than self-adornment and in 1899 countenanced the order to discontinue the wearing of 'osprey' by officers of the British Army. In 1906 Queen Alexandra allowed the Royal Society for the Protection of Birds to state that she herself never wore ospreys, and disapproved of such decoration. But in America as early as 1869 there had been an order for the preservation of sea-birds, entire colonies of which were being wiped out to provide the trimmings for hats. Even at this date the repercussions on the ecological cycle of such thoughtless actions were being discussed.

In 1902 Britain forbade the export of all wild bird skins and feathers from British India, but Lord Avebury's efforts in 1908 to introduce a plumage bill in the House of Lords was stifled in the House of Commons. It was not until 1921 that England assumed a serious protective rôle towards birds, and by then, as must be remembered, feathers were out of fashion: so much for humanitarian principles. In America the Lacey Act of 1900, which put protection in the hands of the US Department of Agriculture, had had teeth.

Perhaps the most interesting point about this early concern with the creatures at man's command was that it stopped at birds and did not include the protection of endangered species of animals, many of which were hunted by equally shortsighted and disgustingly inhumane methods. The only explanation which springs to mind is that feathers were after all totally unnecessary, no more and no less than articles of adornment, superfluous to the fundamental needs of dress; leather and skins on the other hand, like hides and tusks and shells, had not yet been produced synthetically by the chemists and so were not available in alternative, plastic forms. At the same time, the climate was less controllable by sophisticated heating methods, and many actions, travelling for example, exposed the person to discomfort and even danger from exposure. There was thus a practical argument for retaining furs and skins which did not apply to wearing egret plumes on your hat.

The earliest figure associated with the idea of animal conservation must be the enigmatic, not to say ambiguous, figure of Archibald Belaney, who was known to the world as Grey Owl and assumed by the world to be a Red Indian. In fact, although he said he was born in 1888 in Mexico, the man who turned out to be his father was both English and in England at that time. Belaney had gone penniless to the New World, led a life as a trapper which included what some might think equivocal relationships with various women, was adopted by the Ojibway tribe, revolted against the cruelty inherent in killing his beloved beavers, and lived on to preach the ideals of humanity and conservation to the most distinguished audiences. He died in 1938, a revered figure whose befeathered profile decked the first anti-trapping advertisements. How, wondered Grey Owl, could any woman wear a fur knowing that it had come from a creature which had suffered agony in a gin-trap? Still women sported the rarest furs regardless.

Fashion, as those who followed its mainstream soon found out, is a hard master. When you think of the hours of female effort spent until quite recently in achieving a pair of navy-blue shoes and a matching handbag or some such similar 'essential' it is perhaps not surprising that it took so long for the new performers to appear. For nearly seventy years fashion held a large section of society in a thrilling grip; attempts to break away were confined to a few raffia-belted and besandalled 'simple-lifers', although possibly all those fancy dress parties and charity pageants which were such a feature of life before 1939 were symptoms of a desire to escape from an inflexible mould.

In the mid-sixties, however, young people began to opt out of mainstream fashion in a big way. Pottering about the ancient world and the amazing Orient, they once again used beads to symbolise their peaceful intention, only this time they were wearing them, not giving them away. With fluttering ethnic robes, djellabahs, ponchos, kaftans, moujik shirts, Mao tops, blue denims, with flowers in their hair and little on their chests (Rudi Gernreich's topless bathing suit had appeared in 1964), they were viewed by the rest of society not as reformers but as drop-outs, hippies, flower-children and for the most part as irresponsible (**75**). Certainly the motivation behind their clothing was not hygiene, since many of them were overtly dirty. But then they had been brought up, especially in America, in an era of manic cleanliness. Nor can their garments be seen as practical. Modern mainstream fashion, the Cour-règes shift, the high-style place of trousers for women, Yves St Laurent's 'dual garmenture' of tunic dress over pants which in 1968 transformed the potential of bifurcated netherwear for the pear-shaped, all this was practical. Sweeping the dirty pavements with a long, flower-printed cotton skirt, struggling for your bus ticket through a layer of shawls, hitching up the togas of a Buddhist monk, was not.

If not practical, and not hygienic, what was it? Arguably, a protest at the materialistic, plastic-minded society which ruled the world and looked set to desecrate the planet by its unheeding use of resources, its pollution of the upper, middle and immediate air and its careless slaughter of man, beast, fish and flower. These oddly dressed figures wanted no part of the space race and the fights of governments. They wanted hand-crafted things, fashion which was the antithesis of chic and ephemeral, ancient things with a past and therefore a future. It was a rejection of the machine age as strong as the Aesthetic Movement's rejection a century before of the colours and the standards of brash Victorian prosperity.

Human nature being as adaptable as it is, and as bound on survival, very soon the less outrageous principles of breakaway dress became mainstream fashion. The little office dress, which in many businesses held at bay even the mighty trouser vogue of 1968, is now likely to be a sweeping velvet or print skirt hung over with a jangle of Moroccan beadery and a macramé belt. Natural fibres are high fashion because they are felt to be biodegradable and recyclable. Popular reading includes *Only One Earth*, *The Care and Maintenance of a Small Planet*, by Barbara Ward Jackson and René Dubos.

The most effective indication of reform has been the inspiration of legislation against the sacrifice of rare creatures for adornment. The fur trade in particular has been revolutionised. Conscientious furriers imposed first a voluntary ban on endangered species, and conscientious publicisers confined their approval to ranched and humanely garnered furs. In 1970 the United States introduced extensive bans on furs, hides (including crocodile skin), ivory, shells. The Brazilian three-toed sloth and the pink fairy armadillo were rescued from their fashionable destiny. In 1972 Britain banned tiger, snow leopard and clouded leopard skins. Vicuna skins were already forbidden.

Certified or not, spotted furs are shown by a designer at his peril. Christian Dior heard the first hisses in the history of the house when they showed big-cat coats in 1970, and even the Italians, who have always seemed to have a vivacious disregard for wildlife, now allay the fears of couture-going journalists with announcements about the origins of their furs while the cynical wonder what would happen if you appeared behind the scenes with a roll of notes. The pressure of public opinion has done nothing but good for the design of furs, since it has focused attention on originality and make, because the furrier can no longer simply display the miracles of nature; most of them are embargoed, thank goodness. The spin-off has been the invention by the synthetic-fabric firms of materials which in some cases so closely resemble real furs as to be almost indistinguishable. This direction in fabric design has been much supported by the wildlife preservation societies, which seems odd. Surely it would have been better to render the whole idea of wearing anything which even faintly resembled an endangered pelt unfashionable and unthinkable. Presumably the organisations concerned bowed to a weight of public opinion registered in the less conscientious mass market, and opted for a 'better to marry than burn' policy. Furs are the main area in which minority groups have made a significant change in fashion.

How ironical it must be for Grey Owl, or Archie Belaney as he is presumably known in the happy hunting ground where no secrets are hid, to think that legislation whose seeds were sown by him has been enacted on behalf of his animals and yet been unable to save an equally endangered race, the Indians by whom he was adopted. Ironical too that, while the rights of animals were recognised in 1970, it was not until the publication the following year of Dee Brown's definitive history of the American Indian, *Bury My Heart at Wounded Knee*, that majority concern was galvanised for the plight of the hapless redskins, and not for a further two years that the long-dead chiefs could look down on a new warrior champion in the form of the movie star Marlon Brando.

JAEGER'S SANITARY STOCKINGNETTE COMBINATIONS
PATENTED.

BENGER'S MAKE.

Guaranteed pure Sheep's Wool,

FOR

MEN, WOMEN, AND CHILDREN.

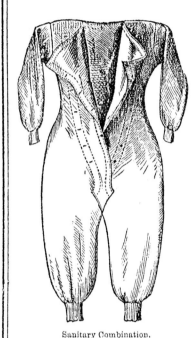

Sanitary Combination.

PRICES.

Sizes	1.	2.	3.	4.	5.
Winter Quality B	15/9	14/6	13/3	11/9	11/3
Summer ,, K	17/3	15/9	14/6	13/3	12/6
Extra ,, KK	20/-	18/6	17/3	15/9	15/3

The Combination Under-Garments will be found particularly convenient for Ladies, and have been widely recognised as agreeable and practical to wear.

Recommended in the *Medical Record*, 15th Aug., 1881.
,, ,, *Medical Times*, 30th July, 1881.
,, ,, ,, ,, 15th Sept., 1881.
,, ,, *Draper*, 1st July, 1881.

JAEGER'S SANITARY STOCKINGNETTE COMBINATIONS

FOR BATHING

REGISTERED.

With short sleeves and legs, fitting close, with girdle.

60. Dr Gustav Jaeger's basics from an 1885 catalogue, issued after their extraordinary success at the 1884 Health Exhibition. Combinations provided all-over protection in wool stockinette and were double-fronted to conserve the 'sanitary emanations of the body'. Also in the catalogue were similarly fabricated shirts, vests, pants, hoods, corsets and dresses, for men, women and children were equally at risk. Such clothes were very popular with intellectuals and dress reformers and the young Bernard Shaw was almost a walking advertisement to their efficacy. Jaegers changed their image in the late 1920s and became a fashion store, while 'combs', having descended to the village trade, provide the outdoor worker or the rheumatic with the cosy comfort of wool next to the skin.

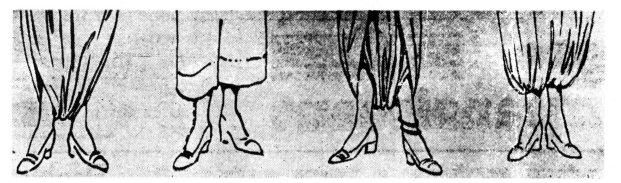

61. Wearing the trousers, the first-ever couture designs for the New Woman by Paul Poiret. They were launched against a noisy chorus of mingled acclaim and blame at the Auteuil races in 1911. Poiret suggested an oriental version, more or less bag-shaped, which fell in gentle billowing folds intended for evening and informal wear. Bechoff-David concentrated on wide and divided skirts for outdoors. The artistic and avant-garde wore them for the evening and during the 1920s they were increasingly adopted for sports and leisure.

62. *Aglaia,* the journal of the dress reform movement, illustrates its view of correct dress for ladies in 1893. The dress reformers of the mid-nineteenth century had deplored on aesthetic and hygienic grounds heavy clothing, tight corsets and garments which squeezed arms and hampered legs, so they devised an alternative based on classical and mediaeval modes. By the late nineteenth century English reform dress had been regularised into something approaching the dress of the Regency and could easily be purchased from the Artistic and Historic Dress department of Messrs Liberty. The preferred colours were the soft, muddy tones of Gilbert and Sullivan's 'Greenery Yallery, Grosvenor Gallery' and the materials were soft-draping 'Liberty' fabrics. The sketch is by Walter Crane.

63. Raymond and Isadora Duncan set up a colony of neo-Hellenists in Paris before the First World War. According to the comment in *Bon Ton* of 1920, from which this illustration is taken, they considered themselves a living expression of the 'rêve de Beauté'. Raymond anyway persisted in his tunic and toga, his hand spinning and weaving, but Isadora occasionally exchanged the classic robes of the truly liberated for the more sophisticated and seductive simplicities of Paul Poiret.

64. A presentation at Court, 1905, an occasion which marked the recognition of the socially acceptable. The 'debs' wear what was probably their first grown-up evening dress, conventionally pale. Though the designs vary, the feathers, train and bouquet were obligatory for all the ladies presented. *(Sketch)*

65. A dress that never was. This Court outfit designed by Mainbocher (1890–1977) in 1938 is a cross-cut, not very daring evening frock, worn with the three feathers and the veil and absolutely according to the presentation etiquette required by the Lord Chamberlain. A very conventional dress for a non-conventional non-occasion, it was designed for the Duchess of Windsor and she never appeared as Duchess at the English Court. *(Centre de Documentation de Costume, Paris)*

66. The clothes recommended by *Bon Ton* for smart mourning in 1920. Conventions were still nominally strict in France, hence the widow's cap and veil, but the concept was beginning to relax and the line and length are fashionably chic. So many had worn black during the First World War through sad necessity that it is interesting that by the early 1920s Chanel had re-established it as the fashionable colour.

67. Dressed for the Royal enclosure at Ascot in 1937. The man with grey topper and morning coat had his decision made some forty years before; the lady on the right has gone for the Ascot-cum-garden-party. Strange as the dress looks to us, it was actually in the height of contemporary fashion. The lady on the left wears a 'Vogue approved', neat matching dress with coat and hat, stable in a breeze and resistant to showers. Nowadays, of course, it is hard to tell some of the guests from the gypsies. *(Syndication International)*

68. When Princess Mary, the Princess Royal and daughter of George V and Queen Mary, married the Earl of Harewood in 1922, she wore a dress designed by Queen Mary's favourite London dressmaker, Reville and Rossiter. It was a fashionably long-waisted tunic of silver and crystal-beaded marquisette, girdled with pearls and orange blossom and worn over an underdress of cloth of silver. The train, also of silver, was embroidered with the emblems of Empire ranging from the wattle of Australia to the lotus of India. The material was specially woven by the firm of Warners.

69. The romantic bride, Barbara Cartland, in 1927, in layers of gauzy frills. Her dress, long of waist but full of skirt, looks back to the 'twenties and forward to the 'thirties. One of the first fancy wedding dress outfits, it was credited by the *Sketch* magazine to her and by her in *The Isthmus Years* to Sir Norman Hartnell. *(Sketch)*

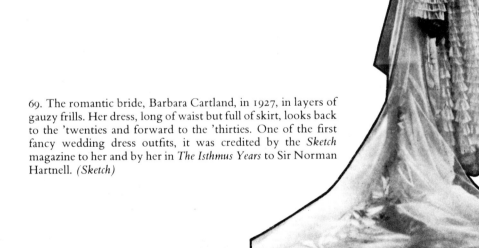

70. Princess Marina of Greece, for her marriage to the Duke of Kent in 1934, wore a dress designed by the patriotically and fashionably acceptable Anglo-French couturier, Edward Molyneux (1894–1974). The dress, simple and traditional, and soon to be widely copied, was a cross-cut sheath with wide hanging sleeves made in specially woven white and silver brocade (the colours traditional for royal brides), and to a design incorporating the rose of England. This is a house sketch from Molyneux. *(John Cavanagh)*

71. The marriage of Princess Elizabeth to HRH the Duke of Edinburgh, now Prince Philip, in November 1947, provided a much-needed excuse for a glamorous royal occasion in tired post-war England. The dress, by Sir Norman Hartnell (1901–), had a heart-shaped neckline, long sleeves and a wide, flared skirt. The silk thread was British, the dress was made from a soft Scottish satin and the train from a stiffer quality of silk; since the occasion was as nationalist as it was fashionable, even the silk worms were British-born, at Lullingstone, Kent. The dress was covered in embroidery, pearls and crystal, Botticelli-inspired. A blend of York roses, ears of corn, syringa and orange blossom, it was, in the words of the late James Laver writing at the time, a 'symphonie en blanc maieur... the occasion demanded a poet'. *(Camera Press)*

72. Princess Anne, who married Captain Mark Phillips in November 1973, wore a dress designed by Maureen Baker, then design director of Susan Small Ltd. It was a high-necked princess line, with a stressed shoulder-line and wide 'Tudor' sleeves, the shape emphasised by rows of pearl-trimmed tucks. The material was 'Annello', a pure white satin specially woven for the occasion at the Sudbury Silk Mills, Suffolk. The train was of net embroidered with clematis trails. Princess Anne wore the same tiara that her mother had at her own wedding. Her bridesmaid, cousin Lady Sarah Armstrong-Jones, wore a pinafore-styled dress of white silk organza with mesh sleeves, and a Juliet cap decorated with narrow white satin ribbon enriched with tiny pearls. The bride's small brother, Prince Edward, wore traditional Highland dress. The groom wore his formal uniform, characterised by the extreme elegant tightness of the trousers or 'overalls'. *(Sport & General)*

73. In Jacqueline Kennedy, the United States found its first lady of fashion. She was fascinated, even obsessed by good dressing. As wife of the President, she patriotically patronised Oleg Cassini, a United States designer though Paris-born, but also extended her custom to Givenchy, Courrèges and Chanel. The top-stitched, understated clothes, the pillbox hat, the sleek pumps and the short white gloves (of which she had hundreds of identical pairs) were widely copied. Her children wear neat asexual coats, purchased from Rowes in Bond Street, which since the 1920s have been the unchanging uniform for all young heirs to fame and fortune. Mrs Kennedy is photographed at the inauguration of the memorial to the late President Kennedy at Runnymede, 1965. *(Keystone Press)*

74. Avant-garde wedding dress of 1969 by designers Mia Fonsagrives and Vicky Tiell, fresh from dressing an Elizabeth Taylor film, *The Only Game in Town*. The wedding dress top is actually a direct copy of the Rudi Gernreich topless swimsuit of 1964 applied to a mini-skirt. But if the dress looks all the more vulgar for being old-fashioned the shoes look forward to the cross-gartered clogs launched in the mid-seventies. The 'groom' (the designer Simon Boyle) wears the soft-style suit of the 1960s when jewellery first became acceptable for men. *(Keystone Press)*

75. The nonconformists of the 1960s retreated to a 'natural' way of life, non-competitive, contemplative or lazy depending on one's point of view. They divorced themselves from artificial aspects of modern technology which, in the case of this couple photographed at a pop festival, apparently covered detergent and shampoo, as well as the Pill. They preferred natural fabrics, the ethnic and the cheap, and turned for their clothes to jumble sale and Indian shop, undeterred by the occasionally over-pungent Afghan jacket. *(Keystone Press)*

Punch

The nature of PREJUDICE

76. A *Punch* cover of 1967 which visually encapsulates the mainstream and the breakaway in dress. The 'city gent'—the Establishment—wears the short black jacket, the striped trousers and the bowler hat which have been the uniform of commercial respectability since the 1920s and are now adopted by the ambitious, emergent Third World. The long-haired 'hippie', with his headband a mark of mourning for the dead of Vietnam, his Afghan coat suggesting a sympathy with the problems of the Indian sub-continent, his sandals and his jeans, carries his bed roll and guitar. He is the nomad, not the man of property. *(Punch)*

Part Two

Special Clothes

5

Royal Command

Even if further evidence were needed that Bessiewallis Warfield Spencer Simpson would have been quite unsuitable as Queen of England it could be supplied by the fact that she was obsessively chic. There is hardly a reference to her in any memoir which does not contain the details of what she was wearing and at the age of seventy-five she was still tripping round publicity parties at Maxim's in Paris, wearing her colour—Wallis blue from Dior. References to her jewellery are even more numerous: 'I led in Mrs Simpson, in a simple black dress with a green bodice and rippling with emeralds, her collection of jewels is the talk of London,' says Sir Henry Channon in his diary; and again, 'Someone at Cartier's foolishly told Bertie Abdy that they are resetting magnificent, indeed fabulous jewels for Wallis and for what purpose if she is not to be Queen?' Barbara Cartland records the frisson generated by the gossip that Mrs Simpson's diamond clips were centred with the huge stones from the earrings left as a personal legacy by Queen Alexandra to King Edward VIII. Certainly her grasp of elegance was formidable, but perhaps her greatest triumph was that she, with her protuberant eyes and froggy mouth, had by the end of her life convinced everybody that she had been a beauty (**82**).

But history suggests that queens who are too intent upon their fashionability come to a sad end, and one could argue a connection between over-indulgence in dress and unsuitability for the throne. Cleopatra, for example, fared badly despite the scented sails, and Zenobia of Palmyra, whom Gibbon lauds as equally lovely and more clever, and whose specific charms he moreover lists in *The Decline and Fall of the Roman Empire* under the flimsy excuse that 'in speaking of a lady these trifles become important', well, Zenobia came apart at the seams when confronted with the nastier aspects of Roman life. There remains of course the Queen of Sheba, whose ensemble or lack of it rocked Solomon to no small effect, but then she, with a spice trade to protect, was a political dresser like Queen Elizabeth I of England. There is surely a rewarding scenario to be worked out as these two formidable dames calculate with their couturiers the exact number of pearls and the exact degree of décolletage needed to get the King of the Jews to back off the trade routes, or to convince the Spanish ambassador that England could fight the Armada. Forget Queen Elizabeth's connection with silk stockings. For a start, she was exceptionally nasty and unhelpful to the poor Reverend William Lee, the inventor of the stocking frame, since she thought his modest machine would put handworkers out of business, and in any case the first pair of silk stockings was almost certainly given not to Bess but to her sad little brother, Edward VI, by Sir Richard Gresham, and poor Edward died miserably.

Marie-Antoinette must be the prime warning of the need for royal restraint. The Empress Josephine was a more than snappy dresser before she fell from the high life, and then there was the extravagant Empress Eugénie, who was said never to wear a pair of shoes twice. Fortunately, her feet were so small that her footwear went on to a charitable after-life, but the Empress herself was dethroned. Elizabeth of Austria led a wretched life watching her son ill handled, despite all those ravishing diamond stars and tulle crinolines from Worth. One must suspect that Mrs Simpson, in her angular Schiaparelli outfits ('She did make some rather extraordinary things'), her little Mainbocher tailleurs and the family jewels, might have had an equally troubled reign.

Since she is a woman of such innate elegance it is of course fascinating to speculate what Mrs Simpson would have done to royal style. Would she have had to dress British—she who remarked, so gossip goes, that the best thing the new Queen Elizabeth, consort of George VI, could do for British fashion was to stay at home? Barbara Cartland relates that with the abdication 'the young decorators who had been busy with plans for modernising Buckingham Palace tore them up'. What plans? To paint over the cream and gold with mauve stripes? And what part did Mrs S have in these plans? Although she later became as obsessive over her décors as she was over her clothes, her taste in her early life in England is assessed by Sir Henry Channon, who moved in the right circles, as banal. 'She invited us for a cocktail at Bryanston Court where she was living in a dreadful, banal flat.' It is hard to imagine the Duchess of Windsor tolerating anything banal or dreadful. Perhaps her influence would have been all for the best, and might have established England as a centre of couture long ago. After all, not only the chic fall heavily. No-one could accuse the poor last Tsarina of Russia of being ultra-smart, and she perished in a cellar.

By far the most interesting aspect of royal dress must be its advance towards and its retreat away from ordinary high fashion, for in retrospect it can be seen that the monarch and the mortal have come together and grown apart again in their dress in elliptical curves which met in or around the reign of Queen Alexandra and have ever since been getting further and further away from each other. At the point when the monarchical system was both widespread and apparently secure, when the constitutions were established and the inheritances fixed, royalty could afford to look ordinary. At every other time their special nature has had to be implicit in their dress. A king must be recognised, so only he may carry certain accessories; his status must be upheld, so only he may wear certain clothing; he must have ready access to finance, and diamond buttons are easier to move than a deposit account; he must overawe potential enemies with an exhibition of the national wealth—what was the Field of the Cloth of Gold but a sartorial expression of what was in the coffers? There is a mystical significance attached to certain items, particularly the crown or head-covering, worn even in battle, for if kingship denotes power it also denotes sacrifice; the king must die that his people may prosper.

By the time of Queen Victoria it was not necessary for the king to die, since that dubious prerogative had been delegated to others whose demise would not disturb the delicate balance of international power. Kingship was at once less necessary and more emotive. The warrior had become a symbol, the statesman was turning into a cypher. Aware perhaps of this increasing irrelevance, the people of Britain railed at the frumpy old queen in her mourning weeds and wanted more, not less, indication of kingly pose in her dress. They were right. In 1880 there were fifteen monarchs on their thrones; currently there are only six. The British wanted their monarchy secure in appearance as well as in position.

Queen Alexandra has the dubious distinction of being regarded as the last royal fashion leader, which in the context of this book is tantamount to saying that she reflected a society so secure that she could expect and afford to dress as any other highly privileged woman might do (**77**). She still had ideas of her own, being, for example, more humane than many of her contemporaries; in 1906 she permitted the Royal Society for the Protection of Birds to use her name in support of their campaign to limit the slaughter of rare species. Forced to dress British for patriotic reasons, she ordered her trousseau from Christian and Rathbone of Wigmore Street and thereafter was faithful to Redfern, who, since he had a Paris branch, was presumably somewhat au fait with the niceties of Continental cut. Every now and then the Queen escaped to Paris itself and then she could be found in Doucet, employer of Poiret, or in Fromont in the Rue de la Paix. Queen Alexandra was divinely beautiful and sweet-natured, with her cloudy frizzy fringe, her deafness and her unpunctuality, and she was loving in the face of the most hurtful infidelities. But she had spark, too.

Proffered some bizarre historical costume for her coronation, she replied to Sir Arthur Ellis: 'I know better than all the milliners and antiquaries. I shall wear exactly what I like and so will all my ladies. Basta!'

The Prince of Wales, who was to reign briefly as Edward VIII, must have longed to say the same thing when he was confronted with his rig for his Investiture at Caernarvon Castle in 1911. Aged seventeen and a midshipman at Dartmouth, the unfortunate youth was paraded before his loyal subjects 'in white satin breeches and a mantle and surcoat of purple velvet edged with ermine. When he first saw this costume, which he later called "fantastic" there ensued what he has described as a family blow-up,' wrote Frances Donaldson in her book *Edward VIII*. 'He complained that whereas the costume of the Garter was historical this preposterous rig would make him a laughing stock to his friends in the Navy.' Queen Mary, his mother, knew better. Since the whole Investiture had been dreamed up by the arch-enemy of inherited privilege, David Lloyd George, whose Celtic empathy with what people wanted saw him through a political life of considerable achievement, she, consciously or not, absorbed the need for a king in future to look less like everybody else's nicest uncle and more like a king.

It was indeed Queen Mary who first led the curve of royal dress away from contemporary fashion. As a girl, she had been conventional and subservient to a rôle which exposed her to engagement to two brothers in succession, the Duke of Clarence and then the Duke of York. The betrothals were not initially to do with the heart, although George V grew to love her so that his voice would crack when he got to such passages as 'when I think of all I owe her'. She owed him her style of dress, immutable as the seasons, a very rock of princely clothing, while all around her thrones exploded. Her long dresses, her toques, her parrot-headed brollies and her button-strap shoes became in her lifetime the symbols of something admirable and enduring in the British monarchy, but they bore no relation to what everyone else was skipping about in (**83**). She wore long gold lamé by day (Queen Alexandra had had quite an eye for spangles, too) while everyone else was wearing the briefest jersey. She was never seen in the cloche, which might have concealed the increasingly regal features, and what she wore gave absolutely no clue either to the charm of lack of it in her figure—everything was loose and straight up and down—or to her emotions. It is said that King George looked at all the sketches sent to the Palace by the industrious Mr Reville and Miss Rossiter, and only those he approved were ordered.

As a girl, Princess May of Teck (as Queen Mary then was) was dominated in her choice of clothes by lack of cash and by her mother's advice. In *Shops and Shopping* Alison Adburgham records that the Tecks, who lived at White

Lodge, patronised a London dressmaker, Madame Mangas, in her 'tiny pied à terre in Mount Street' for their town clothes but that Princess May had her everyday things made by the local dressmaker, possibly a Mrs Mason, in Kingston-on-Thames. Bonnets, considered by Mama to be very smart and not too expensive, were provided by Madame Valentine Meurice, and the bride included in her trousseau sensible things from Linton and Curtis and from Scott Adies (who had satisfied Queen Victoria's passion for tartan as well as that of her family). By now she had moved up to Redfern, though Madame Mangas got in on the act with one or two items. Describing her own ensemble for dinner at Osborne, Princess May, now the Duchess of York, uses the word 'tidy' of her tiara'd and otherwise bedecked person. It is easy to see the adjective as family shorthand or as a joke, but in view of Queen Mary's future fashion rôle it is possible that she meant what she said. She looked the part.

His long apprenticeship for the throne gave Edward VIII plenty of time to investigate fashion, which he did to his father's exasperation. George V, who had a sense of chaff many less sensitive young men would have found hard to take, laid traps for his dapper little son about which decorations were worn where, and fussed about his clothes. The Prince, who as a child had had the traumatic experience common to nanny-kept infants of having his trouser pockets sewn up—was it terror of masturbation or terror of the look of idleness, one wonders—went in for odd hats, Fair Isle sweaters, the Windsor knot to his tie and wearing his top hat at the wrong angle. This last put him out of court with his own set, for it was the irredeemable mark of the cad. He pioneered the cutaway collar and had the trousers of his suits made in America. He was, in fact, passionately interested in clothes, as his book *Family Album* shows. Published in 1960, this innocuously titled volume, which one would expect to be filled with sepia snaps and sepia vignettes of his relations, is in fact an extended essay on contemporary and historic dress for men, illustrated at first hand by the Duke's own preferences and those of his family.

The Duke opens his fashion notes with the letter from Queen Victoria to Edward VII, then aged ten. 'Dress,' she informed this incipient hedonist, 'is a trifling matter . . . but it gives also the one outward sign from which people in general can and often do judge upon the inward state of mind and feeling of a person; for this they all see, while the other they cannot see. On that account it is of some importance particularly in persons of high rank . . . we do expect that you will never wear anything extravagant or slang, not because we don't like it but because it would prove a want of self-respect and be an offence against decency, leading as it has often done before in others, to an indifference to what is morally wrong.'

From which the Duke concludes that clothes make the prince. In her

biography of him, Frances Donaldson writes: 'Another of the Prince's personal qualities which was to emerge at this time [he was at Oxford] was his
extraordinary interest in clothes. Later generations have learned that a fondness for personal adornment is a leading masculine characteristic held in check
for a short time at the beginning of this century by the unnatural fashions of
the day; but the Prince had an interest in clothes far deeper and more extensive
than a mere desire to dress himself up. . . . His personal tastes were for
informal clothes and he liked bright colours and large patterns. Some people
thought his taste very vulgar and first among those to whom it made little
appeal was the King.' Lady Donaldson refers to the Duke as 'returning
compulsively to the subject of clothes again and again' in *Family Album*. The
Duke himself is at pains to point out in his memoir: 'Let it not be assumed that
clothes have ever been a fetish of mine.'

Family Album is possibly most interesting for the light it throws on formal
clothing of the times; to dine with his parents the heir apparent would don
white tie and tails and Garter Star, which can hardly have made for an intimate
evening, and in the daytime whenever he visited his father he would put on, 'of
course', a morning coat. Coats interested the Duke, and he traces the evolution
of the long-skirted cutaway into the formal morning coat via the portraits at
Windsor Castle. His tailor for forty years was Scholte, and his choice of
rope-soled ankle boots and suède shoes (popularised in the Eastern Empire
during the 1914–18 war), which he wore in the 'twenties, got him looked at
askance for effeminacy in America. Perhaps the most electrifying revelation of
royal dress in *Family Album*, and one which does rather throw doubts on the
Duke's sense of humour, is the passage in which, discussing the charms of the
bearskin, the towering fur headdress of the Brigade of Guards, he points out
that it is 'not as uncomfortable a form of headgear as might be supposed, once
it is properly broken in to the head. I used,' reveals the Duke guilelessly, 'to
keep my head in training for the bearskin, by wearing it in moments of leisure
and privacy during week-ends at the Fort.' Tableau!

With the accession of Queen Elizabeth (now the Queen Mother) royal
fashion found what Norman Hartnell describes as 'its first star'. Combining in
an extraordinary way the greatest simplicity, approachability and charm,
George VI's hard-won bride very soon established herself firmly in the mould
of ikon dressing vacated by Queen Mary. Her 1937 coronation robe (**81**),
executed by the efficient Madame Handley Seymour, a great Court favourite,
is much what you would expect and does not compare with the sensational
design done by Hartnell for Queen Elizabeth II. As Elizabeth of Glamis
moved into the spotlight which had been destined for somebody else had not
that somebody else proved quite unacceptable, Norman Hartnell, probably

116

the most underestimated of English designers, was waiting in the wings to realise in clothes for this adored little figure the nation's yearnings for a stable and visibly different king. This different king, the admirable and nervous Albert, Duke of York, had his ideas on what queens should wear just as his father had done, and indicated to Hartnell that a return to the crinoline dresses shown in the Winterhalter portraits at the Palace would be in order. The Duchess of Kent, who was both spectacularly beautiful and supremely chic, is sometimes credited with the renaissance of the crinoline in the summer of 1938, but in royal memoirs the credit usually goes to the King on behalf of his queen. The crinoline might properly be seen as the last trend set by royalty, since after the interruption of the war there was a burst of bare-shouldered or strapless dresses and bouffant skirts. The small waist, however, was a natural reaction to the straight clothes of the preceding decade and it had not caught on before the war.

The royal tenue had caught on with individuals; Rose Fitzgerald Kennedy, wife of the American ambassador, found herself entangled with her grand guests when they came to dinner in 1938. After the meal, and before the Walt Disney films, the Queen and the ambassadress, the former in pink satin with paillettes, the latter in turquoise satin with the same garnish, were photographed together. Their decorations meshed, and Mrs Kennedy reports rather tartly that in the pictures it is her gown which is rather pulled to one side. She had had other sartorial setbacks in the illustrious set. Staying at Windsor Castle for the weekend, she noted that the two little princesses 'were in rose dresses with checked blouses, red shoes with silver-coloured buckles, white socks and necklaces of coral and pearl'. Mrs Kennedy, however, was in her tweeds, only to discover all the other ladies in afternoon frocks.

Though defeated by Madame Handley Seymour for the coronation robe, Hartnell's turn with the new queen came soon; three weeks before the state visit to France which was to be a major event of the new reign, the Countess of Strathmore, mother of the Queen, died. Hartnell was left with the task of re-making an entire wardrobe for the bereaved lady. He had already wrestled with and mastered the problems of colour which are imposed by the orders and ribbons worn by royalty for full-fig occasions. But what could he do with black crape or, even more daunting, the traditional mauve? A flash of the inspiration of his stage-designing days came to him and he asked whether white was not in order, too. It was, and thus was born the famous white trousseau which took the Parisians by storm (**80**).

The success of that wardrobe, the extraordinary way in which Norman Hartnell understood the people's innate desire for spectacle, and Queen Elizabeth's uncalculated but sure sense of what dressing as a star was all about put Hartnell into a cul-de-sac of design from which he never escaped. One might see it as a very cosy cul-de-sac but one might also spare a passing regret for a brilliant talent which was never allowed to bloom naturally. The demands of royal dress—and they continue to move away from fashion—are tremendous. The need to be seen, the need to be able to sit or stand or kneel discreetly and comfortably, the need to decorate the stage, the need to impose the personality of the wearer and to back up the world's most sensational collection of jewels, all are items in the brief held by a couturier to a British queen. The publicity generated by the royal warrant is more than offset by the time and labour involved and by the endless red tape—which still exists—about who is going to wear what for when.

Hartnell was first spotted by a gossip columnist, or rather *the* gossip columnist—Miss Minnie Hogg, Corisande of the *Evening Standard*. Stuck for copy, she went to see a Cambridge revue and liked the frocks by young Mr H. (Mr H. is now Sir Norman). He then underwent the traditional soul-searing period of indoctrination into the world of fashion, which included being knocked off wholesale by the ageing Lucile and always being stuck for cash. At last came the breakthrough—an order for a high-society wedding dress, upon which if upon nothing else the English like to splash. Like the suit for the Mayor in Beatrix Potter's story, *The Tailor of Gloucester*, the Hon. Daphne Vivian's dress for her marriage to Lord Weymouth, heir to the Marquess of Bath, established the fortunes of its maker and turned him overnight from an innovator into an institution. But then who but he, or Hardy Amies, could dress the Queen in an evening gown for eleven o'clock in the morning and do it with dignity, integrity and credibility?

The growing interest in the monarchy has exposed areas of family life to the media which had previously been closed to them. Subjects generally rejoice at a queen's pregnancy. No comments are made on this delicate subject, however. Although Queen Victoria apparently never wore the crinoline which spanned so many years of her reign, she seems to have concealed her interesting condition from the publicists of the time. Likewise Queen Alexandra, perhaps because the full, loose dresses of the times of her pregnancy would have hidden away an elephant. The future Queen Mary, enceinte in the mid-1890s, would have been an object of interest because of her connection with the dynasty, but then the royal schedules were much less arduous and the paparazzi photographers had not made their appearance. Those revealing frocks of the 'twenties had no royal babies to conceal as the bachelor Prince Charming wound his way through London society, and little Lillibet and Margaret Rose were safely deposited in the nest before the limelight hit their family. Queen Elizabeth II has produced four children without anyone recording so much as a bulge—perhaps she has been fortunate in not having Sir Henry Channon around with his sharp eyes to note in his diary that 'Princess Marina's trailing black velvet tea-gown half hid her pregnancy'. Certainly the author can recall no mention and no picture of an incipient prince or princess.

Royal grief is less private. The unfortunate widows are forced to appear in the full trappings of sorrow and to watch that most unnerving of ceremonies, the carriage of the dead spouse's coffin on the shoulders of a bearer party. Perilous steps are negotiated, impossible lifts and drops accomplished, so far without mishap, while the royal woman stands in black from head to foot and thickly veiled. There is little of the fortitude of 'the King is dead, long live the King' in their garb.

Weddings, on the other hand, have a style all their own. The most publicised wedding of the century was that of Princess Elizabeth to the handsome Prince Philip in 1947. Her radiant dress, provided by the faithful Hartnell, and the charming quality of her personality, allied to the fact that she would one day be Queen, eclipsed all other runners in the marriage of the year stakes. Hartnell knew this and did her proud with a dress which combined just the right degree of magnificence for the daughter of a king but after the years of austerity with a touching youthfulness which was a gesture to her years and her size (**71**). When Princess Anne, her daughter, came to be married in 1973 the choice of a run-of-the-mill wholesale house—Susan Small—to provide the gown raised eyebrows, but the dress was pretty and suitable, though hardly original (**72**).

The place where tradition plays perhaps the strongest part in royal dress is the head. Since time immemorial women's hair had been credited with mystery and power and invested with a special significance—possibly because hair seems to continue to grow after death—and the cropping or revelation of hair has always been associated with vengeance or the granting of particular privilege to the viewer. By 1890 Marcel had invented his wave and in 1904 the German–Swiss Nessler had an improved version called Nestlé, the French presumably being thought smarter. But while royalty adopted the fashionable crimp to the hair they continued to hide it on all possible occasions. Two explanations suggest themselves: the first is that headgear has always had formal indications of rulership, the second that royal dress was again moving away from the contemporary styles adopted by most women. As for those British royal headscarves, they represent surely no more than a natural desire not to appear impossibly windblown when pursuing favourite outdoor sports with a State banquet to go to in the evening.

It is said that Queen Elizabeth I was deeply jealous of Mary Queen of Scots because the latter was very tall—nearly six feet high—and height in women was regarded as signifying superior powers. Queen Victoria never seems to

119

have minded being a little body and wore neat, practical bottines for walking at Balmoral. Edward VII propped up his bulk with high heels, though his grandson Edward VIII, who was small and only half as wide, never resorted to this boost of stature, as he tells us in *Family Album*. The last two generations of royal ladies have, however, been notable for their footwear, which especially in the case of Queen Elizabeth the Queen Mother owes nothing to prevailing fashion and everything to the gaining of a few inches. It is hard to see this as a conscious desire for superiority, and easy to see it as an innate understanding of what being royal is about these days—you must be seen, and if you are five feet nothing high heels are a help. To relieve the pressure on the foot of being so jacked up, the favoured style has a peeptoe, even when the rest of the world was wearing Gucci brogues.

In 1975 the Member of Parliament, William Hamilton, wrote what he called the first criticism of monarchy to be published in Britain in this century. The book is an out-and-out attack on the concept of monarchy and argues in great detail—financial, constitutional, religious, moral, personal—why the present system is unacceptable. The book is marred by Mr Hamilton's anti-feminist prejudices, which reveal themselves in the most subtle and presumably unconscious ways. But it is well argued that monarchy is irrelevant if nothing worse. Mr Hamilton ends his book a frustrated man because through what he calls apathy, or through what others say is the desire for more monarchy not less, the Queen remains entrenched in the English heart. One of the major factors rehearsed before the referendum on whether Britain should stay in the EEC in 1975 was the question of sovereignty. In parliamentary terms this meant of course self-determination, but to the man in the street it meant interference with their Sovereign Lady Elizabeth, by the grace of God mother of four, the middle-aged exemplar of the low-profile liberated woman.

The question most often asked about royal dress is why it appears to be stuck in the 1950s. The answer is that the positions of royal and normal dress are moving apart as the position of royalty changes—which indicates that Mr Hamilton is either right or totally wrong.

77. Queen Alexandra with two of her daughters, wearing full formal dress in 1905. The elegant, elongating line owes much to stout boning and corsetry. Jewels and bead embroidery give a coruscating gleam to the whole figure. They wear the jewelled 'dog-collar' which Queen Alexandra made fashionable. These tight, graduated necklaces, carefully tailored for each wearer, were introduced only in the late nineteenth century. They enhanced the beauty of the genuinely swan-like and had the additional advantage, for the more mature, of distracting from saggy chins and concealing ageing lines and blemishes. *(Sketch)*

78. Princess Marina, Duchess of Kent, at Ascot in 1938. She wears a tip-tilted 'Eugénie' hat of the kind that she and milliner Aage Thaarup launched to well-deserved popularity. It combines fashion and the essential royal visibility with a unique charm, and emphasises the resemblance between the lovely Duchess and her great-aunt, Queen Alexandra. *(Keystone Press)*

79. The Duke and Duchess of York, later Queen Elizabeth and George VI, on their country-house honeymoon in May 1923. Both wear well styled conventional clothes of their time. Elizabeth wears a braid-bound tweed suit, long and loose as contemporary fashion demanded, with a V-necked jumper and the string of pearls which was still the only acceptable jewel for county/country wear. Possibly the suit is part of her trousseau from Mrs Handley Seymour. The Duke wears a tweed suit of which the trousers, neatly tapered to shoe-top length, are particularly well cut. *(Press Association)*

80. Queen Elizabeth the Queen Mother in the gown she wore for the Paris Opéra during her triumphant state visit to Paris in July 1938. Designed by Sir Norman Hartnell, inspired by Winterhalter, and white in accordance with conventions of royal mourning, it was of draped satin trimmed with silver lace and camellias and mounted on a new-style crinoline. *(Original sketch by Sir Norman Hartnell)*

81. Queen Elizabeth dressed for her coronation in 1937. She wears a fashionably cross-cut gown made by her favourite dressmaker, Mrs Handley Seymour. The white satin is embroidered with the emblems of an Empire unchanged since the same symbols, roses, thistles, shamrocks, leeks, lotus, maple leaf, fern and mimosa were used to decorate the Princess Royal's wedding dress in 1922. With it she wore the traditional purple velvet robe with ermine cape and borders, the edge gold-embroidered with the national emblems. It was lined with white satin, more comfortable and just as economical as Queen Mary's compromise in 1911—hers was lined with white rabbit instead of traditional ermine. This drawing was made by Irene Segalla, style artist of the 1920s and 1930s, who made the original publicity sketch for Mrs Handley Seymour in 1937.

The Queen Mother's dress and robe are now in the Museum of London and some of Irene Segalla's work can be seen at the Victoria and Albert Museum.

82 (*below*). Wallis Warfield Simpson was accepted as one of the best-dressed women of her time. For her marriage to the Duke of Windsor at the Château de Condé in 1937, she wore a dress designed by Mainbocher in a specially blended shade, 'Wallis blue'. A two-piece which was so strict, even severe, as to be almost governessy, it was implacably neat, as was the Duchess's style. The only design feature was the tight corselette waist which Mainbocher launched publicly in his 1938 collections. With it she wore a small halo hat—and her underwear was probably blue too. Sir Cecil Beaton was there as friend, guest and the only official photographer, and in this rarely reproduced photograph he has emphasised the essential loneliness of the Duchess in her predicament. He has also, incidentally, hidden her hands, which he considered her least attractive feature. (*Sir Cecil Beaton*)

83. Queen Mary seen in 1949 in her long, form-fitting gown and her toque. She adopted the style sometime during the First World War and thereafter remained immutable through a generation which saw a revolution in dress and society. Invariably and impressively royal from neck to toe, she was not too tolerant of those who preferred more revealing garments. (*Keystone Press*)

84. Three Queens at the lying in state of George VI, February 1952. All wear strict royal mourning, and the traditional long black crape veils perform a very necessary function when a public duty must be performed at a time of private grief. Queen Mary, eighty-six years old, wears a widow's cap peaked in Tudor archaic style and floor-length coat and dress, the Queen Mother a modified widow's bonnet, and her daughter Elizabeth II an updated smaller version. *(Keystone Press)*

85. Formal royalty: the English royal family with the Emperor and Empress of Japan on their state visit to England in 1971. Like Queen Alexandra and her daughters, modern royalty on full-dress state occasions blazes with family jewels, orders and bead embroidery. But, under all the glitter, the clothes are simple and functional in cut, crease-resisting sheaths which usually just zip up the back, entailing a minimum of fuss and maintenance. Built-up shoulders support medals and orders. Queen Elizabeth II wears a straight-cut dress which has the effect of making her seem taller, while the Queen Mother inclines towards the styles of her youth with a modified full skirt and a softness at the neck and hem which with the skilled assistance of Sir Norman Hartnell she has made particularly her own. *(Press Association)*

86. A royal garden party, 1962, and 'regulation' formal summer dress. For the men, morning coat and grey top hat (similar garb is suggested in etiquette books already a century old), and for all the ladies gloves and—perhaps demonstrating a basic kinship of spirit—almost identical floral finery for both the Queen and her lady guests. Fifteen years later the clothes differ but little, for this is the as yet unchanging backbone of England. *(Syndication International)*

87. Charles, the new Prince of Wales, and Queen Elizabeth II at the Investiture in July 1969. The staging of the ceremony demanded a rare skill in the blending of tradition, nationalism and fashion. Here the Prince of Wales wears a crown of Welsh gold, made to specifications laid down by Charles II, designed by Louis Osman and donated by the Goldsmiths' Company, with the uniform of the Colonel-in-Chief of the Royal Regiment of Wales and the robes originally worn by his uncle for the 1911 investiture. His mother is in an afternoon outfit, designed by Sir Norman Hartnell, of pearl-banded gold silk, topped by a Tudor-style matching hat from Simone Mirman. *(Press Association)*

88. An informal royal family at the Windsor Horse Trials in 1974. The Queen wears a strictly 'country' tweed suit, boxy, hardwearing and warm, fashionably acceptable for at least five years either way and with a hundred years of tradition behind it. She also remains loyal to the inevitable country sweater, the single row of pearls and the flat-heeled brogue shoes. Princess Anne, in plaid shirt and flared hipster jeans, American-style imports only recently acceptable to the country scene, is as conventional for the younger set as is her mother for an older generation. Prince Philip looks back to the fashions of the 'fifties in a comfortable baggy sweater and slacks, while Captain Mark Phillips compromises with somewhat old-fashioned drainpipe jeans and a tweed jacket with poacher pockets. *(Press Association)*

6

Menswear

Students of the 'What if?' school might like to ponder what would have been the effect on the British national style if Wellington had died after winning Waterloo and if Nelson had survived Trafalgar. Even a cursory knowledge of their characters suggests that things might have been different if the little admiral had gone on to become the hero and image and trendsetter of an age. For a start, the English might not be so buttoned up—before they were stamped with the dour stiff-upper-lip imprint of Wellington, it has been said, the inhabitants of this island were just as emotional and demonstrative as other Europeans and went about kissing each other with as much fervour.

Without Wellington, would Lord Shaftesbury have needed to pass a law against the use of stolen boys as chimney sweeps? Would school have been less brutal? Would society's attitude to women have been less patronising and paternalistic? Or would Nelson, whose attitude was distinctly adult, have been considered too much in the mould of the wicked uncle to find favour with Queen Victoria? However it came about, even though Wellington himself was quite a dandy, little can have been more depressing in the national style than late Victorian decorative taste and late Victorian menswear.

True, at the end of the nineteenth century men, or some of them, had flirted with the idea of dress reform, with knickerbockers and knee-breeches as special areas of interest. In 1894 a new magazine, *Aglaia*, suggested designs for a more elegant male evening dress which might have got one thrown out of one's club (**89**), and in the same year Mr Henry Holiday's designs for improving working clothes might have performed the same service for the equivalent of the humbler brethren. They were nothing if not effete. In each case, the conventional trouser legs—the hated 'tubes'—were replaced with a neat britch to the knee. The considerations behind these changes were both aesthetic and hygienic. Dr Jaeger was anti-trouser to a passionate degree, stating that 'by leaving the legs too cold, while keeping the abdomen too warm, i.e. by causing a faulty distribution of the blood and consequently an unequal nourishment of those parts of the body, the modern trousers are responsible for the sparrow-like legs and protruding stomachs which are so common with men'.

Unhygienic trousers were, perhaps; unaesthetic, surely not. It is hard to feel that the sparrow-like legs and protruding stomachs appeared to greater advantage in knee breeches than they did tucked into the seemly tube of the trouser leg. Indeed, it would be interesting to know which came first, men less well endowed by nature and fed up with putting sawdust in their calves, who designed something which obviated the chore, or prudish Victorian attitudes to the human body which led them to conceal the legs even of their pianos. During the preceding Regency, men's netherwear had been as explicit as the damply clinging muslins of the women. On the other hand, one could argue that the tighter the pants the less mobile the wearer without risk of a split, so the provocation must have been more a fashionable gesture than a declaration of intent.

The history of bifurcated garments is thought to have begun among shepherding peoples who wrapped their legs and feet in skins and kept those skins in place with thongs cut from the same source. Presumably, the colder and muddier the climate the higher up the legs they twined. By the Middle Ages, stockings made on the separate, seamed principle, or like modern tights, were being worn under tunics so brief that the Church denounced them as lust-provoking. That did not prevent Dr Jaeger, whose portraits at least bely any such scandalous intentions, from advocating much the same lines as the 'hygienically correct ideal' for Victorian manhood. The Iron Duke had long ago been trundled to St Paul's in his amazing hearse, but even so Dr Jaeger's theories on legwear were regarded as too much, or rather too little, for the average man.

Thus in 1900 we find the average man wearing trousers, shirt, front-buttoning jacket of thigh length (the morning coat, with its distinctly aristocratic overtones of the riding coat of the past, was confined to the upper classes), some form of tie or scarf or cravat at the neck, and almost certainly a waistcoat. The most surprising thing is that seventy-five years later the average man is still going about in very much the same amalgamation of garments, and the hottest mid-seventies trend, the breaking down of the formal suit into two different though still toning materials, is a reversion to an even older idea. No-one seems to know just who invented the matching suit—perhaps one should just call it the suit—but a shrewd guess is that it emerged from the uniforms made by the American factories which had been mechanised and geared in design for the Civil War. These factories switched swiftly to civilian clothing and took many of their traditions with them. In England there were men such as Montague Burton to feed the ideas through to the new white-collar class.

Burton set up a retail shop in Sheffield in 1900 on £100 borrowed from a relative, and like others of his date he was both a brilliant merchant and an idealist. The squalor of the trade appalled him, and he was imbued with the wish to raise the standard not only of those who made the clothing but also of those who would be clothed by him. His idea was that neat and well-looking suits, so essential to a man's pride and profession, should be easily available to the masses; but at the same time he rejected the idea of totally ready-to-wear garments because he thought they militated against human individuality. Thus Burton founded that English phenomenon, the cheap, mass-produced yet in a sense made-to-measure suit which was still with us after the Second World War. By then it could be said that Burton's inspiration had become an albatross. The sheer impracticability of making to measure at a price rather than buying in bulk in a really good range of sizes has slowed up design improvement and customer service in terms of stock.

What makes the lack of change in menswear especially surprising is that, while women have usually been prepared to accept some degree of inconvenience for the sake of appearance, men's clothes are dictated by social and economic logic. These used to be inextricably bound up with work, mobility and status. But few people now travel on horseback, trades are still very varied and, if there has been a levelling out of life-styles, why has its sartorial expression levelled out around English outdoor riding clothes of the late nineteenth century? Consider the waistcoat, now an object of fashion, originally a sensible way of protecting the chest under a wide-fronted jacket. Double-breasting meant that when one side was dirty it could be buttoned up the other way (no-one seems to know where sex segregation in buttoning comes from). The tie is the last vestige of the neckcloth, useful for absorbing the sweat and keeping it off the uncleanable silks and velvets of outer dress once people began to worry about such niceties. The suit jacket has or has not vents, according to fashion, though the whole idea of vents derived from the fact that when the longer coat evolved from the cloak and the surcoat some means had to be devised to let you get your leg over the back of your horse. One might have thought that with the coming of the cheap car in 1920, the urbanisation of the population, and the new and radically altered means of transport for the new fashion-conscious man (the bus or the train), all vestiges of the saddle would have ridden off into the sunset. Not a bit of it; at a time when most men have never been nearer a horse than their TV set, to have or not to have vents in your jacket is still a major fashion topic.

The story of double-breasted overcoats is similar. Gentlemen of leisure wrapped themselves in capes and coats, but the workers and the soldiers, who had to have a degree of mobility in a life without central heating, needed an overcoat. Derived from a cloak, whose double thickness in front ensured extra warmth, the coat buttoned across the chest. It still does, when fashion dictates, though it is women who have really come out the losers for nothing is less commodious than a coat which only looks smart fastened up.

Beside the basic shape of men's clothes, the other factor which has remained largely constant is colour. Less black is worn now, it is true, but the average colour in 1900 was drab, and it is drab now. Why? The colour of women's clothes was revolutionised by the introduction of easy-care materials and processes for cleaning, a revolution brought about by customer demand. Men could have darn-free socks, iron-free shirts, shine-free suits, throttle-free collars, but they do not. Even though 90 per cent of shirts sold (and who needs to iron undies and pyjamas—answer, every brainwashed housewife) can be drip-dried and worn unpressed, men remain a bastion of the valeting ideal, even if the valet is home-grown. Then, with so many of the male population sedentary at work, the idea of a garment such as trousers which presents precisely the same area of cloth to be polished by the chair every day is absurd. A full robe would make more sense. It is only in recent years that conventional offices have not looked askance at the executive who takes off his jacket—it is still comme il faut to ask the Chairman's permission to do so at grand committee meetings—yet what could be less comfortable to sit and write in, with the skirt of the coat creased and the arm holes and shoulders strained to accommodate the arms stretched forward on the desk? All these discomforts are compounded by the fact that the favourite cloth by far for the average man remains the traditional woven style, i.e. that with the least amount to give. Knitted fabrics, which offer far more flexibility and ease, are wrongly regarded as somewhat cheap and nasty, and need to be made to look as much as possible like an English tweed or a Yorkshire worsted to find favour with the discriminating male.

Both the slow change and the comparative inconvenience of men's clothes are additionally strange because, if the position of women in society has changed as much as we think it has in this century, it has changed not in a vacuum but in relation to that of men. Is it that the liberation and the new interests of women have been overstated, and does there remain in fact a thumping majority happy to iron shirts and darn socks and take that old grey suit to the cleaners? Having at last begun to temper the climate themselves instead of just adapting to whatever climate males ordained should prevail, are women now going to find that men are impervious to prevailing currents? Is the fashion phenomenon a purely female manifestation? When in the technology-minded 'sixties designers such as Pierre Cardin, Rubin Torres and Rudi Gernreich started putting men into jump suits, battle jackets and Chairman Mao collars and doing away with ties, in fact trying to make menswear ergonomic, economic, snug and modern, it never caught on. All that happened was that the trendies in their white polo-necked evening sweaters were banned from the stuffier restaurants.

The answer is surely that the suppression of change in men's clothes over the last century has been an aberration. Women had more ground to make up, but the position of men has also changed in all sorts of fundamental ways in and out of the home, so we can expect now to see a spurt of interest in male clothes as that in women's declines, followed by a settling down into development at much the same pace. Whether the two lines will ever converge—will it be the kilt or the toga?—remains to be seen.

The classical inspiration for male clothing, based on the observation of nature, is usually argued to be sexual allure or the territorial prerogative—the offer of the safe nest. Depending on the social climate of the time, these two prime factors in dress takes turns of prominence, going in and out like the little figures on a weather clock and charting the temperature.

In 1900 the sun shone benignly on the mature man. Paterfamilias ruled supreme at home, the commercial world was dominated by men who had arrived via years of their own efforts, heads of state were shrewd with age. The Prince of Wales was fifty-eight and not even King Edward VII yet; Bismarck, architect of modern Germany and then Europe, had died two years before at eighty-three. From their sleek macassar'd heads through their grave beards to their neat pointed boots they were the images on which millions of men from vastly different surroundings cast themselves for their leisure moments. Miners changed into suits for Sunday best, and when the Prince of Wales left one waistcoat button undone, through either negligence or flatulence, it was an occasion for a fashionable note. A whole new working class was born—the clerks and the white-collar workers whose aspirations led them to dress in approximation of the boss, not to reflect their trades.

Without any doubt this was the dress of territorial assertion. Having beaten off Dr Jaeger and his mediaeval tights, men were ensconced in the solid and sombre cloth of material prosperity, even if the tenacious doctor had got a grip on their underwear. What those frock coats and morning suits and snug overcoats said to women was that the men who wore them were sure of their possessions in this world, sure of being able to provide a well-appointed nest in which the females and young could be tucked up safely. Trespassers entered upon the hearts and laurel shrubberies of these men at their peril.

Some men wore corsets until the 1914 war, but they must have been intended as a gesture of vanity and self-gratification (or to please their tailors) rather than to enhance the masculine physical allure. It was after all a time when 'ladies' were not permitted to regard sex as a pleasure. There is nothing, though, to suggest that women felt deprived by the eclipse of the male figure. Indeed, being realists they probably preferred the security and respectability which seemed to be promised by the unchanging gear of their menfolk to the elegant and wanton dress of the Regency beaux, which was all too often accompanied by wanton manners. To many, however, the dark suits of the late Victorian period must have been redolent of the suppressed emotions and repressed talents of a life as restrictive as the clothes they wore.

The First World War certainly made men's clothes less formal but it did not bring about a youth boom, perhaps because so much of the youth had been killed. For the same reason the bias of men's fashion did not change from territorial assertion, or status direction, to being more overtly sexy. There was no need. Women outnumbered men now, so those who had fought to make a land fit for heroes and the mothers of heroes were issued with a demob suit so hastily scrounged by the government's agents because of the speed of demobilisation after 11 November (to meet the coming general election) that many of them were shoddy rubbish, and the heroes found themselves clad in the rags of a scandal. Blue, brown and grey were the suitably drab shades chosen for the standard suit which the government then tried to introduce, 'of thoroughly sound-wearing properties to retail at 57/6', with the help of a shadowy entrepreneurial figure, a Member of Parliament called James Mallaby Deeley. To do him justice, Mallaby Deely is said by contemporary observers to have suggested plum as an alternative colour.

Although the First World War had so many incalculable results they were not apparent in the dress of the period. For the next twenty years clothes varied only in details from those of happier times. Men had nervous breakdowns (called neurasthenia), contracted marriages in which sex was to play no part (the Trefusis and Russell cases, for example), went bankrupt on chicken farms, danced and tried cocaine, stood in the dole queue, went on hunger marches and failed signally to provide for their families, all in much the same garments as had for their grandfathers been signally the uniform of provision. Jack Buchanan wore a double-breasted dinner jacket on stage in 1924, and the Prince of Wales, the Pragger-Wagger, had old ladies scrabbling about in their knitting baskets for ends of coloured wool to make Fair Isle sweaters (**97**). But on the whole it was a dull scene.

King George V, confronted with a Labour Government in 1924, rallied like the decent, bluff soul he was and commanded that these new men—not

133

gentlemen, but still the government—must not be embarrassed by the cost of formal dress appropriate to their elevated rôle. Inquiries were therefore made from that most discreet and invaluable establishment, Moss Bross of Covent Garden, whence it was found that a Household, Second Class, Levée Dress could be had for £30 complete with cocked hat and sword. By the next coronation, in 1937, people were borrowing tiaras like cups of sugar and hiring their robes from theatrical costumiers (presumably in stock for *Iolanthe*) at such a pace that the Countess of Dudley was in danger of going improperly dressed until she revealed to Nathan's that she was their own old customer, the delectable actress Gertie Millar.

Meanwhile, back in the Empire things were more solid. In India in the 'twenties and 'thirties conventions were most obviously observable in evening clothes. 'It was absolutely de rigueur to change for dinner. It was only natural to change after the day's work and what was more easy to change into than a dinner jacket. If you did not want to do this then you could "dine dirty", but it was not looked upon with favour.' Remember that India was a country where servants were still in plentiful supply. Reginald Savory recalls: 'If you dined out pre-1914 anywhere in India privately, it was a tail coat, a boiled shirt and a white waistcoat with a stiff collar and white tie.' (Mind you, laundry was removed every morning by the dhobi and returned all ironed and neatly folded in the afternoon.) Savory continues: 'I even remember in the Himalayas where we had to ride about five miles to get from the camp to the station club where we danced, we would ride in on ponies in our tail coats. We'd put our tails into our trouser pockets and trot in and dance there. Then we'd stick our tails back into our trouser pockets and gallop home in tails, white waistcoats and boiled shirts, the lot!'

Having said that men's dress changed only in detail and not in essence, one should not forget to record the two most extravagant of those details, both of which affected the trousers. The first is plus-fours, a garment derived from the rural habit of protecting the lower leg over the trouser with a buttoned gaiter in fashionable circles and at a more humble level with a bit of string tied round to keep the fullness out of the mud. Plus-fours as a new garment began, practically enough, for shooting when that became a 'ranched' sport which included otherwise city-dwelling gentlemen pounding over unaccustomed rough and bristly terrain. It was then found that the same shooting costume was useful for golf, perhaps because chic amateurs found themselves forced to negotiate a great deal of rough, or because golf, an ancient and democratic game, had a tradition of democratic dress, or possibly because the neat stockinged leg gave a better view of the ball. Anyway, plus-fours were worn as part of the casual-look clothes after the First World War and, though certainly suggestive of sports, they were not so strictly classified that the moment the game was over you had to change.

The really amazing detail in the cut of trousers was the style known as Oxford bags. Their zenith, when they hit the ordinary man and *Punch*'s satirical pages, was reached in 1925 (**96**). They were revived for both men and women in 1972.

If outerwear was conformist, the Men's Dress Reform Society, whose founders were the actor Miles Malleson, the psychologist Flugel and an avant-garde gynaecologist, Norman Haire, did its best to make it otherwise by encouraging open necks, sandals and knickerbockers (those knee breeches again). Fabians and vegetarians seem to have been the only practitioners of this draughty style.

The availability of alternatives, or rather their unavailability, no doubt accounted to a great extent for the slow change in menswear between 1900 and 1939. On the other hand, history has proved that unless some superior force intervenes what the customer is asking for the customer can eventually get. Thus when the men's fashion explosion hit the market in the mid-sixties, it found John Stephen of Carnaby Street with the roots of a whole new way of merchandising a man's wardrobe. Until that time, men had bought their clothes from the best tailor they could afford (who carried out their instructions) or from that British phenomenon the multiple tailor, the poor man's answer to Savile Row. In America, they bought from grand English tailors and shirtmakers and topped up their accessories in Italy and France, or bought ready-mades from a highly sophisticated range of fittings at home. On the Continent, nearly all the work was done by individual tailors, from the most elevated to the tiny one-man backstreet businesses where the craft was none the less an art. This highly personalised aspect of the way men dress is one of the reasons why it is so hard to be sure whence new men's styles come; the patrician customer patronises a tailor in league with him, not being dictated to as women are by their couturiers, and the mass market traditionally goes for safety first. Even now, the idea that a neat suit will get you a job and a mortgage dies hard. One trendy boutique owner interviewed confessed to owning one dark suit—to wear to impress his bank manager.

The effects of the Second World War may or may not have been more cataclysmic than those of the First, but they were certainly much more clearly reflected in clothes. It is almost as though the shock of the First World War was so numbing to those who had been in it and so incomprehensible to those who had not that all everyone wanted was to look as though the status quo had been re-established. The atmosphere in 1945 was very different. To begin with, world war was not a new phenomenon; it had happened before. Secondly, although there were fewer casualties, many more people—especially civilians—had been involved. Women, already more emancipated than in 1914, had been particularly active. Whole nations had been galvanised into action to resist the Nazi oppressor and there was a real sense of community between people. Crisis is always a leveller of the artificial barriers of class and wealth and after the Second World War most of the remaining social compartments were either flooded or infiltrated gradually by new blood.

The immediate effect of this in clothes was to give the impression that a lot of people did not want the war to end. It was not need alone that dictated the wearing of British Warms, the duffle coats of the heroic Navy, the cavalry twill narrow trousers favoured by the smart regiments off duty, nor the soft suède desert boots known colloquially as brothel-creepers. A great many men who had been accepted into the previously closed officer ranks during the war found a gentle hint of their service glory useful in civilian life. Also, the suggestion that you had been one of the boys (even if your flying jacket was brand new) gave you an added cachet with liberated girls, who might otherwise have thought you had shirked at home instead of toiling bravely alongside all the super chaps they had been meeting in their war work.

Just as crisis flattened the social barriers, the youth boom of the 'sixties flattened the professional ones. Instead of going into the family firm as a manager, instead of going into the City, young men began to look around for more exciting jobs with quicker prospects. So too did young men who had no family firm and no introduction to a modest clerk's desk in the City. A whole mass of young and not so young men was suddenly projected on a market which was itself changing radically. The idea of what was an acceptable job had largely gone by the board and in any case some of the most profitable jobs were in television and the advertising and marketing media, which had been unknown before the war. Youth was at a premium in these new industries, perhaps because the industries themselves were so young it was felt that youth was needed to understand them. Gone was the authority of age, the stature of the dark suit. The pursuit of youth was on: flowered shirts with flowered ties, jackets off in the office, new creaseproof materials for Atlantic-hopping executives aged under thirty, new lightweight suits for the broiling central heating of modern offices.

Along with the need to look young for work came the need to look young for sex. Before the Pill gave women the chance to be the aggressors instead of the quarry in the mating game (the early 'sixties), most men believed that women liked the solid father figure—at any rate off the screen. The average man washed his own hair in the bath, used unscented talc if he used any at all, pooh-poohed deodorants, probably had scurf on his coat collar and never gave a second thought to his expanding paunch. All of a sudden the ladies were less available; they were not forming proper lasting relationships with good, kind, scurfy men who would provide for them and be henpecked by them in the proper old-fashioned way. No, they were darting off with whizz-kids in foreign sports cars, living with them quite openly, and quite openly having lots more fun than the poor doormat man was.

So how to compete? Now that there were plenty of men around, how to make oneself attractive sexually after years of getting by with the dress of territorial assertion? Obviously clothes were vital, but all the fashionable clothes were suddenly too tight or too short or had no room for paunches and flabby thighs. So began the new romance of man with his God-given shape, a romance which can be studied in health farms and gyms all over the emerged world. The contents of the average man's bathroom cupboard changed too. Alongside the bicarbonate of soda, Dr Scholl's spray for athlete's foot and a mangy toothbrush, one began to find the bottles of Old Spice, of Brut, of Braggi, of Factor for Men, of a whole battery of beauty aids. By 1970, unisex hairdressers were blow-drying and styling and colouring far more male heads than would have been thought possible fifteen years before. There was also a discreet trade in men's make-up, usually labelled with some euphemistic title or some purported therapeutic value—foundations might be 'bronzing tan creams', and night moisturisers 'as used by high-altitude skiers' (some sporting rub-off was deemed masculine). One waited for the moment when a hand cream to alleviate the callouses of honest toil would be advertised: 'as used by the Oxford and Cambridge Boat Race crews'. Estée Lauder, doyenne of cosmetics now, was honest: 'Why shouldn't a man have a little help with his looks too? It gives him confidence when he goes for a job, especially when times are hard.'

For the first time since the war, in the 'fifties and 'sixties there were more than enough men to go round. Having spent so many years conforming to ideals of feminine charm established by men, women got the option on their own sex life; men began to dress to attract a new type of girl, and it seemed for a while that what this girl wanted was not a lover but a son. During the 'sixties the neat, self-confident young woman in her Courrèges carapace was escorted by a very young (looking), slender, boyish type in a velvet or satin blazer, silk shirt, Missoni cravat, hand-knitted Fair Isle gilet, soft corduroy or grey flannel trousers, with blow-dried hair and some pretty jewellery. With his acne and his B O subdued by the new toiletry wonders, he was like a beautiful, caponised chicken—no sexual threat at all. Platonic friendships blossomed, the young of both sexes shared flats in which living together really did mean just and only that. Some thought this preoccupation with little boys was a bore and

137

said so. Mary Quant, deploring the effete and bowdlerised bodies she saw, stated that men 'ought to smell of fresh sweat, not after-shave'. It was as though women who were freed from the necessity of having unwanted children were reacting to this novel situation by falling in love with the least mature adults they could find instead. By the 'seventies the situation had evened out and men, like women, had the chance to dress 'to do their own thing'.

Something else which changed the shape of men's fashion in the 'sixties was the growing tolerance of and sympathy with homosexuality and the changes in legislation affecting it. When the British designer Tom Gilbey showed short swagger-back jackets in 1971 together with little knitted pull-on hats and soft raglan sleeves it was a look which could have been thought equivocal (**105**). By the mid-seventies it raised no eyebrows. Indeed, the most interesting point about the new ways of tailoring for men is that they illustrate that it is wrong to think that unisex clothes means that women borrow from men—we now have unisex clothes but they are derived in fact from women's.

Reference has already been made to the difficulty of tracing the source of men's styles which is a result of the intimate nature of the way men get their clothes made, even now. But there is no doubt that lately most of the imaginative trends have arrived from the young, who have a flair for fashion and who simply create a new look out of their heads. Men's fashion only really began to move when their new spending power enabled young men to buy their own clothes. Now, it is Lurex-threaded evening sweaters for the disco, feudal tweed suits for the pub.

The desire for fashionable and individual dress has gone right through society and is especially noticeable in the determination of unskilled workers not to sacrifice style for practicality. Thus long-haired machine-operators defy regulations and prefer the very real hazard of getting entangled to conforming with their dreary elders, and lads on the building sites turn out to mount ladders and play lunchtime football in high-heeled shoes of multi-coloured leather.

Shoes seem to have a special significance for men. Mediaeval dandies risked falling flat on their faces in their exaggerated pointed toes; a good pair of boots is the fundamental pride of the coster; the right boots are an essential in certain gangs. In the days when wives and mothers bought their menfolk's clothes the lad on the building site would have had, whatever else he lacked, proper footwear.

Despite the influx of immigrants into Britain, their colourful native dress has had no effect on the men alongside whom they work—rather the opposite. The new arrivals soon became as drab or as flashy as their peer group dictated. Ritual costume had its problems, though. In Sheffield, the bus crews refused to work with Sikhs wearing turbans, and when it became compulsory to wear a crash-helmet for motor-cycling those turbans got in the way again.

One of the most intriguing areas of men's clothing must be uniforms. Uniforms embody the two basic criteria of male dress, territorial assertion and sexual allure, to a degree where it is hard to see if or when one or the other is in the ascendant. The First World War, unique in so many ways, was also unique in the drab and utilitarian costume provided for the combatants. Not so long before, the Crimean campaign had provided a splendid opportunity for men to die accoutred in the panoply of regiment and colour. Their sacrificial garments were grand indeed, but unfortunately a great many died not in the fight but from heat or cold occasioned by the unsuitable nature of their dress. On the other hand, that dress was a powerful recruiting agent in the country (for hearts as well as soldiers). In the slums and the rural areas a man had few other chances of dazzling the girl of his choice.

By the middle of the 1914–18 war, recruitment was out and conscription was in, war was no longer confined to the professionals, and a civilian army was not concerned with glamour. Formerly, one of the purposes of designing a uniform was to inspire terror in hand-to-hand combat. With high-powered guns you never got close enough to frighten anyone except your own side. The whole art now was to blend as nearly as possible with your surroundings so that the location of your expensive piece of equipment was not betrayed and you yourself were as hard as possible for the deadly new weapons to pick out. Personal camouflage had arrived. In a war of such scale and which was so unselective in its targets—how does a telescopic rifle know when its target wants to give in?—the elements of humanity and the fair chance were eradicated. When the settlers, in green drab working clothes, fought the British redcoats in the American War of Independence they were considered to be showing bad form, not quite to be playing the game, because they slipped through the green undergrowth picking off the all too conspicuous scarlet-clad troops. By 1914 the slaughter had been nicely depersonalised.

An ironic flash of military splendour in the streets came in the late 1960s when the least martial types—hippies and pacific students—wore bits and pieces of old uniforms in a jumble, garnished with the medals of long-gone campaigns. This manifestation was certainly not the result of pride. It was more likely an expression of sympathy for the draft-dodgers and a gag at the expense of America's involvement in Vietnam (**103**).

Military uniforms are not the only sort. Many groups, whose interests range from Scouting to terrorising the streets in gangs, like to feel that they 'belong', that an affinity of dress makes them part of a larger and therefore more powerful entity. The shy boy welcomes the anonymity of dressing like others, the ruffian enjoys the identification with physical strength that his black jacket and silver-studded skull decoration give him. Some of the most violent gangs have been the most scrupulous dressers—the British skinheads with their obsessions with every detail of their dress (**102**), the American hell's angels in their glittering and deadly gear (**101**). Just as creatures of the same species seldom fight one another and recognise one another by their appearance, so dress protects (usually) members of these cult groups from attack by their peers. Heaven preserve the stranger on their territory though; the very fact that these characters feel the need to pack together betrays, in adulthood anyway, an inability to live at peace with the majority of the community, as we must on our overcrowded planet.

Finally, there is paramilitary uniform, the definition of which is most complex. In 1936 Britain banned the wearing of such dress under a Public Order Act as a direct result of the activities of Sir Oswald Mosley's black-shirted Fascist followers. The Act then seems to have lapsed, but has been revived as a result of violence in Northern Ireland. In November 1974 *The Times* reported the conviction of persons for parading in berets and dark glasses, the dress which signalled sympathy with the Irish Republican Army, membership of which was shortly to be banned. At the trial it was pointed out that such a costume might equally well be worn by a French onion-seller as by a committed political fighter. No-one seems to have explored the even greater complications which may ensue if defendants claimed that their outfits were the new spring line of some well-known couturier. For the legal record, context was held to be the deciding factor.

One point is certain. The suppression of change in menswear is finished for all who want it to be, just as the suppression of emotions is no longer held to be the only key to upright behaviour. Even so, 1976 saw a universal move back to formal dressing, with the two or even three piece 'office' suit the best-selling item in all age groups. After the flowering of velvets and frills of the mid-sixties, when the aggressive emancipation of women gave men a chance to be the more elaborate sex, we seemed to be back at square one. But this temporary regression was not surprising. The economic climate was harsh and jobs had to be looked for and dressed for; women had enjoyed a fling of freedom and were now, in many cases, settling down to a more feminine life, illustrated by their softer, more curvaceous clothes. Above all, the return to conventional suits may be seen as the reaction of men in a welfare state, with a much more permissive attitude to marriage and with an increasing number of women able to support themselves by working. It was time to re-establish the status quo, or paterfamilias might find himself largely superfluous.

89. Evening dress suggested by the Reformed Dress Society. Henry Holiday, who wrote the article accompanying this proposed design in *Aglaia* in 1894, hated the idea of trousers and his concept had something of the eighteenth-century exquisite about it. The young Oscar Wilde wore a similar suit plus a green carnation and it remained a stock variant for the slim-ankled aesthete like Gilbert's Bunthorne in *Patience*.

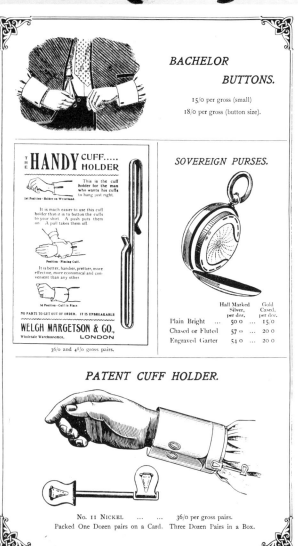

BACHELOR BUTTONS.

15/0 per gross (small)
18/0 per gross (button size).

THE HANDY CUFF..... HOLDER

This is the cuff holder for the man who wants his cuffs to hang just right.

1st Position—Holder on Wristband

It is much easier to use this cuff holder than it is to button the cuffs to your shirt. A push puts them on. A pull takes them off.

2nd Position—Placing Cuff.

It is better, handier, prettier, more effective, more economical and convenient than any other.

3rd Position—Cuff in Place

NO PARTS TO GET OUT OF ORDER. IT IS UNBREAKABLE

WELCH MARGETSON & CO.,
Wholesale Warehousemen, LONDON

36/0 and 48/0 gross pairs.

SOVEREIGN PURSES.

	Hall Marked Silver, per doz.	Gold Cased, per doz.
Plain Bright	50 0	15/0
Chased or Fluted	57 0	20 0
Engraved Garter	54 0	20 0

PATENT CUFF HOLDER.

No. 11 NICKEL ... ... 36/0 per gross pairs.
Packed One Dozen pairs on a Card. Three Dozen Pairs in a Box.

Improved Scarf Securers.

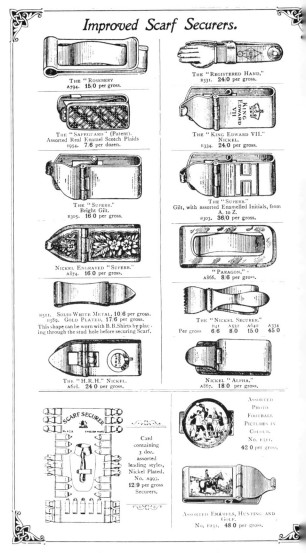

THE "ROSEBERY."
A794. 15/0 per gross.

THE "REGISTERED HAND,"
B331. 24/0 per gross.

THE "SAFEGUARD" (Patent).
Assorted Real Enamel Scotch Plaids
1954. 7/6 per dozen.

THE "KING EDWARD VII."
NICKEL.
B334. 24/0 per gross.

THE "SUPERB."
Bright Gilt.
B305. 16 0 per gross.

THE "SUPERB."
Gilt, with assorted Enamelled Initials, from A. to Z.
A303. 36/0 per gross.

NICKEL ENGRAVED "SUPERB."
A874. 16 0 per gross.

"PARAGON."
A866. 8/6 per gross.

B511. SOLID WHITE METAL, 10/6 per gross.
B589. GOLD PLATED, 17/6 per gross.
This shape can be worn with B.B.Shirts by placing through the stud hole before securing Scarf.

THE "NICKEL SECURER."
B41 A532 A640 A334
Per gross 6/6 8 0 15 0 45 0

THE "H.R.H." NICKEL.
A628. 24 0 per gross.

NICKEL "ALPHA."
A867. 18 0 per gross.

SCARF SECURER.

Card containing 3 doz. assorted leading styles, Nickel Plated. No. A993.
12/9 per gross Securers.

ASSORTED PHOTO FOOTBALL PICTURES IN COLOUR.
No. F511.
42 0 per gross.

ASSORTED ENAMELS, HUNTING AND GOLF.
No. F251. 48 0 per gross.

90. The precise elegance of the Edwardian man was not too easy to achieve if you were not in a position to have everything made to measure. For the average man coping with imprecise ready-to-wear sizing and a workaday existence there were slipping starched collars and cuffs, crooked cravats and popping braces. For him the Welch Margetson catalogue of 1908 provided a variety of helpful hardware. The modern man, with everything bonded or welded into place, does not need even the humble collar stud. (*Welch Margetson*)

91. Pillars of society recorded by Sir Benjamin Stone (1838–1914) outside the Houses of Parliament. These whiskered representatives of Birmingham industry, as respectable and affluent as they could possibly be, are wearing the uniform of the early twentieth-century plutocrat, complete with well polished top hat, high starched collar, silk-faced morning coat, striped trousers and neat shiny shoes. The illustration is from Sir Benjamin Stone's *Pictures*, a selection culled from the thousands of photographs made by this Birmingham businessman, MP and pioneer of record photography.

92. Working men, as recorded by Sir Benjamin Stone at a hiring fair. These three men, advertising their availability for employment by the nosegays in their buttonholes, are wearing country Sunday best and look commendably smart considering the condition of agriculture in Edwardian England and the low standard of living in the rural cottage. Men's clothing was available ready-to-wear in the small towns but was comparatively expensive and paid for after harvest or by instalments. Second-hand clothing, the standby of the town's artisan, was not easy to come by in the country, though the older man in this picture seems to have equipped himself with a warm extra jacket and wears a snug double-breasted waistcoat. The clothes have a rough and ready fit and the trousers, the first part to wear out, do not match. The younger men wear their wedding or Sunday collars but the older the ubiquitous muffler.

93. The smart and sporty from Minister's Report of Fashion, 1910. The suits have long jackets and are worn loose and slightly draped, while some of the trousers taper to a neat turn-up. There is a breezy American flavour to the styles: the turn-up was still avant-garde and controversial since it implied careless dressing and no carriage (a turned-up trouser did not dangle in the mud). The men look comfortable and the turndown collar and even the self-supporting trouser were just becoming adopted. Single or double-breasted, all the suit types we know today were already in existence.

94. The businessman as dressed for 1921–2 by the *Sartorial Gazette*. Ten years have changed the fashion line and the suits are tailored closer to the figure. They are much higher-waisted and the trousers are narrower. The more conservative and professional still wear a morning coat and striped trousers with spats and patent boots, though it was becoming a trifle old-fashioned. For the man on the way up, the dark jacket and striped trousers, later the invariable outfit for the shopwalker, were more correct. For leisure wear and the young and trendy there was the double-breasted tweed suit. Hats and gloves were still almost invariably worn.

95. 1926 and modern man is with us, wearing suits with loose-cut jackets, double and single-breasted, straight-cut trousers and even suède shoes, new in 1926 and still fashionable in 1978. The style was set in the late 1920s and is confirmed by the current taste for reaction and plagiarism. Only the crumple, inevitable in old suiting fabrics, reminds us that this is a cloth of the past. *(Radio Times Hulton Picture Library)*

"GOOD HEAVENS, THERE'S A FELLOW IN OXFORD BAGS!"

"GREAT SCOTT, THERE'S A FELLOW NOT IN OXFORD BAGS!"

"POWERS ABOVE, THERE'S A FELLOW STILL IN OXFORD BAGS!"

96. Oxford bags, exaggeratedly wide-bottomed trousers, came into fashion quite suddenly in the spring of 1925, the first youth gimmick to hit modern men's dress. They were supposedly based on a custom at Oxford University where sporty young men wore wide-cut trousers to accommodate plus-fours which were forbidden by the university authorities. The style spread among the young of all nations, then as swiftly disappeared; perhaps the economic climate of the late 1920s was just a little inclement. But the style left a tendency towards the wider, straighter trouser which lasted until the 1950s. *(Punch)*

97. The sportsman Prince at Muirfield in 1927. Like all the clothes he preferred, his golf outfit is bright, loose-fitting and comfortable. More than any other individual he brought men's knitwear into the fashion field. His pullover is most complicatedly Fair Isle, a trend which brought much-needed additional income to the Scottish knitters, and stylistically interesting—the neck is low and the pockets are a new (and useful) 'steal' from contemporary feminine fashion. He wears plus-fours, a style he did much to popularise. They are no baggier than those of his contemporaries and are in the large Prince of Wales overcheck, a pattern which he himself credits to his grandfather, though his own fondness for it added greatly to its vogue. The dashing Argyle socks and the check cap are a dizzying sight and precede the 1976 Bill Gibb mix and match by almost half a century. (Press Association)

98. The Prince of Wales, formally informal at the opening of the Ryder Cup in 1933. He wears a light flannel double-breasted lounge suit, smart and conventional for the time with its long jacket and wide-cuffed trousers. His panama is a sensible if somewhat transatlantic innovation. Like many men he became set in his ways: even at the end of his life, a generation and a royal world away, he still wore the long, square-cut, double-breasted jackets and the baggy trousers of his young manhood. The hand nervously straightening the tie remained a characteristic gesture. (Camera Press)

"Must be a soldier"

99. Jon's 'two types' epitomised the combatant soldier of the Second World War. They were expert survivors with a flair for adapting Army issue. The pride in individualism and improvisation was recognised by commanders of the quality of Montgomery and Wingate, who found in them the strength and spirit of a citizen army as opposed to an Axis military machine. The extreme climate and conditions of the Western Desert and Italy, where the 'two types' were stationed, made warmth and comfort essential—hence the scarves, the long pullovers and the suède desert boots. After the war the style persisted, providing a heroic top dressing for the struggles of civilian life. (*Jon*)

100. This cartoon of a 1957 barrow boy shows the unappeased post-war appetite for sharp dressing, at first ignored by the conventional tailors. The style originated with the 'zoot suit', which was born in the jazz-mad Puerto Rican slums of the USA in 1941 and which made a delayed appearance in Britain among the Soho wide boys or 'spivs' in the immediate post-war years. The suit's broad coathanger shoulders, loose draped jacket and baggy but tapering trousers were adopted and adapted for the Shaftesbury Avenue style of menswear. It was not the first time that styles had been set by the rough and tough; almost exactly the same thing had happened after the French Revolution. (*Nicolas Bentley*)

'And would you mind also telling me who your tailor is?'

102. 'Bovver boys' or 'skinheads', one of the British youth gangs of the late 1960s, were characterised by their uniform appearance. Their shaven heads, braces, jeans and thick-soled work boots were an exaggeration, precisely studied, of a stereotyped working-class image. Too easily identifiable in case of 'bovver', and hobbled and disarmed by the police who removed braces and boots (clothing and armament), they first blurred their identity by growing their hair and becoming 'suède-heads', then merged unidentifiably with the rest of their contemporaries. *(Camera Press)*

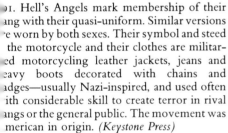

ɪ. Hell's Angels mark membership of their ɑng with their quasi-uniform. Similar versions ɾe worn by both sexes. Their symbol and steed the motorcycle and their clothes are militar-ɛd motorcycling leather jackets, jeans and ɛavy boots decorated with chains and ɑdges—usually Nazi-inspired, and used often ɪth considerable skill to create terror in rival ɑngs or the general public. The movement was ɑmerican in origin. *(Keystone Press)*

103. The Army Game in St Tropez in 1974 was the degenerate end of the army surplus trade—you paid extra for real blood. The fad for wearing ex-Vietnam uniforms and U S army badges chaotically intermingled demonstrated an equal sympathy with both sides and a conscious antagonism to war in all its aspects. More practically the trade has provided generations of young people with cheap, hard-wearing clothes as well as grounds for a healthy cynicism about both the accountability and the accounting system of ministries of war. Those uncom-promisingly against society still cull their gear from somewhat spurious Nazi relics. *(Sunday Times)*

104. The space-age look by Pierre Cardin (1922–), the most relentlessly inventive of couture designers working in France. He trained as an architect and designed women's and men's clothes in the 1960s. These ergonomic jersey suits owe more to the space man of science fiction than to the dress of the astronauts, but the idea makes general practical sense and variations of it turn up in every student show—but not in the High Street. *(Pierre Cardin)*

105. Tom Gilbey (1939–) described himself as the first man's couturier. This young Londoner, who opened on his own in 1967 when he was only twenty-eight, trained as a tailor and matured in the Carnaby Street era. His inventive, easy-fitting, somewhat unisex styling has brought him large design consultancies with European menswear firms. Here, in 1971, he shows the swagger-back coat, the jelly-bag hat, the colourful tweeds and bright knits hitherto only to be found in the feminine market. It amazed at the time but it was the start of a new trend. *(International Wool Secretariat)*

7

Sporting Dress

Before the First World War, sport was the prerogative of Gentlemen and in some instances, such as golf, of Players. Gentlemen (and ladies) were well bred and sporting by their upbringing, and to lose gracefully was counted a necessary quality. Small children in their nurseries were adjured by Nanny not to be a bad loser, and smacked if they showed spite and chewed up the halma board. Britain had the monopoly of top-level nannies and it was doubtless from this that there sprang that fatal national characteristic which has ruined so many English competitors, the idea that it is better to be a good loser than to win, indeed that there is something not quite nice about winning. ('Nobody speaks to the runner-up in America,' reported Billie-Jean King, holder of nineteen Wimbledon titles, in 1974.)

When the Americans appeared to play at Wimbledon just before the 1914 débâcle they were regarded as hopelessly barbaric because they practised for the matches, which other people might not have had the opportunity to do. 'Tennis was played by ladies and gentlemen and all the crowned heads of Europe,' recalls Ted Tinling, the only designer ever to become famous purely for sports clothes; 'it simply was not done to try to appear to win.' Suzanne Lenglen changed all this in 1919. Quite sure she wanted to win, she did away with the cinched waist and constricting neat tie advocated by the formidable Mrs Sterry in 1909. Above all, Lenglen did away with the exhausting and unaerodynamic underpinnings thought indispensable by previous champions. Gone were the decent petticoats which slowed the wearer to a trot. It was all a far cry from the 'tennis apron of peacock-coloured plush' offered free by *Queen* magazine in 1881, which was to be embroidered with 'cobwebs and spiders' webs' (did *Queen*'s copywriter know of some difference lost to us?) and with dainty twigs on the pockets.

It is interesting to speculate whether the reason why tennis fashion has been able to advance is that it is comparatively so modern a game that male domination and the desire to keep women subservient is less well established. It is after all only for a hundred years that cows going in at one end of Chicago have had the option of emerging as a steak or a tennis racket. Like riding, tennis has become one of the great television spectator sports but, while riding has traditions of dress which have evolved solidly since a man first got his leg across the wild brute, tennis—once it had been established that it was all right to try and win—was a virgin fashion court.

Lenglen (**108**) was the first to recognise the spectator needs of a game played on an area so confined in space and colour. She also knew that she was a star and was prepared to dress to please her public, and the public is always grateful for a spectacle. In her early days Lenglen was content with the services of the little dressmaker of French folklore, but when she became well-known she was dressed by the charming and gifted Jean Patou. It was, however, Ted Tinling who dressed her for her re-entry into tennis in 1937, just before her untimely death. 'The world had closed against her,' he wrote. 'She was the epitome of feminine grace, but now it was the Alice Marble image, all shorts and jockey cap, which was fashionable (**109**). Lenglen wanted to arrive at a compromise, so we made her a pleated skirt, front buttoning, over shorts.' Shades of 1971!

Until the arrival of Ted Tinling, players who wanted to be smart patronised an established designer. Eileen Bennett, with rich parents, had pretty things in satin from Molyneux. The disciplines of designing for the game are not all ergonomic. When Helen Jacobs appeared at Forest Hills in America for the Wightman Cup wearing the same as she had worn at Wimbledon she was sent off by Mrs Wightman as not suitably dressed. Queen Mary disliked bare legs, so white stockings were de rigueur at Wimbledon. Perhaps the most famous furore on those suburban lawns, though, was caused by Gussie Moran's lace-edged panties in 1949. Miss Moran, the Gorgeous Gussie, claimed that she had Red Indian blood and she wanted something spectacular, with colour. With his famous tact, Tinling explained that colour was out. With his equally famous flair for the novel he made her a very brief dress with matching panties edged in lace which just very occasionally might be glimpsed as she ran about the court (**110**). In retrospect, the whole concept is unexceptionable, but at the time Tinling was castigated for bringing sex into sport and had he spent the winter sowing dandelions into the turf he could hardly have been held a more dangerous man. Gussie's pants were not even the baby kind with rows of lace across the bottom which 90 per cent of club tennis now reveals. They were just close-fitting knickers with a yard of lace round each cuff. 'I see myself as the

Amelia Bloomer of this century,' said the designer modestly; 'she revealed the instep, I applied the same principle two feet higher up.'

By 1974 Tinling could dress Billie-Jean King, Madam Superstar, in a dress of sheer lace which, although it looked more suitable for tea on the lawn, never came apart as she served her dominating aces. This choice of something so super-feminine by a woman usually regarded as very tough is indicative of another split character. Billie-Jean King, close to, is slight and yielding. In public she is a virago, pulled between the quotes 'In America you've got to win' and 'Women are taught to lose to win. If you're too good at a sport men won't want to love you.'

By 1974, too, sequins and spangles and gold lamé were being worn by tennis stars, who played for the most part under the lights of the indoor stadium and the eye of the TV camera. The new patterns of leisure have transformed tennis into an evening sport which millions want to watch, and the stars no longer want to play in the afternoon. As Tinling explains, from our earliest days we are taught that there is something special about the night, it is a treat to stay up for dinner, and we know that the matinée performance is only for old ladies.

Women's golf clothes were revolutionised not so much in order to allow a competitive spirit as by the relaxation in fashion which came in with Functional Chic. Golf, after all, had been played by women from an early date: Mary Queen of Scots is said to have been gambolling on the links unseemly soon after her friends had blown up Darnley, they had a proper club at St Andrews by 1867, and the Ladies' Golf Union was founded in 1893. Instead of fashion producing designs to accommodate the popular sport, however, the ladies were thrust into all the most uncomfortable bits of men's tailoring wear. Heavy skirts edged in leather clogged their progress, as did the male chauvinist attitude reflected in the remark that ladies' holes were shorter because 'The postures and gestures requisite for a full swing are not particularly graceful when the player is clad in female dress'.

'She would hurry in, eager to be on her way, wearing a heavy circular ankle-length skirt, high-collared shirt blouse and a long, swinging red-lined cape. This was considered the correct costume for the game and we all thought her very smart,' wrote Edna Woolman Chase, describing the wife of her boss, Arthur Turnure, who was a ladies' golf champ in America in the early 1890s. The voluminous garments had some uses, though: the staff of Mr Turnure's new magazine, *Vogue*, were amazed when Mrs Turnure suddenly produced a baby son.

One man who did think women should have a better chance at the game was the tailor Thomas Burberry of the Haymarket. He seems to have been a man most sympathetic to the new female craze for speed and sport, and was forever kitting out the ladies in ulsters and duster coats and mica veils so that they could roar about the countryside in their automobiles (it was recommended to carry a small pistol in the box under the seat along with your necessities) or putting them into unexceptionable divided skirts for bicycling. Looked back at now, the Edwardian craze for cycling strikes us as rather overdone, but it must be remembered that until the advent of the machine nobody could travel faster than he could walk or run without recourse to an animal or to a machine which would almost certainly need another person to power it. The costume for cycling was still a source of comment at the turn of the century (**106**). In L. P. Hartley's book, *The Go-Between*, there is much speculation as to whether the little boy's new bike, a bribe for his message-carrying, will be ridden into the hall by its donor wearing bloomers.

Thomas Burberry's gift to golfing women was the Ladies' Free-Stroke Coat, with Patent Pivot Sleeve and Adaptable Skirt which seems to have been taken up and down on drawstrings. By the time of the immortal Joyce Wethered, who was eighteen in 1920 when she first won the English Ladies' Championship, post-war relaxation in dress and above all the widespread use of jersey fabrics made patent pivot sleeves unnecessary. Miss Wethered was both shy and modest, and it is an interesting comment on the atmosphere of the times that it was only because of the persuasion of her brother Roger, who was captain of the Oxford golf team, and his friends that she ventured into the limelight.

The golf clothes of the 'twenties were both practical and attractive—indeed, one could wear them now, as the picture of Diana Fishwick, the mother of the Walker Cup player, Bruce Critchley, shows (**111**). Her stockings have charming clocks finished with an arrowhead, her cardigan is like those now produced by St Laurent and her skirt, pleated so that in repose it is all patterned and then swings to reveal plain panels, is as pretty as Bernard Nevill's work in the late 'sixties. But for fashion, golf had to wait for the arrival, if that is not too drab a word, of Babe Didrikson Zaharias in 1936. Mrs Zaharias was as different a character from Miss Wethered as you could imagine. A superb athlete, totally extrovert and filled with confidence ('Forget it, I can beat any two players in this tournament by myself,' she told an unconfident partner nervous of spoiling the score), she was the first to wear a tight skirt. She said she liked to be able to 'sit' in it to putt. That this was radical is illustrated by Ted Tinling's story that the golf-skirt buyer for Lillywhites in London used to take all the models offered for her inspection home for the weekend—if she could not get over a stile in them, they were out.

Changing patterns of wealth and leisure produced the package holiday tour,

154

some of the earliest being for winter sports. In 1898 Dr Henry Lunn took a group to Switzerland. No special boots were worn, and ladies who ventured to wear the rational dress of knickerbockers had to run the gauntlet of abuse from the Swiss peasants. Alison Adburgham points out, however, that the canny natives soon learned to curb their disapproval of so lucrative a trade in spite of improper dress. By the time Paul Poiret was epitomising women's desire for liberation, a Mr Symons was making trousers which were worn under skirts by the lady skiers, who removed them (the skirts, not the trousers), handed them to a gallant escort to put in his knapsack, and cascaded blissfully down the snowy slopes. As with golf, it was the war which really freed women for skiing and allied active sports because it made the idea of trousers, and the revelation of legs, acceptable. In essence, all developments in costume since then have been technical.

A sport whose mores have changed considerably is riding. Originally the preserve of the wealthy, to whom a good horse ranked—or perhaps one should say rankled—above most other chattels, including a dutiful wife, riding changed from being a necessary form of transport to a leisure luxury in the space of fifty years. Strangely, the kit deemed suitable for the performance of the equestrian art remained fixed in the Edwardian image, although in the hunting field riding trousers gave way to breeches and boots, a good example of democratic, ergonomic adaptation; gentlemen who had served in India brought back jodhpurs, strange-shaped trousers with narrow nethers and spreading uppers which were seized on by children and by women newly emancipated by the 1914–18 war and the realities of life without servants. Dress for showing and hunting remains formal to this day (**113**), with even ambitious toddlers, inspired by their TV heroes, dressed in fawn breeches, black boots and navy jackets, topped with a 'hunting' cap. Headwear, as traffic and tarmac roads take their toll, has become the major item of a riding outfit but, au fond, little girls on recalcitrant ponies are ensembled on much the same lines as were the farmers who poked at fat cattle at agricultural shows years before anyone had heard of a bending race. Tweeds are more permissible, and no longer incur the question Edward VII is supposed to have asked Lord Harris at Ascot. Confronted by the surprisingly rural outfit of his chum, the King inquired of his lordship if he was 'goin' rattin'?'—whence the term ratcatcher.

The other great change in riding clothes has been brought about by the demise of the side saddle. This dangerous, elegant and expensive method of keeping women in their place survived as an anti-feminist anachronism long after horses had ceased to be used purely as transport when it was convenient for a full-skirted lady to sit sideways on a mini-howdah. As late as 1930, the

Master of a smart pack of hounds might indicate his preference for ladies to come out side-saddle. The dangers of being dragged by voluminous skirts catching in the pommel (which seem to have been no deterrent to the intrepid Victorian and Edwardian huntswomen, a comment perhaps on the lack of alternative thrills in their lives) had been mitigated by the efforts of such as C. W. Davis and Joseph Smith to produce 'safety' habits. The chic names to wear were still Busvine or Maxwell.

In the end it was not a change of heart on the part of Masters or a yard full of sore backs after a particularly vigorous house party which changed society's attitude to riding astride, it was sheer economics. The First World War created a new class of poor; taxation, death duties, unemployment, disastrous business schemes, all bit into an area of the middle classes hitherto quietly comfortable. The Stock Market crash and the Depression starting in 1929 hastened the process. The whole paraphernalia of the side saddle, its weight and cost and limited use, became anathema to the New Woman. If she had to feed, muck out, groom and exercise her horse she saw no reason why she should not ride it any way she wished. Interestingly, riding at the most competitive and nerve-testing level has been a sport in which women have consistently equalled or outstripped men. Olympic show-jumping teams have contained women members since 1956, when Pat Smythe rode at Stockholm, and in 1964 the American Lana Du Pont was included in her nation's team for the even more arduous Three-Day Event at Tokyo. In 1976 the Queen of England's daughter was selected for the British team for the same event at the Montreal Olympics, but to the dispassionate observer there seems to have been more fashion movement in what the horse wears than in the rider's dress.

106. Cycling, the new sport for the new woman of the late nineteenth century, required clothing that freed the leg from cumbersome petticoats. Bloomers had been known since the 1850s but in England were the perquisite of the eccentrics of the Rational Dress movement. The average Englishwoman preferred to compromise with a heavy but ankle-length tweed skirt over flannel petticoats or over neat but well-concealed knickerbockers. Daring Continentals preferred the 'knickers', without the cumbersome camouflage, as shown in this view by Jean Béraud of the cycling club at the Bois de Boulogne in 1895.

107. The early motor car was an expensive toy for the upper classes, many of whom took pride in driving and even servicing the vehicles themselves. Cars were open, winds cold and country roads dusty and often unmade, hence the warm protective clothing, with men and women equally worried about the ravages of dust on face and hair. Will concern with atmospheric pollution from the internal combustion engine, still with us seventy years later, again put drivers and pedestrians into protective masks and goggles?

This drawing for *L'Illustration* in 1905 was from the perceptive hand of Sabattier, who chronicled so much of the fashionable life of his time.

108. Suzanne Lenglen, shown here in 1922, brought a new chic and ease of movement to dress worn for tennis. In her first press interview she made an endearing attempt to reconcile the English public to such revealing styles by stating that she was simply wearing what she had been accustomed to wear as a child. Her bright cardigan and bandeau were copied all over the world. Oddly enough it is her long white stockings, attempts at decency intended to appease Queen Mary, which would be considered the most dashing part of her ensemble today. Less static photographs show a titillating glimpse of thigh between garter and skirt. *(Keystone Press)*

109. Alice Marble, American winner of the ladies' championship at Wimbledon in 1939, played like a man and dressed like one, in her all-white, neat, functional outfit of sports shirt, straight-cut shorts and eyeshade cap. Her style set the trend until feminity returned with Gorgeous Gussie in 1949. *(Keystone Press)*

110. 'Gorgeous Gussie' Moran won the Wimbledon ladies' singles in 1949 wearing a controversial outfit designed for her by Ted Tinling, then at the beginning of a new fashion career. She wore regulation white, a decorous two inches above the knee in length, but new were the frilly trimmings, the first post-war attempt to bring back prettiness to tennis clothes. The material was an experimental British celanese soft rayon jersey and Tinling, in his book *White Ladies*, says he added the notorious lace trim to the panties just as a decorative afterthought.

This photograph, from Associated Press, won Bob Ryder the award of Photographer of the Year. It was a shot for which dozens of photographers were lying in wait.

111. Diana Fishwick drives off in 1932, wearing clothes that have become classic golf style and are the sort of thing of which Mlle Chanel would have approved. They owe much to the ordinary country garb of the 1920s and on the whole have not changed much in the last forty years. Ted Tinling was responsible for the post-war restyling of golfing dress, when he promoted the use of fine cashmere and West of England flannel for the English ladies' team of 1952. He also got rid of the traditional, masculine-style collar and tie. As the game becomes more popular and suburban, more women have taken to wearing trousers. Initially an American trend, this is now accepted by all but the most reactionary of the clubs.

112. Erté designed these ride-astride habits in 1916 for the magazine *Harper's Bazaar*. 'L'Amazone du Demain' on the left wears 'grey chamois with a cardigan of blue silk. . . . The gaiters which are one with the breeches fasten with conspicuous pale blue buttons.' 'Promenade Matinale' on the right is 'a striking habit of beige cloth with the breeches cut in one with the skirt of the coat. The black silk stock wraps about the neck and is knotted at the back'. Daring when ride-astride habits were just becoming accepted, and then only with all-concealing coats, these drawings were probably more a design exercise than a suggestion for actual wear. Chamois was the traditional material for the upper part of breeches. *(Erté/Charles Spencer)*

113. Judges in a ladies' hunter class in the 1960s wear women's riding dress at its most formal—the side saddle habit with breeches and boots, neat masculine-style collar and tie, a protective bowler and veil. Skirts worn since woman first perched herself on a horse in a position more decorous than secure have here reached a final and uneasy compromise between decency and convenience. They are so cut about, to rob them of possibly dangerous weight and bulk, that they are mere aprons fastened into place with a variety of straps and snaps and supposed only to give way in extremity or an accident. *(Barnaby's)*

114. Elegant winter sports of 1912, illustrated in the somewhat avant-garde *Bon Ton*. Most dressed for warmth rather than ease of movement, but as the unconcealed knickerbocker, at first a German fashion, became socially accepted, only the really skilled lady skier tended to retain her skirt. Even then it was more or less as a mark of prestige. The knitted cardigan coat, cap and pullover were worn for most chilly active sports and were among the inspirations of the young Gabrielle Chanel.

115. This ski outfit was designed by Lord Snowdon, then Tony Armstrong-Jones, in 1958. It was an elegantly revolutionary contribution to the post-war winter sports world. He used the new stretch and waterproof fabrics to design clothes which the *Sketch* magazine described as 'the first really modern space-age fashions'. Above is his 'balloon line'. Interestingly, he has looked back to ski clothes of early days and put his girls in knee-length breeches. *(Lord Snowdon)*

116. At the turn of the century bathing suits were saggy, baggy and discreet. They provided, at least when not wet, an opaque cover between neck and knee; the stricter beaches demanded stockings as well. The most popular materials were serge and jersey, neither notably quick-drying. Only children, the emancipated and the skilled swimmer wore the one-piece 'regulation' or 'Annette Kellerman'. This form-fitting costume, which left bare both arm and calf, was named after the ebullient Australian exhibition swimmer who from 1904 did so much to promote aquatics as an aid to the body beautiful. The lady in the foreground of this seaside snap of 1913 wears an old-style suit, but the ladies of the group are more daring. *(Syndication International)*

117. Bathing suits became noticeably scantier in the 1920s, when sunbathing became a popular craze. The suits bared necks, backs and legs, but it was not until 1934 that the first two-piece suit appeared on a popular beach. Bare-chested men were still chivvied by American Leagues of Decency on the eve of the Second World War. This satirical drawing dates from about 1925.

118. Bathing suits were radically reduced in 1964 when American sportswear designer Rudi Gernreich introduced his topless design. Initially a not too serious comment on fashionable suits of all gaps and straps, it was topical enough to become a trend. The same designer was responsible for the tiny 'thong' in 1975, a development of the 'string' of 1974. This bare-breasted bather actually wears the bottom half of her bikini, a minimal two-piece bra and pants suit. Originally called the Atom, it was introduced from the French Riviera in 1946, and was the precursor of the two-piece suits that now dispute world beaches with the more traditional one-piece. Her shocked audience wears the sort of summer dress current on any English beach, home-sewn and crumpled, a debased Courrèges shift. *(Camera Press)*

8

Children

'The tailor was here to help dress little Frank in his breeches. He looks taller and prettier than in his coats,' wrote Lady Anne North in 1679, recording an important step in masculine development, the moment when, aged about seven, the male child was transferred from frocks into trousers.

The classical explanation for dressing boys in the same clothes as girls is not calculated to appeal to feminists. One might be entitled to think that the only reasons are the obvious ones: that since the sex of the baby could not be predetermined some sort of neutral garment was necessary; that since children grow so fast it was more practical to dress both sexes alike on the hand-me-down principle of large families; or that a loose dress was, as Rousseau thought, less cramping to the growth and movement of the child. 'The best plan,' he writes in *Emile*, 'is to keep children in frocks as long as possible and then to provide them with loose clothing without trying to define the shape which is only another way of deforming it. Their defects of body and mind may all be traced to the same source, the desire to make men of them before their time.' This revolutionary theory, expounded at a time when children were still being swaddled, is about the only expression of concern for a child's comfort or attempt at dress reform to be found for the next one hundred and fifty years, and the publication of *Emile* caused a sensation. It is also worth noting that in the last quarter of the eighteenth century not only was the predilection for nautical dress for children of the Victorian and Edwardian periods anticipated by the matelot loose trousers of the boys but the promotion of breast-feeding by mothers in public, one of the more advanced current interests of the Women's Lib movement, was in full swing.

The actual explanation for putting boys into frocks is that male children are so much more precious than females and so inherently superior to them that the jealousy of the malignant spirits who haunt the primitive superstitions might be aroused by a boy child and they might be inspired to harm him. By dressing a boy indistinguishably from his sisters, one threw the spirits off the trail. If it does not say much for the intelligence of the goblins, this theory does in fact provide an answer to those who point out that even in royal or noble and wealthy households with no need of economy children were dressed alike when they were small.

If the idea of taking the child's convenience into consideration is a twentieth-century one, so too is the idea of clothes designed specifically for children. Throughout history children had been dressed in miniature versions of whatever adults were wearing; if the adults were in rags or skins, so were the children. Responsibilities fell upon their shoulders young, for their life expectancy was much less than ours. The teenager is another product of the twentieth century, bred out of enforced education and the improved standards of living, feeding and health which have built a whole new period, 'adolescence', into the greatly extended human lifespan. By the close of the nineteenth century, reformist opinion was sufficiently advanced to deplore corsets for girls, even if they still had to endure the back board or walk about with books balanced on their heads. This immediately made the silhouettes of women distinguishable from those of children for, while their elders creaked and fainted in their stays, little girls wore loose smocks and enveloping pinafores (**120**).

Developments in education also played a part in establishing a separate clothing identity for children. The Education Act of 1870 provided for the setting up of elementary schools by local boards and in 1876 education was compulsory to the age of thirteen. In 1891 further legislation provided the possibility of free education for all. Private girls' boarding schools and colleges evolved that lasting horror, the school uniform, a cul-de-sac of fashion if ever there was one, and when R. A. Butler's Education Act of 1944 raised the school-leaving age to fifteen and offered secondary education in grammar, technical or modern school free without means test or restriction, the whole state had the dubious privilege of being able to join the élite of the uniformed.

Since the egalitarian principles of a uniform for school are well founded, and since the fact that competition is impossible outweighs the élitist aspects in all but the most biased view, the astonishing thing is that the standard of uniform design remains so bad. In London in 1978 you can see small boys wearing heavy corduroy knee breeches, a bulbous cap like an Edwardian motorist's, and a mustard fisherman's sweater—all this for walking down Sloane Street. These boys belong to one of the most select private preparatory schools. If your son attends the much-publicised Gordonstoun in Scotland, his manly thighs will be revealed, despite the icy winds which blow near Inverness, by little-boy shorts. Dresses of lilac synthetic jersey and scarlet and mauve capes may be had from the totally respectable John Lewis Partnership. It is hardly surprising that in 1970 there was serious trouble in many schools over what might be worn in class, with children being sent home for their rebellions. At the same time, many sixth forms did away with uniform altogether and some schools, such as St Paul's Girls' School in London, one of the most distinguished day schools in the country, abandoned uniform in their entire senior school.

The wheel had come full circle. Rescued by education and enlightened thought a hundred years earlier from the slavery of a factory or the often sad fate of the child-bride, given a whole new period of protection and opportunity in their lives, it was as though young people now kicked against the enforced safety nets that held them and longed to get out into the wicked world earlier. Where there is a demand there will be a supply, and it was not long before the merchants discovered that the extension of childhood had provided them with a new market. With the prosperity which followed the Second World War, that market suddenly had lots of lovely money, disposable money, money which had no other direction, no mortgages, no bills, no household responsibilities to meet. The teenage market was born. Make-up and clothes appeared as if by magic to lure the pennies out of the purses. Magazines such as *Honey* (launched in 1961) and *Petticoat* (1966) were founded on the exploding young market and were powerful weapons in deciding how the cash should flow. So was *Seventeen*, in America; like *Mademoiselle*, it was quick to change its image to meet the new spenders' tastes.

Perhaps because the traditions of good motherhood and praiseworthy housewifery placed so much emphasis on provision for children, perhaps because many women who enjoyed sewing no longer needed to make heavy adult clothing now it was available ready-made and so could content themselves with the preparation of tiny garments, the style of children's clothes changed very slowly even when it had its own identity, and continued to demonstrate a noticeable preference for hand-made touches. To dress your children in elaborate, smocked, starched and frilled clothes indicated leisure and servants and a full wardrobe. So too did pale colours and delicate materials and a deliberate disregard for ease of care. Since Little Lord Fauntleroy's mother, Dearest, had only one old servant to help with all the chores, one might guess that she was less concerned with status than was the noble household to which the child was removed to be groomed for his inheritance. Once he started galloping about in a velvet suit and white collars his costume must have been a nightmare both to put on and to look after. Even Christopher Robin, by no means the child of a grand family and, indeed, probably

166

viewed by his creator as an idyllic picture of carefree childhood, must have taken some dressing, with his felt hat, his smocks, the braces which caused such excitement to Pooh and Piglet, his little tweed coat with the velvet collar (very much as worn by the Queen's children and President Kennedy's and still going strong in 1978 in shops such as Rowes of Bond Street), and his long, multi-buttoned gaiters (**121**, **122**). The gaiters have gone, it is true; they proved almost too much even for Rose Kennedy, the mother of the President, who recalls the hours spent doing up and undoing nine children for New England winters.

Convenience dressing began when the majority of women had no leisure and no servants, and it began with a revolution in the least convenient clothes a child has, baby clothes. Fumble-fisted young mothers, graduates in all but the maternal arts, struggled with little arms and little vests, nappies and more nappies, dresses which rode up and diminutive suits which rode apart in the middle. They wept into their sinks and the eagle-eyed buyers of tots' departments, catering on the one hand for indulgent and chore-liberated grannies and on the other for frantic young mothers who were changing Granny's presents for yet another pair of denim rompers, reported a swing to practicality. After all, what was the point of a washing machine if the bulk of the washing—baby's—could not go in it? Science was the fairy godmother, and the one-piece, stretch-towelling, pop-fronted baby suit was with us (**126**). So too were plastic pants, which seared the legs of the badly managed child but gave Mother another hour or two of dry lap, and some strange things called nappy liners which purported to allow wet to travel outwards only. At the height of the bonded-fibre (paper-style tissue) dress excitement, one enterprising firm launched a whole layette in its perforated and disposable fabric. It may well have clogged the lavatories from here to Ohio, but I never saw a child wearing the material. But disposable nappies, like disposable sanitary towels, were here to stay.

How children are dressed reflects to a great extent how they are viewed in their home surroundings. A theory was once mooted that you could discover the nationality of any little girl by giving her an ice-cream. In a Catholic, sensual country such as Italy, where a child is still brought up to play a rôle which is traditional, the little girl will already be conscious of both her looks and her chic. Therefore, in accepting the treat, she will arrange her frilly petticoats so as not to crease them and then, leaning well forward, enjoy her ice without any fear of getting a drip on her frock. An American child, possibly equally elaborately dressed, will sit down without preamble and munch the cornet without minding if the dress is dirtied, because free expression and true spirit are more important to the non-conformist conscience than a preoccupation with femininity. The theory never got as far as considering English children. Perhaps if it had it would have found that they would not accept the ice at all, on the grounds that Nanny thought it was unhealthy.

Despite their slow changes in style, children's clothes have proved a profitable platform for some designers. The classic illustration must be Jeanne Lanvin, who founded a house which is still successful by making pretty dresses for her daughter before the First World War (**128**). Cardin, Daniel Hechter, even Dior, have turned an eye on the mini-market, but what sells reflects once again the attitudes and the priorities of different countries. In a country which still regards children as a blessing and a gift, the expenditure on short-lived clothes is correspondingly higher taken in relation to income. The British damp down their boys' inherent love of colour and texture as soon as possible. Many parents dress their children to indicate their standing or their own beliefs. Some, it is hard not to feel, dress their children from pure spite. Romily John, son of Augustus John the painter, recorded in 1974, 'We were all terrified of him. He forced us to have close-cropped hair and wear loathsome knickerbockers and pinafores and I grew up a shy, solitary child who had nightmares.' So much for swinging Bloomsbury.

Perhaps the most interesting aspect of minors' clothing remains its position vis-à-vis surrounding adults. As we have seen, until the latter part of the nineteenth century children wore scaled-down versions of adult dress. True, between the death of George IV and the accession of Queen Victoria clothes for women had had a childish quality, but it was the twentieth century which really witnessed the arrival of mother-and-daughter dressing the other way about, i.e. with parents clad to look like the sisters of their own children. Among designers, Jeanne Lanvin was famous for her mother–daughter outfits inspired by a much-loved child, and in high society it was Mrs Dudley Ward, for seventeen years the intimate friend of the future Edward VIII, who, around 1920, had the witty chic to wear gingham dresses exactly like those of her two little girls.

No such coming together was visible on the masculine front, where little men began the century dressed (once they were out of skirts) in diminutive sailor suits of imperial-colonial cut, moved in the 'twenties and 'thirties to the comparative comfort of shorts and smocks, but all through the century have been put into replicas of daddy's suit—preferably in drab grey or prickly tweed—just as soon as was feasible.

It was Norman Norell, who might have known better, who began the mass-market mother–daughter trend in America. In 1964 he designed a suit for his (women's) collection which was inspired by a boy's outfit from a firm called Merry Mites. 'The paragon of the sixties,' wrote Marylin Bender in *The*

Beautiful People, 'became the nymphet.' We had already been exposed to the delights of Lolita, the twelve-year-old anti-heroine of Vladimir Nabokov's highly equivocal novel. Now the focus of the modelling world was Twiggy, aged seventeen, British, Cockney, and discovered by the photographer Barry Lategan and the hairdresser Leonard in London. 'We used to dress like Jackie Kennedy; now we're dressing like Caroline,' the TV personality and former Miss America, Bess Meyerson, is quoted as saying in 1966. The urge to dress young imposes a terrible strain. The old term, 'mutton dressed as lamb', is none the less apt for usually being spitefully employed.

Not all the dress-alike hopes were commercially fulfilled. In 1963 Miss Bender records that the buyers caught a cold in their efforts to mimic the adult trend for floor-length hostess dresses. The grannies thought they were good fun but mothers returned them next day. By 1974, however, English style included wistful Kate Greenaway pinnies and smocks even in the chain stores, and little girls were wearing long frocks like their mothers. Little boys could look like Daddy, too, but it was the process in reverse, since while many adult women met their daughters half-way in girlish dress, little men continued to be dressed remorselessly as just that. In fact, England never was bitten by the dress-alike bug to the same extent as America. True, all sorts of women too old or too plain took advantage of the mini-skirt, but this was as much a statement of their own feelings as a desire to be identified with the baby market.

To delve into the motivation which persuades a mature and elegant woman that she is more attractive dressed as a snotty schoolgirl is to risk objections from those trained in psychoanalysis, but all dress is predicated on the emotions or freedoms of the wearer, so any book on clothes must at any rate try to explain a period which, it is to be hoped, is being left behind.

Two factors motivate the desire to appear youthful even in an age when, as the Italian film director Franco Zeffirelli has pointed out, the real phenomenon has been the spread of the middle period, not the problem of youth. In his view, innocence, in the sense of not having experienced certain things, stops now at sixteen when it might have been twenty-five. Similarly, medical advances have extended the fertile and vigorous life of many to sixty-five or more, when previously illness or accident or war might have carried them off long before. Couples are thus confronted with an immensely expanded period which they can expect to spend together. At the same time the obvious reasons for monogamy—security of the nest, provision of food, certainty of parentage of the children who were the inevitable outcome of sex, religious mores—have all been undermined by the realities of the modern state. The welfare offices take care of the house and the food, the Pill prevents the conception of unwanted children, abortion takes care of those dubiously sired, if necessary, and the grip of religion has slipped. Thus the hunt becomes one of sexual pleasure. Man is by nature polygamous; the younger mate is biologically the more fertile; many people are trapped in lives so dull or so disastrous that their natural instinct is to try to re-live time ill spent. Small wonder that to many women their cycle seems inexorably set in the conquest-consolidation-decline pattern.

The second factor which has been crucial in the unhappiness of countless women has been the concentration of the suppliers of consumer goods on the young, rich market. Nobody really wants the older, more tricky, more discriminating customer when the money is easy. Hence the production of publications such as 'girlie' magazines like *Playboy*, which mix the natural nostalgia for what has been missed with the supposition that sex is a consumer goody too, and suggest that—oh most insidious!—it is only possible to be sexy if you are young (because the young have the money to buy what the advertisers are selling). The peddling of vicarious youth and the demolition of years of useful happy contribution to the community by women hooked instead on sad tranquillisers and bitchy bridge parties seem a high price for society to pay for an easy-care life. It is to be hoped that the breaking up of communities into more human groups, which could be a future pattern, will re-establish the charm and sense of self-worth all older women should enjoy. After all, the septuagenarian Madame de Maintenon was moved to write to her father confessor that she found the twice-daily attentions of Louis X I V in bed too arduous, and to ask if she might now give them up. He, chauvinist beast, told her that she had to put up with her lot, but there is no record that she was dressing like a nymphet to retain the royal favour. On the contrary, she looks a dour old puss, for all the diamonds.

VELVET SUIT. HIGHLAND SUIT. HIGHLAND SUIT. KENSINGTON SUIT. PRINCE ALBERT SUIT. WHITE DRILL OR GALATEA BLOUSE. NAVAL SUIT. NAVAL SUIT. VELVET SAILOR SUIT. KNICKER MIDDY SUIT. COVERT COAT

VELVET PATIENCE. TWEED SULTAN SUIT. CADET SUIT. KENSINGTON SUIT. MAN O' WAR SUIT. SAILOR SUIT. SAILOR SUIT. GIRL'S SAILOR COSTUME. GIRL'S SUMMER BLOUSE. BOY'S SUMMER SERGE REEFER.

RUGBY SUIT. RUGBY SUIT. RUGBY SUIT. ETON KNICKER SUIT. GREENWICH SUIT. YOUNG LADIES' COSTUMES. YOUNG LADIES' REEFERS. FOOTBALL JERSEY. FOOTBALL JERSEY. BOYS CREAM FLANNEL SHIRTS.

RINK JACKET AND VEST. REEFER SUIT. REEFER JACKET AND VEST. ETON JACKET SUIT. YOUTH'S MIDDY SUIT. NORFOLK SUIT. RUGBY SUIT. YOUTH'S RINKING SUIT. MORNING COAT & VEST.

119. Aspiration, and probably perspiration too, marked these clothes as typical of those intended for the average middle-class child of the late nineteenth century. Available reasonably cheaply, both ready-made and tailored to order from a large manufacturer, they are romantically titled, durable and must have been almost unendurably stiff and stuffy. They were clearly aimed at the status-conscious parent rather than the active child. Although seventy years have passed, taking with them the 'velvet suit' (top row, extreme left) and the 'highland suit' (top row, second from left), the 'reefer' (third row, fourth from right, and bottom row, second from left) is not far from the two-piece suit which is still the staple of youth outfitting departments. *(Stationery Office Records)*

120. Liberty children's dresses, like this one from their 1904 catalogue, were always easy-fitting and comfortable in keeping with the dress reform movement, an important factor in the firm's fashion policy in its early days. They were often made in soft washable fabrics, another Liberty speciality. This loose-fitting dress owes something to the countryman's smock but, worn with a blouse, it is obviously related to the modern tunic or pinafore dress which schoolgirls still wear.

121 and 122. The typical child in the books of A. A. Milne, illustrated by Ernest H. Shepard, is dressed like most other middle-class children of his time—and far more easily and comfortably than he would have been ten years previously. In the picture from *When We Were Very Young* he wears lightweight and washable short trousers (knickers) buttoned to a blouse top, and ankle-band shoes. Listed among the delights of 'Growing Up' in the Milne poem of that title are 'I've got shoes with grownup laces, I've got knickers with a pair of braces'. A loose smock or blouse kept Christopher Robin reasonably clean outdoors, the only difference from the strictly establishment child of today being the gaiters to cover the little short white socks.

123. Upper-class Edwardian children, like these little girls photographed in Hyde Park in 1911, were small monuments to the theory of conspicuous consumption, clad almost invariably in white starched dresses whatever the season. The eyelet-embroidered borders on these frocks are clearly visible. Warmth, on a chilly March day, is provided by diminutive bunny fur coats and mountainous matching hats—surely a trifle ostentatious and *nouveau riche* even at the time— while legs are covered with button-up gaiters. Nanny wears her proud badge of servitude, her uniform bonnet. It is consciously archaic in style, recalling the hats of the 1880s. (*Radio Times Hulton Picture Library*)

124. These working-class children queueing for free food in Cheapside in 1901 wear dark hard-wearing clothes. They are ill-fitting and some are probably cast-offs which have been clumsily cut down or taken up. Two of the girls wear the ubiquitous pinafore, washable protection for their heavy stuff dresses. The children all wear boots and they are by no means the poorest of the poor. If they were, they would have been barefoot, for boots were the largest cost item in the working-class's clothing budget. (*William Gordon Davies*)

125. The baby of 1909, clothed from this Woollands catalogue, would have been dressed for show rather than for comfort or hygiene. The long day gowns, of which this christening gown is only a slightly more elaborate version, were made from fine lawn, lace and insertion, and often stiffly starched. They provided plenty of employment for the working woman whether nanny, washerwoman or sweated sewing hand. The long gown looked graceful when the child was carried in the nurse's arms (baby carriages were at this time relatively little used) and gave an illusion of warmth more reliably provided by layers of flannel petticoats and a woollen carrying cloak over all.

No. 43.—**Handsome Christening Robe**, exquisitely embroidered Panels, trimmed Imitation Valenciennes Lace Insertions.
PRICE **£6 . 19 . 6**

126. The baby stretch suit, introduced in the early 1960s, was a development of the one-piece sleeping suit of the enlightened 1930s which had been intended to provide a flexible, draught-proof covering. It tended to tangle and shed buttons until post-war technology added stretch, drip-dry fabrics and machine-washable snap-fastenings. *(Warners)*

No. 36.—**Exquisite Lingerie Frock**, finely tucked, trimmed with many Lace Insertions, Hand-embroidery, and Real Crochet Motifs. For girls of 16 years.
PRICE **8½ Guineas.**
Other designs ranging in price from **63/-**

127. Teenage fashion hardly existed before the First World War but the sixteen-year-old, poised between schoolroom and début, was for one brief year permitted a special dress. She could lengthen her skirts to the ankle but not yet put up her hair. In this 1909 Woollands fashion plate of a dress for a sixteen-year-old, the hair is held back in a big 'flapper' bow. With her hair up and her skirts ground length, the seventeen or eighteen-year-old was labelled mature for marriage.

128. Jeanne Lanvin (1867–1946) was the first designer to blur the distinction between clothes for girl and woman. By 1920 it is the adults who wish to look like children and in these dresses, designed for *Bon Ton* in 1920, she deftly exploits the robe de style, with its tight bodice and full skirt, which she introduced in 1915 and was to keep fashionable throughout the 1930s, making it something equally suitable for mother and daughter.

129. These school uniforms are taken from a 1934 Lilley and Skinner catalogue and only the material —thick grey flannel then, polyester mixtures now—would distinguish the wearers from their prep-school descendants two generations later, despite forty years of continuous educational reform. Blazers and shorts were then seen as rational and comfortable, which they were, especially when compared with the tapering knickerbockers which they had replaced in the 1920s. The school cap is still proudly unchanging, utterly impractical except as a badge of belonging. Stiff and formalised, it has long lost whatever function it had as a Victorian games cap when it was soft, warm and shady for the eyes.

130. Children of today wear clothes so specifically designed to last that they are all more or less based on those worn by manual labourers, for example blue jeans or bib and brace overalls. And whereas in 1900 every little boy was once dressed as a little girl, now (in keeping with women's lib?) the trend is reversed. Tough toddler styling was originally American and was naturalised in England along with the chain store and the washing machine. *(Access)*

Part Three

Fashion as a Trade

9

Fashion as a Trade

It is a regular mark of a society which feels itself secure and prosperous that it accords to production of the three basic needs of life—food, shelter and clothing—the status of creative arts and considers them a legitimate field of opportunity for sincere talents. What one might call the more compulsive arts—literature, music and painting—need no such luxurious soil. They can exist if need be in the gravel of the fascist or the concrete of the totalitarian state. Thus from the outset fashion is a reflection of society: its very existence tells us something about the nature of the times.

In the past hundred years, however, two major, interlinked developments have affected clothing and seem to have distorted its place irreversibly. One factor is the invention and exploitation of machinery for clothing manufacture which has brought dress fashion for the first time within the reach of almost anyone who cares for it. The second factor is the immense change in the pattern of distribution of wealth in many parts of the world and the greatly raised standard of living of many populations. Thus, although the twentieth century has seen two global confrontations and a series of major economic crises, and although many countries have felt anything but optimistic and secure, clothing has retained the elements of fashion, of a creative art, and the problems of societies have been reflected not in its disappearance but in its nuances over the years.

In 1900 the moment was propitious for fashion. In the West a new class of women had been made rich by the efforts of their men in commerce. They had neither the aristocratic traditions nor the country interests of wealthy women of previous generations, and their lives were newly urban. Often high-minded and intelligent, often the reverse but now leisured, they found their outlets for leisure hemmed about with considerations of social nicety which might have been ignored by those with the confidence of birth and breeding. On the

179

throne of England sat a queen, the model of propriety and domestic rectitude. A woman's place was at home.

At the same time the husbands and brothers and fathers of these women worked in a new way. They were not the colourful military adventurers, the great landowners, solid squires or courtiers of an earlier date. These new men made their money through management and organisation, were often unknown to those who worked for them and few actually saw what they made their money from. They worked in offices and warehouses in filthy cities where the chimneys belched out the news of an economic boom. They dressed in sensible, sober, dark colours which inspired confidence and did not show the smuts, and it was left to the women to express the security and prosperity of industrial revolution in their clothes. The success and relative status of the man were exemplified by the sumptuous and impractical attire of the females of his family.

Thus at the end of the nineteenth century was to be found the conglomeration of factors which signalled the start of the boom in mass fashion, namely commercial optimism, mechanical opportunity, the product and the customers. There was a whole new section of society with money to spend and the leisure to indulge in dress. Its members were for the most part restricted in their other interests, and the mechanisation of manufacture was getting under way. In 1900 haute couture, as opposed to mere clothing, was included in the Paris Exhibition at the Palais des Fils called 'Tissus et Vêtements', a hitherto somewhat mundane display. Fashion was about to become Trade.

The birth was not an easy one. By 1850 the Singer sewing machine was a commercial proposition but it was curiously slow to make its impact on the clothing industry, especially in Britain. For many years the machines were confined to men's and outwear garments and the majority of fashion was made by hand, frequently in appalling conditions. If fashion is an art it must be the art which has extracted the greatest toll of suffering, both human and animal; for while the pursuit of gastronomic gratification can furnish some disgusting examples of man's inhumanity to bird and beast, for the purposes of inessential self-adornment innumerable creatures have been sacrificed and men, women and children have worked as virtual slaves. The sewing machine reached Europe too late for the eyesight and the lungs of a generation of wretched seamstresses.

Their plight did not go unremarked. *Punch* carried many cartoons which were pointed reminders to women of fashion that their finery was the product of cruel exploitation, a favourite technique being to juxtapose the idyllic scene in the gratified lady's boudoir, as she dons her gown and chooses her jewels, and a sketch of the emaciated and exhausted producer of the gown slumped by her single candle. *Punch* also printed, in 1843, Tom Hood's famous poem 'The Song of the Shirt', but the main concern among the grand clients seems to have been that their dresses were not contaminated by the diseases of typhus and consumption or by the lice which raged in the tailoring sweat-shops (**131**).

On the other hand, the historian William Lecky, in considering the situation of women in 1869, saw terrible hardship ahead and even fates worse than death for the unmarried because machinery was replacing women in the sewing trades. The fact that in these trades the squalor could hardly have been increased by any number of machines did not prevent Lecky from regretting that 'the distaff has fallen from the hand. The needle is being rapidly superseded and the work which from the days of Homer was accomplished in the centre of the family, has been transferred to the crowded manufactory'.

Not all that work was being transferred by any means. At the start of the twentieth century the greater proportion of women's clothing, especially blouses, lingerie and dresses, was made by hand, often by outworkers, and the makers were extremely badly paid. In 1908 an investigation entitled 'The Makers of our Clothes' by Mrs Carl Meyer and Clementina Black included case-histories of teenage girls in good dressmaking houses who were earning 4s 6d (22½p) per week and of home-workers getting no more than 1s 6d (7½p) for making a cheap coat. The elaborate Edwardian blouses which were such a feature of fashion at that time were sewn for a wage of 10d (4p) per garment, while plainer blouses commanded only 1s 2d (6p) per dozen. Feminists will see in this deplorable situation yet another example of the exploitation of women; sociologists will note another instance in another industry of the use of predominantly female labour and of the lack of a proper career structure and pay opportunities.

'The Makers of our Clothes' had itself been inspired by an 'anti-sweating' exhibition organised in London in 1906 by the *Daily News*, a paper owned by the Cadbury family. In America the situation was just as bad, though it was mainly her immigrants, swarming from the hungry Old World to the hopeful New, who bore the brunt of fashion's need for cheap labour; in England the exploited for the most part were themselves British. It is perhaps worth pausing here to consider why the clothing trade should have been so harsh an employer and should continue even to this day to be unsatisfactory in many respects.

The point about fashion when it becomes industrialised is that it is very tempting to try to apply normal industrial rules to it while it remains a firmly individual and wayward creative business. Although it may be tempting to plot the connection between what people will want to wear and how they are feeling at the time, experience has shown that only in retrospect is that connection visible. There is an element in what makes successful fashion which has so far defied the most ingenious attempts at diagnosis. As soon as there was enough machinery to make, and enough customers with money to buy, clothes which were fashionable as opposed to merely answering the calls of necessity, the potentially enormously profitable new commercial avenue revealed itself as not straight and lined with the shady poplars of established practice, but tortuous in the extreme; anyone negotiating it needed a real seat-of-the-pants driving flair to keep going. The need to guess all the time what the customer might want to buy makes for a very nervous industry, which hardly encourages conditions of stability of employment or temperament.

More seriously, as Lecky pointed out, clothes had from the dawn of constructed garments been sewn by hand. Clothing was traditionally a manual industry, labour—as opposed to capital—intensive, and furthermore it was a trade requiring minimal skills in its workers. Many of the immigrants who went to New York were family groups of people of peasant stock, but they could sew all right. In England, it was the urbanisation associated with the industrial changes in the country which provided the hapless human fodder for the sweat-shops. They could sew, too: witness the adage, 'while you can sew you will never starve'. Or not quite.

The industry developed differently in different countries. In America, the mass-market trade was founded on the factories which made the uniforms of the Civil War, which coincided with the advance in technical and mechanical expertise. Thus from the start the industry was oriented towards bulk and towards the mass-production of similar styles rather than the innovation of new trends. The size of the market, the diffuse nature of the country and the lack of traditions all pushed the American garment business to the reputation it still holds, which is for fine, efficient reproduction at an excellent price. Cheap American ready-to-wear is probably the best in the world.

The American clothing workers' unions were and still are very powerful, engineering historic strikes in 1909 and 1910. In 1909 twenty thousand women workers walked out in New York but, despite much sympathy and the support of the *Evening Journal*, the first strike did little more than pave the way for the second in the following year. This second strike had immense repercussions on the labour movement in the country and an agreement, called optimistically the Protocol of Peace, was signed between workers and employers. Within a year, however, the conditions of work in the garment quarter were once again the subject of news when 145 women died in the Triangle Shirtwaist Company fire in March 1911. Pockets of sweating continued to exist and still do, but the garment workers' union is powerful enough for a New York Mayor such as John Lindsay in 1972 to pay well-publicised visits to Seventh Avenue, the heart of the rag trade area in Manhattan.

There is an ironical twist to the protective power which the American unions exercised on behalf of their members, for by the very act of pushing up wages and conditions of employment they encouraged retailers to look overseas to cheaper and less intransigent sources. Indeed, a major preoccupation for store buyers is now the location and exploration of new sources of fashion. This is engendered partly by the mania for exclusivity which motivates competing shops and partly by the mania for novelty which motives this country of well trained conspicuous consumers, but, put all together, the pressures to look overseas have been strong enough to found the textile industries of several less developed countries and to support that of France to an astonishing degree.

A good example of American enterprise in the pursuit of the right merchandise is Hong Kong. This British Crown Colony had a textile industry which was founded in the 'fifties, really on the lowest possible labour rates—the labour being provided by the Chinese who escaped across the China border—and on the system of Imperial Preferences operated by Britain. England bore the brunt of the first waves of crude produce and so Hong Kong got itself an image for providing the cheap and nasty end of fashion; this image, understandably, was not precisely counteracted by the British manufacturers. The Americans arrived later and with a much surer idea of what they wanted. In addition to buying in Hong Kong, they buy their raincoats and shoes in Poland, shirts in India, sweaters in Taiwan and suits in Finland. South America is a prime area for examination in the 'seventies and it remains to be seen if the African continent can prove politically stable enough to earn valuable exports.

The attitude of the American union is interesting. When recession hit many parts of the world in 1975, it was noticeable that the British began to agitate for a ban on imports, while efforts to export remained especially unimaginative, but the International Ladies' Garment Workers' Union, grasping the fact (which seemed to have eluded the British) that fashion is an inessential which has to be promoted in the consumer mind, was helping to finance a film on the history of American style.

For fashion to the American woman is not a part of a cultural heritage, an innate need to be surrounded by the nicest and most elegant things; it is a heavily merchandised and advertised method by which she can buy the good life in the materialistic sense. France's traditional interest in women, whether

183

as glacial ideals or erotic objects—or as everything in between—trained the less intellectual and more puritanical Americans to look to France for messages about what women want. At the same time, America was far too big and too diverse in its societies to foster that unified taste and that sympathetic single-minded audience which the designers needed, nor could it hope to gather in one place all the talents which stimulate each other so successfully in Paris. Also it was already too developed to have those pools of hand labour in small, flexible workrooms which trendsetting demands.

Instead, fashion was sold to the Americans by the most intensive and ingenious Madison Avenue methods, which included the invention of a whole social group, the Beautiful People, to wear it. It was all part of the consumer dream, and the factories boomed with the reproduction of millions and millions of copies of French models because France held authority in the minds of the customers. It was fashionable to be fashionable, but events have shown that, when the advertising man's patter grew stale and Americans began to fumble for more fundamental values, fashion was one of the first grafts on the consumer society stock to wither.

Germany, with no couture tradition and repressive economic and political conditions for much of the century, still took advantage of the necessity to rebuild her smashed factories with an eye to the future. Germans have no pretensions to design originality, though they have become consumers of design on a huge scale. Instead, their textile industry concentrates on superb quality reproduction of tailored clothing which it is now virtually impossible to get made by hand. For value and finish, German coats and suits take a lot of beating. They lack flexibility, and there is a certain inexorable quality about what they produce which sometimes seems more suited to ball bearings, but with so fine a technical start they must, as hand labour becomes ever more expensive and hard to find, always be in a strong position.

For so artistic and innately so elegant a race the Italians came into the fashion game late. From before the Second World War only Mariano Fortuny, he of the crinkled silk tunics, is remembered. The man who eventually created the alta moda Italiana, Giovanni Giorgini, managed to get only four American buyers to go to Florence for the showing in 1950, even though that most astute and dedicated champion of Italian fashion, the Marchese Emilio Pucci, was opening up tasteful palazzi for the presentations and, more important, was himself designing a revolution in clothing (**133**). It was Emilio Pucci who introduced that essential of modern itinerant life, the knitted silk jersey shift dress (which folded as flat and small as a handkerchief and emerged unscathed from a dozen suitcased journeys), the complementary 'palazzo' pyjamas (actually rather narrow by modern standards) and tunic-length skirt top. His clothes were made in brilliant colours which reflected the warmth and gaiety of his sunny country, and the prints were novel in that they were originally meant for scarves; all, on examination, proved to be made up of squares or panels, and each square bore, in a tiny black scrawl, his signature. They were to become the uniform of a whole generation of jet-setters, as much as were Gucci pumps and handbags a little later. No wonder some cryptic writer coined the phrase 'the Gucci-Pucci syndrome'. It was indicative of a whole way of life.

It was not as a rival to French couture that Italy developed. It was as a source for beautiful fabrics, magnificently coloured, as a producer of incomparably lovely leather, and above all as the country which first made knitwear high fashion. Italian knitwear became a byword for chic, and managed to hold its own through the continuing brilliance of designers such as the Missonis even in the face of intense copying and price undercutting, notably from the Far East. As the industry grew, so the occasions for viewing it multiplied, and there are probably as many fashion fairs today in Italy as there are anywhere else. Italian couture retains a unique flavour, a national character which less creative, even if more efficient, nations look for in vain. Italian fashion is quite different from that of France, and no less the product of the society which bred it. French clothes seek to overwhelm with smartness and a perfection of detail which makes the well trained perfectionist exclaim with pleasure. The allure is based on an attention to grooming which can be chilling, even daunting, to the uninitiated. Italian clothes, on the other hand, just go all out to seduce you in as many of the senses as a dress can. To see the best French couture is to be awed by a technical masterpiece; it is an appeal to the intellect. I suspect the appeal of Italian design is for women that they want to put it on, and for men that they want to take it off.

And what of England? Back in the 1920s, S. P. Dobbs in his *Clothing Workers of Great Britain* expressed what is probably the traditional English suspicion of fashion. He regretted that 'constant capricious change' prevented firms from being able to manufacture in bulk, having instead to work seasonally and thus wastefully in order to meet the demands of different styles. This was particularly bad for mechanised firms, who needed long runs. While the good Dobbs might be castigated for not making the necessary leap of imagination from clothing to fashion, thirty years later there are many floundering industries who would see sense in what he said.

Having exploited her own people initially, the British fashion business never took off in the way that the Americans did, for of course the market was nothing like so large, nor did it develop the creative cachet of Paris. Poised uneasily between France and America, Britain never accepted good fashion as an integral part of civilised life, as did the French, nor was it peddled by quite such high-pressure methods as the Americans had developed. Instead, fashion ground along in genteel grooves and was and is for the most part under-capitalised, fragmented and dependent on the outworker system of labour far more than is desirable for consistent quality or efficient delivery. After the Second World War it quickly became apparent that wages and conditions did not compare with those of the munitions factories from which most of the work force had come. For an industry less endemically shortsighted, this ought to have been the moment to invest heavily in mechanisation processes, on the theory that labour was going to become ever more scarce and expensive. Two factors seem to have been particularly relevant in preventing this; the first was that unlike some other countries not all our factories had been bombed flat, so the incentive to rebuild was not paramount. The second was the arrival of an influx of unskilled labour from India, the West Indies and such countries as Cyprus, much of which found its way into the textile trade.

However, it was discovered after the war that despite a traditionally suspicious attitude to the value of design, especially in fashion, we in Britain could be really rather good at making it. Efforts were put in train to get the industry onto a more secure and professional basis. First the old war-horse of British couture, breastplated by Norman Hartnell and helmeted by Hardy Amies, was ambled out onto the fashion battlefield. He sniffed the air, performed a few decorous half-passes in suitably high society (everyone connected with the Incorporated Society of London Fashion Designers seems to have had a title, except of course the designers, whom it would have been most suitable to honour) and then retired to his quiet English field unmourned by the skittish mares who were now placing orders for couture models. A better stayer was the Fashion House Group of London, founded in 1958. This was the cream of British ready-to-wear—Susan Small, Frank Usher, Dorville, Polly Peck and others—and there is no doubt that this group was responsible for building Britain a fine reputation for well made, well priced, efficiently delivered and sympathetically interpreted top fashion. The manufacturers ventured abroad on selling trips, British Weeks invaded the calendar, Ambassadors were persuaded (by the figures on the bottom line, no doubt, for it was the time of Export or Die) that fashion was not some silly female preoccupation but a valuable industry, and they lent their gracious presences to promotional events much as they would if they had been pushing the sale of tractors. In 1966 the Clothing Export Council was formed to co-ordinate what had become a jumble of overlapping groups, and in 1972 the London Fashion Fair was added to a buyers' schedule which was fast filling the whole year. In 1975 exports of clothing from Britain totalled £365 million.

To anyone concerned with the development of a British national style as opposed to a Britain geared for manufacturing, two factors must have given early cause for alarm. The first was that many of the manufacturers who provided so efficient, well priced and sympathetic an interpretation of fashion to the world's markets were, as first-generation European immigrants, immersed in the tradition that Paris is the only true begetter of fashion trends. The second was that when in 1946, in the heady post-war days of a new Labour government, the appointment of a working party for the heavy clothing section of the industry was announced, two of its objects were to investigate the causes of seasonal fluctuation—in fashion!—and to try to eliminate them; even more ominously out of touch, it was the intention to establish a central information and design centre, from which presumably every manufacturer would draw his new ranges. There is no more bizarre example of the attitude of England to the potential of native design.

Yet at almost the same time—in 1948 to be precise—fashion was added as a separate subject under Mrs Madge Garland, erstwhile fashion editor of *Vogue*, to the departments of the Royal College of Art. Thus began a new era in design education which has provided observers with plenty of cause for both delight and despair. The selection of the fine-arts-based, semi-academic setting for fashion training is open to criticism, so it is worth recapping how the decision was arrived at. In 1936 the Board of Trade set up a committee to examine how best designers might be trained. It was anxious to give status to fashion because its findings pointed up the low esteem in which designers were held by manufacturers. However, before the report of the committee could be published the war intervened and it was not until 1945 (while the Trades Union Congress was suggesting central design registers) that its recommendations were released. When it was found that the committee had decided to place training for what, if not entirely a commercial art, was certainly an 'art mineur' in the classic arts training spectrum, there were those who felt that this would engender a sense of second-classness among fashion designers, and insulate those who were going to have to make a product with a form, a function and a price necessarily determined by the realities of business life. On the academic front the arrival was not welcome either. In 1967, when the Royal College of Art was granted university status, fashion was specifically excluded from the recherché group of subjects for which degrees could be awarded. A monumental row ensued and the advocates of fashion won the day, though in retrospect it can be argued that this victory cemented a defeat for the sensible approach to training which has never been reversed.

At the level below the RCA, fashion design courses proliferated, ranging from those offering a Diploma in Art and Design to those promoting vocational training or highly specialised technical education. With hindsight it can be said that the courses were both too many and too similar, but much more serious was the fact that they developed along a course parallel with that of the industry they were planned (if that is the word) to serve. There was, and is, a gulf between designers and industry, a suspicion and distaste of one for the other which is part ideological and part political, and which the most strenuous efforts by individuals have only partly bridged. That the fault lay in placing training for a commercial art within the fine arts sector of education is the view of many competent observers.

On the other hand, it is worth noting that in countries where the emphasis is more firmly on the practical side the design element is usually inferior to that in the work of English students. The two famous schools in New York—Parsons, with a more intellectual approach, and the Fashion Institute of Technology, largely financed by the trade—appear to turn out well rounded workers, but this may be because competition for places is very much fiercer than under the state system of education in Britain.

However it has come about, the gap between home-grown designers and quality manufacturers has had a wicked effect on the British fashion industry. When the youth boom of the 'sixties erupted, Britain, with a clutch of iconoclastic new designers, artists, pop singers and photographers, was in theory perfectly placed to change the world's theories about her own standing as a creative nation. London became 'swinging'. In practice, it all collapsed in a welter of tacky, trashy clothes which were promptly returned—if they were ever delivered—by their orderers. Fly-by-night businesses flew before ever a sleeve was completed. Of all that hopeful crew, only Mary Quant remains known, a monument to hard work, shrewd management and good timing. The poor reputation which other amateur operations attracted to England rubbed off on the whole industry. Worse, it hardened the hearts of those careful copiers of Paris who had served British exports so well in a previous decade. They wanted no student designers.

By the mid-seventies Britain was importing 50 per cent of her clothing and textiles, and the industry was on its knees begging Harold Wilson, the Prime Minister at the time, to impose restrictive quotas. But Mr Wilson was caught in the classic dilemma of all highly developed countries: should not an industry traditionally labour-intensive and simple to promote be left to the emerging nations so that they could generate the cash to buy our sophisticated hardwear?

So the British fashion industry learnt some bitter lessons indeed: the lesson of the post-war refusal to intensify mechanisation, at which Britain was adept and innovative, although even then it must have been apparent that we would always be susceptible to undercutting on price; the lesson of the continual promotion of fashion as a lightweight subject in which the customer was never educated to quality, only to price; and the failure to take top-level British talent sufficiently seriously for designers—even those without production facilities—to be used as laboratories for valuable ideas (even though so many of the new generation of students preferred to work in a small way on their own, which indicated a new turn in the direction of fashion).

Let us return to the opening years of the century when fashion became trade, a consumer commodity to be marketed to the mass rather than a service industry for the aristocratic and autocratic. Private enterprise was quick to recognise a new commercial avenue and the pressures of trade soon became apparent. Fashion had to change with a speed which, if it seems leisurely to us, was unprecedented. What is more, the ripples of these changes reached right across the social structure. What traders needed was designers with a recognisable personality, who could regularly create newsworthy and sufficiently desirable styles. It was a far cry from the time two hundred years before when the gossipy Mrs Papendieck could record in her *Private Life in the Time of Queen Charlotte* that one puce satin dress had done duty for six years and been revamped no less than three times.

Paris, that crucible of elegance, convenient geographically, sympathetic to the arts mineurs to say nothing of la vie grand luxe, greedy, venal, chic, with its unmatched craftsmen and standards in the couture industry, Paris was the natural centre for the trade of fashion. Endless analyses have been made in an attempt to find out why, so maddeningly for other countries, Paris retains the crown of authority in things to do with feminine style. To generalise, it might be said that in the past, less sophisticated but richer countries have turned to France for guidance about women because women are obviously of such importance in the community there. Where fashion is concerned, it is the priorities of Frenchwomen themselves which keep it sacrosanct. There are, in fact, more women judges and doctors in France than in America, but while American women seem to equate feminism with a need to prove themselves above such fripperies as chic, and the English, who always (according to Hardy Amies) put comfort first anyway, are gratefully slipping back into frumps when they are not rejecting fashion as anti-liberationist, French women clearly see no mutual exclusion between feminism and being intensely feminine. L'art de plaîre (of pleasing men), far from lowering the status of one's sex, is seen to be eminently worthy and mutually pleasurable. Of course it has changed, but only to the extent of a general loosening-up of style and an adoption of the younger, less dauntingly smart designers. But that too is part of pleasing in the modern idiom.

France, with a history of couture for the few and the little woman to copy for everyone else, was slow to mechanise its fashion industry. The wages for seamstresses in the early years of the century were as meagre as those in England, but conditions seem to have been less loathsome, perhaps because of the inherent pride in making clothing and the higher standing of the craft. Until the 'sixties France remained basically an innovative laboratory and purveyor of ideas rather than a mass-producer. When it did start to mass-produce, it was to the highest standards and well mechanised. Though expensive, the clothes have found a ready market. In 1969, ready-to-wear, though employing only 80,000 against couture's 465,000, generated more than 1,011 million francs. In 1975 the figure was 2,884 million francs. The most powerful fashion fair in the world is held twice a year at the Porte de Versailles in Paris, where houses show their collections while 'named' designers show, with the greatest possible inconvenience to all concerned, in their private ateliers. In 1961 only 100 manufacturers patronised the Porte de Versailles; in 1971 there were 780 exhibitors, at least 500 of them French.

The American store buyer was early on the Paris scene. In that classic of its genre, Edna Woolman Chase's *Always in Vogue*, there is an account of a buyer from Wanamaker's (it was Wanamaker who coined the phrase, 'the customer is always right') arriving in Paris on the eve of the First World War, bent, poor soul, on buying gowns while the old world crumbled. It makes fascinating reading because it recalls which designers, now obscure, were fashionable and also illustrates how little idea the Western world had of what was in store. Mr Hoffman, the buyer, was distraught at the prospect that American women might have no Paris fashions for the autumn—and after he had come three thousand miles and all—but instead of darting home and suggesting that the store should finance a field hospital or a battleship, he applied his tenacity to gathering up what he could. Callot was not ready, but Madame Cheruit said, 'Women must have clothes, war or no war, and those who make them must have a way to earn their living.' Paul Poiret was surrounded by weeping helpers and dressed in the uniform of the French Infantry. His comment, 'An artist is nothing when a soldier is wanted. France needs men today, not artists', makes two pleasing points. The first is that Poiret regarded himself firmly as an artist, not a dress designer; couture had come a long way since the humble vêtements of 1900. (In the Second World War the English solved the tricky artists versus men equation with the neat compromise of getting anyone remotely arty to paint camouflage.) Second, the juxtaposition with Cheruit illustrates the author's maxim that the two real characteristics separating the sexes are the idealism of men and the realism of women.

At the atelier of Worth, the Wanamaker buyer was met by the brothers

Jean-Philippe and Jacques, also in uniform. At Doeuillet's in the Place Ven-
dôme the few gowns already finished were eagerly procured by the American,
but his best bit of luck, 'my greatest opportunity', was the discovery that the
house of Bechoff-David had been forced to close by the summons to arms of
its head, so Mr Hoffman was able to buy the entire two hundred garments in
the collection at war prices, 'half the usual figures'.

The poignant contrast of the efforts of a no doubt humane man to snap up
bargains for his trade with the imminent collapse of the era which those
bargains represented hardly needs to be underlined. Mrs Chase also quotes
1914's most apposite fashion advice. It came from a wounded soldier who told
the sweet young woman sent to entertain him in hospital and who pondered
over the new line for spring that it would be 'mourning, Madame, mourning'.
In retrospect, it is more astonishing that after only a few months the French
fashion business was apparently back to normal and *Vogue* was able to feed the
geographically secure Americans with the latest delectable chiffons from
Paris. Meanwhile countless Amélies were praying for countless Georges 'who
was lying on his face, dead, with a bullet through his heart'. Or, a little later,
the poison gas in his lungs.

When important buyers got to Paris they found ready to welcome them the
expansive arms of the Chambre Syndicale de la Couture Parisienne, a useful
body founded in 1868. By the time the author began to attend couture shows
in 1966 she found it a mixed blessing, a mob of aged and ageless women who
sat in tiny cubicles at the top of an inadequate lift. In exchange for a fee they
issued a pass which got one into all sorts of houses one had no intention of
seeing, but they were quite inadequate to cope with a crisis at, say, Dior or
Balenciaga. But, fiercely—enviably—chauvinist, the Chambre was invaluable
to the secure foundation of the French couture business. It organised schedules
of showings, defeated only when Chanel entered the scene and insisted on
clashing with whomever she most disliked at the time; it ran a design school,
with the accent on techniques to fund the couture's workrooms; it organised
the system of cautions or entrance money; and with its identity-card system it
kept tags on who might legitimately be allowed in—heaven preserve you if
you were found not fit to be among the elect.

It was the pirating of designs that the Chambre's lists were sedulously
combed to prevent. In 1920 the French parliament had enacted a law which
gave registered fashion designs legal protection—possibly as a result of the
agitations of Paul Poiret, who as the first star in the new firmament got the first
dose of what mass-production was all about when he went to America and
found his models being sold everywhere, unlicensed. But it is very hard to

stop copying. Toiles were secreted away from the ateliers; photographic memories could reproduce the vital statistics of dozens of models though the viewing fee covered the reproduction of one only; not all journalists were above passing on sketches. It is said that Christian Dior himself once evicted a lady who was blandly photographing his new line with a little camera hidden in her hat. Being fastidious, he donned white gloves to show her out. The idea of imposing an embargo on picture releases was perfectly sound, for it was intended to allow time for the wretched designer to deliver his orders and so reap the benefit of his creative work. Given the modern spying apparatus available since the war, the protection of designs is remarkable, although in 1965 André Courrèges' revolutionary new space-age clothes were pirated in toto (**135**), causing the sloe-eyed Basque to retire in a huff for a year.

Designers in other countries were even less fortunate since on the whole their prestige was not enough to encourage the crediting of their name or the acknowledgement of their influence on an industry which was founded on copying and not on origination. In 1975 the wholesale dress house of Radley in London won a historic legal victory against the deliberate pirating of a mass-produced model, and membership of the European Economic Community brought some benefits of international copyright which applied to fashion design.

The Chambre Syndicale, chaired always by a distinguished designer or appropriately informed figure, proved that if the French are not clubbable they are groupable when their commercial interests are involved. This solidarity and seriousness of purpose was to invest French couture with an authority which even the Germans acknowledged in the Occupation. It was the then President of the Chambre, Lucien Lelong, who had to go to Berlin to discuss the translation of the French fashion world from Paris to the capital of the Reich and to Vienna. What the effect on the nationals might have been is questionable. In *The Isthmus Years* Barbara Cartland recalls that she had been stared at and followed in Berlin in 1935 because she was wearing make-up (she was also remarkably pretty, let it be added) and Hitler had decreed that women should be homely in appearance. There is nothing very homely about French haute couture. What Lelong managed to do, however, was to persuade the Germans that French fashion was sufficiently important to be kept going—in Paris.

The power of the group also allowed a tight hold to be kept on the change of silhouette. Many observers have remarked how surprising it is that when twenty or thirty more or less competent designers unveil their new line they all turn out to have been thinking in roughly the same direction. There are four explanations. The first is that creative designers in any sphere whose consumer antennae are well adjusted do tend to produce remarkably similar offerings at one time. As Samuel Smiles pointed out in *Self Help*, 'When the demands of industry are found to press upon the resources of inventors, the same idea is usually floating about in many minds.' Secondly, in fashion, which is both an art and a trade, there is a commercial advantage in saying the same thing. Anarchy is bad for business; a concerted cry has more authority and can be more forcefully promoted. Thirdly, a customer, however rich, will easily become disgruntled if she sees her wardrobe rendered obsolete too fast. There is no doubt that the uncontrolled explosion of silhouettes in the past five years, with waists in and out, hems up and down, sleeves off and on, has made many women disillusioned with the whole business of fashion; it has almost driven them into blue jeans. A disillusioned customer, who blames fashion for her innate uncertainty about what she should be wearing, is bad business. Finally, the designers very soon found that the maw of fashion was insatiable; ideas were gulped down by the vast new markets in the way a baby cuckoo disposes of teeny titbits proffered by its adoptive parents, and the producers of fashion titbits were kept equally on the wing. The pressure on a designer to produce four collections every year, each containing some stylistic theme that the traders can grasp and promote, is colossal. They burn out faster and faster—or opt out. Some co-ordination of silhouette was good common sense.

On the surface, the way the French actually presented their collections, at any rate after the Second World War, was anything but sensible. Hardly had the first buyer and first journalist made their ways back to Paris when the fashion industry, helped as always by a government both sympathetic and interested ('You cannot divorce creative art from trade,' the minister concerned with the textile industry at the Ministre de l'Économie Nationale told an English writer in 1946), was fêting its visitors, charging huge cautions, behaving as though Auschwitz and austerity had never been, issuing embargoes, tearing up journalists' notebooks, snubbing the meek and squeezing stout ladies into excruciatingly uncomfortable corners of salons. Just as a good deal of ritual banging and jumping around used to be thought necessary to ensure a good harvest, so, it seems, a successful collection cannot happen without a certain level of crippling rudeness and epic optimism about how much flesh can be fitted into a given area.

Under the surface, consciously or not, the excitement and bezazz of the French showings were just what the customers wanted. To have a seat was bliss, to be on the sofas very heaven. The conviction that it all mattered terribly was what set the cash tills ringing round the world. Many modifications later, it still does.

131. A tailor's sweating den in 1904, showing the conditions under which most clothes in the low and popular price range were made in the days before trade regulations became effective. Home and workshop were one and the whole family, men, women and children, worked as a unit. Prices were low and continually undercut, and the hours were dependent only on demand. Since this is a tailor's workshop, the hand finishing and the machine have an equal importance. The workers in this picture are probably Jewish refugees from Russian pogroms of the late nineteenth and early twentieth century; they formed the core of the trade at the time. Little capital was (and is) required, so unregulated homework appealed particularly to most recent and desperate immigrants. In the mid-nineteenth century, the garment workers were mostly Irish, now they are Cypriot or Asian. *(Mansell Collection)*

132. The clothes of smart Paris, intended for export to the United States and drawn by Georges Barbier for *Bon Ton* in 1915. The dress on the far left looks back to the straight pre-war style but all the rest are in the newest mode, with the revolutionary short full skirt which coincided with, even slightly preceded, the wartime rôle-change for women from passive to active. American *Vogue* was most anxious to avoid United States isolationism in fashion and persuaded the French to show clothes in the form of a playlet, *Sylvia's Wedding*, which toured through a series of United States fashion fêtes.

133. A Pucci pants suit became the epitome of Italian fashion on the world markets in the 1950s and 1960s. Marchese Emilio Pucci (1914–) began his design career in 1947 with his sports and resort clothes, inspired by his own experience of the 'Dolce Vita' at its most elegant. He gave them not only a richness of colour, making blouses and dresses from his brilliantly patterned scarf prints but also a trimness of line by using the newly developed stretch fabrics. He is now extending his creative sphere to encompass all aspects of design. *(Italian Fashion Board)*

134. A Chanel dress from 1932. The useful detail of construction is the result of organised fashion piracy. By various unexplained routes, this design was filched from Chanel, sketched accurately and quickly and found its way to Westbourne Grove where toiles and patterns of all the couturiers were made for those who could not or would not afford either a journey to Paris or Chanel's price for a model. This pirate house flourished throughout the 1930s and their sketches, now in the Victoria and Albert Museum, show the complexity of the 1930s cut. *(Victoria and Albert Museum)*

135. Courrèges clothes, 1965. These line-for-line copies by Alexander's, a large cut-price chain of stores in the USA, illustrate the tremendous American appetite for recognisable and conventional French fashion. The other prominent name in the business of line-for-line copies in America was the Ohrbach chain of department stores. Stark, trim tunics with calf-length white boots became a uniform for the smart woman of the mid-1960s and the Basque, André Courrèges (1923–   ), an engineer whose years of apprenticeship in fashion had been spent with Balenciaga, preferred to go from couture alone to producing his own designs and copies direct. *(New York Times)*

136. In 1969 fashion was poised for a change—but which way? These contestants in that year's Miss World competition illustrate the extremes and the compromises: Miss South Africa, on the left, wears a mini-skirt with midi-coat and Miss Turkey wears a maxi. Shops and customers had their worst year ever as store buyers dithered and purchasers hesitated. *(Keystone Press)*

10

Inspiration and Supply

If you asked women for two words to describe shopping for fashion those words would probably be 'Too hard!' Seventy-five years after fashion became a trade, the problems remain of finding something that fits (standardisation of size is often more of a hope than a reality, and now in Britain we have metrication to confuse the issue further), of navigating through acres of stores which are best described (by Ernestine Carter) as uncharted jungles, and of wandering through floor after floor bemused by the scatter-gun technique of the selector, which includes a small shot at everything and no precise direction. But then, how do you know nowadays what you should be looking for? This is the age of do-it-yourself fashion, which takes an awful lot of doing. The magazines and the papers which used to be so specific, authoritarian even, still show you what is going on in style, but then it is going on in so many different directions. Which are you to follow? Rising prices and see-sawing hemlines make the fear of a mistake more real.

It is tempting to think that it used to be more simple and more agreeable to buy one's clothes. There are all those pictures of lovely fitting-rooms and writing-rooms and helpful assistants and striped-panted floorwalkers. Contemporary evidence, however, suggests that it was just as tedious and frustrating, indeed often more so since usually one was buying only the materials and trimmings, which then had to be made up, probably rather ineptly, with endless fittings and standing about. Nor were those who did the making up any more accommodating then than the girl who tells you now that 'there's no call for grey' or whatever. The trenchant Mrs Ada Ballin wrote in *The Science of Dress*: 'It wants both knowledge and firmness to get a dress properly made; for the maker as a rule has a powerful store of arguments by which she defends her errors and the genus dressmaker is too apt to keep the genus lady in a state of hopeless and miserable subjection.' Mrs Ballin thought it was time for a 'strike against this tyranny' and a boycott of couturiers who would not do what they were told. She further suggested that any garment which could be made by a tailor should be so made, since tailors were not only 'more accurate in their fit but more attentive to instructions and less pig-headed'. Mrs Ballin was writing of English dressmakers, and it may have been similar experiences which led Mrs Asquith, who was very fashionable, to feel the need to give full instructions to the great Paul Poiret when she first visited his salon, a moment he recalls in *My First Fifty Years*.

At the turn of the century, very grand French ladies dressed in their own Parisian couture houses, which were still in essence no more than the little dressmakers at their peak (**137, 138**). The very rich Americans also dressed in Paris, and *Vogue* lists the smart houses as Worth, Redfern and Callot Soeurs. The very grand English, while not immune to the chic of a Paris label, stayed at home and shopped at Redfern, Creed, Lucile in Hanover Square, who is the only English designer to have persuaded her frumpy compatriots that pretty underwear was not a sin (her influence has not lasted), Reville and Rossiter, for whom Victor Stiebel worked much later, and Madame Handley Seymour. The adjective 'Court' which was a regular prefix to 'dressmaker' in those days did not indicate that the house supplied the Royal Family, merely that its customers were acceptable in Court circles.

Since the silhouette of fashion still changed slowly, great emphasis was placed on trimmings and on the fabric of the dress. Both the elaborations of the Edwardian toilette, which must have been irksome to free spirits, and the range of fabrics offered for much the same basic model, can be studied at the Victoria and Albert Museum in London which has the sketchbooks of Madame Handley Seymour for several years as well as some paper dolls with a complete ensemble, the work of Irene Segalla. The Museum also houses guard-books from Worth which make the same point.

The average household still relied on the 'little dressmaker'. A part of the folklore of French elegance, the little woman in Britain was a poor, drab thing, coming in by the day, badly paid and exhibiting less a skill and understanding for the art of dress than the truth of the maxim that while you can sew you'll never starve. A nonagenarian servant recounted to the author in 1976 the jealousy with which the village seamstress, a widow with five children to keep, was regarded by the other staff in her mistress's house. It was the custom of this philanthropic lady to send a joint of meat across to the deserving dressmaker every week; her own servants much resented what they viewed as unnecessary charity and would frustrate her good intentions by pretending to forget to deliver the joint or by wrapping it in filthy paper. So much for mutually supportive class instinct.

To us it seems strange that intelligent women who were badly off did not make their own clothes rather than submit to inelegance by moral blackmail or struggle with inefficient and time-consuming workers. But this is to misunderstand the climate of the times. Labour was cheap and plentiful and, as is still found in developing countries today, the organic viability of the community, to say nothing of the retention of pride in service and crafts-manship, does depend on those on one rung in the financial ladder being employed by those—however immediately—above them and employing those—however immediately—below themselves. It would be interesting to argue whether do-it-yourself was the result or the cause of the impossibility of getting anything done by anyone else in the developed countries.

However it may be, it is surprising that do-it-yourself did not come sooner. Think of all the jokes in *Punch*, especially after the 1914–18 war when the new emancipation of women had eroded the servant class and a special monster, the cook-general, was all most housewives could find: why did not everyone learn to cook and thus be free from discord and tyranny? Perhaps the old traditions of responsibility and paternalism died harder than we think.

They certainly died hard in India, where up until the dissolution of the Raj sewing was done by a little dressmaker, only this time a male called a derzi. Squatting on his rug on the verandah, this nimble fellow would copy anything you wanted in record time, including, if you were careless enough not to point out what you wanted, any patches and tears on the original garment.

If the little dressmaker is part of French fashion folklore, the Singer sewing machine is part of the folklore of the world. The only Western innovation not disapproved of by Mahatma Gandhi in India—he had used one when he was in prison and regarded its influence as entirely beneficial, which was handy for the derzis—the Singer machine was also one of the very first consumer durables available on hire purchase, in 1856. It was used by the Wright brothers to sew the wings of their aeroplanes and by the Italians (if Singer advertising is to be believed) for running up dirigibles in 1912. Finally, its effects on the clothing industry from the largest concern down to the most modest home dressmaker are incalculable. Singer reckon that it was the Depression in America which caused the boom in home sewing (meaning sewing by the housewife or family, rather than coming in to sew or working professionally at home). In this country it was the Second World War which gave women who had never previously done either the idea of making clothes and cooking.

How did anyone know what to sew? Back in 1902 one was constantly admonished to buy a really good paper pattern for one's dressmaker to copy. The magazine *The World of Fashion* had included paper patterns in 1850, the year the Singer sewing machine was finalised, but Ebenezer Butterick rev-olutionised the trade in 1866 with a New York mail-order service which in 1873 was extended to Regent Street in London. Weldons, one of the most familiar names, started up in 1879. Very soon, women's magazines discovered in the provision of free paper patterns a reliable way of boosting their cir-culation. Samuel Beeton's famous *Englishwoman's Domestic Magazine* pioneered popular patterns in 1870 and none was too grand to eschew the method. When the pace and variety of fashion became intense, though—say after the Second World War—so did the competition from the specialised pattern companies, whose merchandise was placed next to the piece goods department in the stores; most magazines turned their attentions to knitting.

The first knitting pattern-book is thought to be that published by Mrs Gaugain in 1842, and John Paton's Universal Knitting Book, produced in 1899, was a bestseller. The whole idea of knitted outer garments being smart was new and made possible only because it was adopted by the Jersey Lily, Lillie Langtry. Strangely, its application to sport was not immediately grasped, though by 1909 there were various shapeless cardigans which afforded more comfort to the emancipated new woman. It took Chanel, who had observed the ergonomic charms of jersey even before the war, to make it a high fashion material and to give it a place in history. Since the explosion of silhouette in 1968, jersey, like trousers, has become an integral part of any woman's wardrobe all the year round, for it is especially suited to manufacture in synthetic fibres.

In the 1950s the whole realm of home knitting was invaded by the knitting machine. Although it had the same revolutionary potential as the sewing machine had had a hundred years earlier, its original launch was marred in Britain by shoddy service, overselling, incompetent training and a host of bad debts; even now, although the trade is on much firmer ground and the range of patterns offered on one machine is truly dramatic, the majority of people who knit knit at home by hand. It remains to be seen whether the worsening economic climate of the 'seventies, coupled with the fashionable desire for self-sufficiency, will push up the sales of the Jones and the Knitmaster.

When it is free to take any direction it chooses, supply naturally follows demand, so it is not surprising that in huge countries with remote com-munities, such as America, and in small countries while travel was still difficult, one of the main streams of retailing should have been mail order. The privileged had always had the service of specialist shops in the cities with whom they had often dealt for generations and who could be trusted to execute an order and send it down to the country if a visit, say to London, was impossible. 'With what interest and excitement the arrival of the case containing the garments was awaited,' Lady Jeune wrote of country life in the 1870s, 'and the new mode canvassed. How quietly but certainly the appearance of the new garments at church heralded a reproduction of the same in the person of the parson's wife and the smaller ladies of the community, who considered the big lady a faithful apostle of dress!' Flora Thompson recalls in *Lark Rise to Candleford* the excitement caused at the turn of the century by the re-appearance in the village of girls who were 'in service' and who turned up in their mistresses' cast-offs, which were similarly aped, and she also notes the growing jealousy between the local suppliers to the migratory gentry, and the London shops. The locals were anxious to extend their range to more luxurious items, for which there was a growing demand, and to supply the bonnets of the lady of the manor.

But mail order on the professional scale was the logical result of the opening up of vast areas of America and the British Empire and—in Britain itself—of an interest in clothing not matched by travel facilities or disposable incomes. While the American giants, Sears Roebuck (founded in 1893) and Montgomery Ward (founded in 1872), furnished ploughs and refrigerators alongside Paris frocks, the Army and Navy Stores (which began as a club in 1872) brought a most surprising range of goods, from portable baths to perishable goods packed on ice, in itself a precious commodity, to the far-flung Raj. In *Plain Tales from the Raj* Vere Birdwood recalls: 'We existed on the Army and Navy Stores catalogue, from which we used to order a great deal to be sent up. Everybody spent hours browsing through it, and one acquired all sorts of useless junk over the years.' (A facsimile of the catalogue was a top seller in 1969.) But catalogues for the home market specialised in fashion—at a price. Indeed, the whole mail-order area of fashion has been irremediably connected with cheapness in the public mind, despite various efforts to give it authority and style by the employment of high fashion names as consultants. The biggest group in England is Great Universal Stores, with an estimated turnover in 1974 of £250 million. Littlewoods is also a dominant name, with a turnover of £175 million for the same year, in which it is estimated that there were twenty-four main catalogue names in circulation. Total turnover in 1975 was £1,100 million.

In *The Beautiful People*, Marylin Bender records a similar search for chic among North American companies. Both Sears Roebuck and Montgomery Ward have been loyal customers of French couture and now of French and Italian ready-to-wear.

The direction in which high style did push free trade was that of the department store. Alison Adburgham, in her definitive book on English shopping habits of the past, states that it was Bon Marché in Paris which the

Americans regarded as the first department store because they had never, in 1855, been to the English provinces and seen Bainbridges of Newcastle or Kendal Milne and Faulkener of Manchester. These shops beat the London stores to it both in diversification of merchandise and in operating methods. By 1900 almost all the familiar names were around, though not all at their present addresses. Exceptions were the John Lewis Partnership (many of whose parts did, however, already exist) and Selfridges, which opened in Oxford Street in 1909.

Gordon Selfridge was American and versed in the ways of American retailing, which was without the feudal, small-trader traditions of most of the English emporia and which is well illustrated by the imposing building he put up to house his 130 departments, his rest rooms and his restaurants. He was also a revolutionary in the fashion trade, not just because his windows were lit up at night, not just because he saw his store as having a total ambience and total facilities in which a customer could spend a whole day of purchase and leisure, but because he saw that the customer who would want to spend her day in this way was not the old-style 'carriage-trade' type but one of the swelling numbers of middle and lower middle classes who were such an integral part of the fashion phenomenon.

The provision of ready-to-wear clothes by the stores had been growing steadily, matched by the growing unwillingness of the customer to wait for fittings or to make intricate choices; more and more garments were available ready-made and what was not to be had over the counter was provided swiftly and efficiently by the huge workrooms attached to all the major stores. They carried on, too, the tradition of posting to their country customers, providing seductive brochures of wares which could be sent for with confidence. It was still a far cry from 'impulse buying' which today affects even the most expensive items, including jewellery and furs, but it was a step in that direction. It was also a signpost to the new customer. It takes not just patience but confidence to commission something, be it a sculpture or a new dress. The emancipated upper class may have been irritated by the time-scale imposed by fashion at the turn of the century; the new money was unnerved by the unaccustomed exercise of choice, and all the opportunities for mistakes that choice offers. But if what you have bought is the only thing available in the shop, then you can always shift the blame to the shop.

This recognition of the new customer is crucial in any trade; by a neat turn of events it was a Selfridges-trained buyer, when he was engaged on the turn-around of a long established but fashionably depleted chain of stores, Wetherall, who remarked to the author in 1974 that the greatest danger was in trying to keep on catering for customers who in fact no longer exist. Looking back at the Selfridge concept of 1909, one can see that in British retailing its only successor has been Biba, which in 1973 took over the site of Derry and Toms in Kensington High Street (**139**). Biba, which is part of British retailing history not only because of its collapse but also because of its origins, was established as a store with much the same idea of ambience, relaxation, purchase and leisure which had activated Gordon Selfridge. Unlike the department store of tradition, though, it offered a very closely written script of taste and preference; it was more the reflection of and the provider for a certain way of life than a department store offering many people the products of many industries in many places. Biba's incarnation in 1964 illustrated a new way of thinking at store level, rare since Selfridge's buccaneer efforts. That is not to say that the other stores had not been active; many of them had, but in retrospect their activities can be seen as no more than tinkering about and fiddling while the market for fashion in the stores burned away.

Two major factors gave rise in England to a change of trading patterns which must have done the department stores incalculable harm in fashion retailing. The first factor was the inability to recognise the needs of the customer. As seasons became blurred and more and more people travelled, the stores still pursued antiquated buying schedules which ensured that whatever garment you wanted was not in stock at that time. Then the arrangement of such merchandise as was available remained—remains, to a great extent—so fragmented by garment, price, colour and by the shop's hierarchy that the force of the fashion argument is never felt by even an enthusiastic shopper.

The second factor was the increasing problem of servicing such customers as you had. The retail trade in Britain traditionally occupies a low place in the esteem of school-leavers and careers advisers. Despite the prospects of promotion, the hours, the idea of 'serving' and the pay have all led to a decline in interest in the profession of selling, and this has not been helped by the almost manic secrecy with which the traders tackle their separate though often similar problems. When other lures were not effective, service—superb service—teamed with the attractions of credit and chic van delivery might have held young customers steady, and it is the steady customer, the one who comes back, who is the backbone of any business. As it was, just as the stores did not grasp the implications of the new clothes they were selling, neither did they grasp the implications of the new customer and the new sales staff.

The result was something called the boutique boom, and this is where Biba comes in again. Biba, the brainchild of fashion artist Barbara Hulanicki and her husband, Stephen Fitz-Simon, was originally a boutique, housed in 1963 in an unprepossessing hutch in Abingdon Road. The other historic boutique is Mary Quant's Bazaar, established in 1955 as a result of frustration with what,

1. In the beginning ... and now. The unacceptable aspect of the male anatomy was designated by God initially and by the police in 1975 when a streaker breasted the pitch at Twickenham Rugby Football Ground. Somewhere in between had come the more extrovert display of manly charms revealed by the mini-tunics and tight hose of the fourteenth century (the Church disapproved) and that aggressive notion, the codpiece, within which it was possible to accommodate, according to one contemporary writer, both pins and small objects; the latter phrase is one of those unfortunate slips of the pen which cause modern females to raise their brows at the social implications of this piece of dress. (*Fratelli Alinari/Syndication International*)

2. Fashion has always had its recorders, verbal, pictorial and now photographic. By the 'seventies Barry Lategan was established as one of the most intuitive and delightfully inventive portrayers of fashion. There seemed about to be a romantic revival in the close-knit artistic world, and Lategan drew from a Pre-Raphaelite exhibition the inspiration for a re-creation of Rossetti's Proserpine (*left*). Some of his best work has been to illustrate Ossie Clark's great skill in combining an extraordinary understanding of how to cut fabric to flatter and cling, a new and very sensual degree of revelation, and the fluid look which killed the space-age message of Cardin and Courrèges. Many of Clark's most beautiful clothes have been made in prints by Celia Birtwell, to whom he was married. This dress (*below*) from his summer 1976 collection is typical, but Ossie Clark's influence penetrated right through the High Street market via his inimitable little frocks, usually in crêpe, which were manufactured by the Radley organisation. Probably his most famous innovation was in 1967, the short sleeve worn over a lóng, fuller one, hitherto an unthinkable sartorial faux pas. (*The Times/Vogue*)

3. Painters have always been important conveyers of fashion and of implicit social mores, and even in the age of the photograph they have a special dimension to offer. The high tide of Edwardian opulence was splendidly caught by John Singer Sargent, who in this 1902 picture of the Acheson sisters presents the British apotheosis of the Gibson Girl with her tiny waist and high, boned collar on a fill-in for a delicious décolletage. Pristine white, and a large black hat with ostrich feathers, must have been eminently unsuitable for the plebeian task of picking oranges, even hothouse-grown, but there is a hint that they are in fact closer to the golden apples of Atalanta, who of course had the race all her own way. The Acheson sisters were the daughters of Archibald Barbazon Acheson, fourth Earl of Gosford and of Louise Augusta, second daughter of the seventh Duke of Manchester and of Louise von Alten, who upon Manchester's demise nabbed another Duke, this time Devonshire, and was thus called the Double Duchess. (*His Grace The Duke of Devonshire*)

4a. The First World War freed many women into channels of which they had never dreamed. It also produced a severe shortage of eligible men. Perhaps inevitably the relationship between the sexes was strained. The fashionable reflection in dress was jokey, women wearing asexual tubes or men's smoking jackets. Some women, though, seized the opportunity to follow their real inclinations and to dress the part. Vita Sackville-West stalked Paris on the arm of the daughter of Edward VII's mistress, disguised (she thought) as a boy. Una, Lady Troubridge was the paramour of Radclyffe Hall, author of the famous lesbian novel, *The Well of Loneliness*, which was published in 1928 to undisguised disapproval. On hand for a sympathetic and brilliant portrait was the equally ambivalent Romaine Brooks, a great painter and a terrifying letter-writer. This picture is dated 1924. (*National Collection of Fine Arts, Washington*)

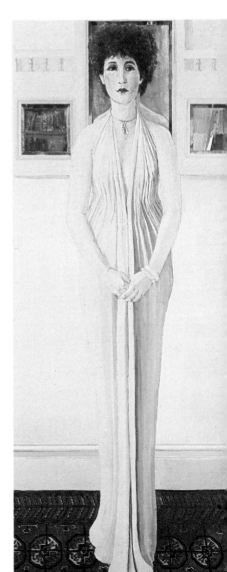

4b. While Kenzo Takada was becoming the most influential designer in Paris, in London the Japanese presence was Yuki, whose calm and decidedly inscrutable way of handling material — the dress in this picture has only one seam — was both a subtle alternative to fantastic extravagance and a technical revolution. The painter, David Remfrey, has fully understood the implications of 1976 dress vis-à-vis its wearer. (*Prudence Glynn*)

5. The reaction to the aggressive, sharp-line clothes of the mid-sixties was the idealised romanticism of Laura Ashley. Impractical perhaps, but recognising a social consciousness and a nostalgia for a more self-sufficient age. (*Laura Ashley*)

6. 'The woman I am interested in is la vraie Femme. Put that with a capital F...' Sonia Rykiel told British *Vogue* in May 1976. One of the most consistently successful of the new wave of French ready-to-wear names which took over from a moribund Paris haute couture in the early 1970s, Rykiel presents an intensely personal, beautifully worked out group of clothes which never outdate one another and yet have something new to add for the addicts each season. 'I cannot understand why other women want my clothes,' Ms Rykiel confessed to *Vogue*. 'They are only an expression of myself in colour and shape.' But then that was the basis of Coco Chanel's talent, too. The photograph, by David Bailey, is of the most famous model of 1976, Marie Helvin. (*Vogue*)

7. A typical refined, clean-cut, all-American Norell idea. Norman David Levinson (1900-72), known to the world of fashion as Norman Norell ('N for Norman, L for Levinson, and another L for looks,' he is said to have explained), was one of the few American designers to become famous in the classical mould of couture/ready-to-wear; the untimely death of Clare McCardell robbed her of the sheer length of service which is strangely such a necessary part of an ephemeral business. Like other famous names elsewhere, Norell had a background of costume design, but he became the Balenciaga of America, and while not the most radical innovator he took the opportunity afforded by the Second World War when America was cut off from the seductive influence of Paris to open an immensely successful business which survived after his more adventurous contemporaries had found themselves abandoned once the fight was over. Norell translated the French concept of intrinsic chic into the dream American lifestyle, and offered American women the chance to sample the quality and intransigence of the hautest of haute couture. The son of a cheap hat store proprietor, Norman Norell died the designer of some of the most expensive and glamorous ready-to-wear clothes in the world. (*Fashion Institute*)

8. The acceptable face of punk. A vacuum is never filled with moderation, always with violence, it has been said. A certain dullness of silhouette in fashion, which reflected an ennui with established leadership in all sorts of fields, produced in 1977 a style called punk. Punk means, literally, rubbish, worthless. There was punk music, punk rock, punk style, which consisted of wearing rags and tatters held together with safety pins and darning stitches, the holes becoming, as the trend spread, more and more self-induced. The pinning craze spread from clothes to flesh, and the bolder punk protagonists pierced their nostrils, ears or cheeks with everything from the statutory safety pin to gold and diamond half-hoops.

It takes both a very stable society and a very clever designer to transform a potentially menacing style into an original and attractive trend. It is thus significant that in 1977 Zandra Rhodes, herself always notable for a surprising choice of dress and hair colour, produced a superb collection of dresses whose tattered hems, exquisitely stitched, and gaping rents clasped by beaded pins created Punk Chic. Much as Yves St Laurent had lent wit and elegance to blue denim a decade before, Zandra Rhodes transformed the principle of old clothes into an exercise in design. In the photograph, Zandra, with green hair, wears Punk Chic from her autumn collection, 1977. (*Robyn Beeche*)

and with how, clothes were available at that time. Bazaar began as a small shop but when it proved impossible to find suitable merchandise even for that Miss Quant turned designer; the need is father to the man (**140**). Many of the boutiques were improvident (if not dishonest), incompetent and short-lived, but they did two things; they removed a considerable volume of the fashion trade from the stores by buying what the young spenders wanted when they wanted it and by providing a sympathetic if sometimes grubby ambience; and they revolutionised the concept of service by specialising in one thing, or things which all went together, all in a small space, all easily available, all with an individual stamp, catering for a new, wide public as effectively as had the intimate dealings of the family shopkeeper, who also knew his customers' taste. Boutiques broke down the old barriers of season and cloth, and, although manufacturers were to tear their hair trying to produce a new range every six weeks instead of twice a year with a couple of mid-seasons if you were lucky, there is no doubt that the maw of the fashion phenomenon could be satisfied with nothing less at the time.

The democratisation of fashion started by Gordon Selfridge was continued apace by the development of the chain stores. Not the cheapest now nor the most fashionable, Marks and Spencer, who in 1975 opened a branch in Paris, remains the classic of the genre, keeping step with its customer so adeptly that she may be anything from a duchess to a cleaner (because that is what society is like now). Marks and Spencer, which began as a penny bazaar, was by 1894 a chain of stores, but between the wars it had a price limit (as did Woolworths) which restricted its fashion sales: five shillings. But the chairman, Lord Marks, came under American retailing influence and so efficiently had the marketing lessons been learned that by the 'thirties it became possible, even for five shillings, to produce fashion that the new working girl wanted. One of the reasons why it became possible was the adoption of intimate relationships with suppliers, who toed what has been felt in creative terms to be both an exacting and a suppressive line. The customer was magnificently served, however, more and more so, and the Englishwoman's predilection for snapping up clothes with the minimum bother is well illustrated by the fact that with an item such as the brassière, surely so intimate and fundamental a garment as to require advice and fitting, Marks and Spencer have one-third of the total market.

America never had a boutique boom because its stores, unimpeded by the feudal hangover, were from the first competitive, alert and high-fashion-minded. All the couture models bought in Paris from the turn of the century were made up in the stores' workrooms, and long after it had ceased to be a profitable concern a store such as Bergdorff-Goodman retained its custom

205

salon to provide for the rich who were too idle to hassle with Paris. Henri Bendel was a brilliant merchant. The Marcus family of Neiman-Marcus of Dallas, Texas, chose to use their money to open a store in 1907 rather than take up the licence for Coca-Cola for that state, and so far as I know have never expressed their regret at the decision. In the often suspicious atmosphere which surrounds the reporting, buying and promotion of fashion in England, it is hard to emphasise sufficiently the push and the vitality which American stores exude. Even a lower-priced store such as Ohrbach's (which is now part of the Dutch Brenninkmeyer empire, familiar in Britain as C and A Modes) attuned its thinking to French haute couture when that was fashionable, producing line-for-line copies which were the uniform of smart New York and of ambition everywhere. (Marks and Spencer bought toiles from France too, but never publicised the fact.) A downturn in the fortunes of the gracious Bonwit-Teller was ascribed by a senior executive of the store to 'staying on the Courrèges balloon after it had been pricked'. Unlike the English, the American buyers went all over Europe—all over the world—with their antennae quivering, and as a result neither the new type of customer nor the new pattern of fashion merchandising threw them. It was a grand store buyer who first told me about Kenzo Takada—'a hot name down on the Right Bank somewhere, you should see him'—as we came out of Dior one sultry August day. Whatever or whoever was in fashion (and in retrospect both seem sometimes pretty silly), your friendly neighbourhood store was throwing parties for it or them, linked with the local smart charity and attended by all the best customers, who had bought new dresses for the occasion.

After the promising start of the Boucicauts and their Bon Marché in Paris, French fashion retailing remained in the grip of the small concern and the couture house. These houses, it is true, extended their activities to include in many instances boutiques on the premises, which sold less expensive clothes and the accessories to wear with them—Schiaparelli's boutique was famous, and Lucien Lelong's 'éditions' department was very influential—and the designers increasingly licensed their names to the manufacture of scent, lingerie, stockings and luggage which were distributed around the country. But French provincial shopping remains much less sophisticated than that of either England or America; Galeries Lafayette, founded in 1895 by Alphonse Kahn and Théophile Bader has only six branches, and Au Printemps, founded by Jules Jaluzot in 1865, has nineteen stores. Both are chic targets for visitors, and for those in search of a cheap variety there are the thirty-six branches of the Prisunic chain. All the major ready-to-wear designers have their own outlets.

Fashion shopping in Italy is even more complex. Thousands of small shops—twice the number per capita of population as those which provide so efficiently for German wants—sell an assortment of odds and ends. Upim and, further up the market, La Renasciente provide chain-store fashion, but the elegant woman dresses in the individual boutiques of the great houses and accessory-makers in the cities.

So much for the supply of fashion to those who want it. But how did they know what to want? The answer is that when fashion became trade and shops began to sell it there emerged the medium in which to promote it. With advances in paper and printing technology, fashion acquired a literature of its own. In 1892 Mr Arthur Turnure introduced *Vogue* to the receptive American public, and in 1909 it was sold to Condé Nast. In 1916, pressed by the impossibility of shipping American issues to Europe, Nast set up British *Vogue* and in 1920 French *Vogue* appeared. The following year *Jardin des Modes* joined the fashionable stable which already included *La Gazette du Bon Ton*, founded by Lucien Vogel in 1912. In 1913 the Hearst Corporation bought a magazine called *Harper's* and began a battle for fashion supremacy which, despite the constant numerical superiority in favour of *Vogue*, has attracted a lively audience and livelier participants.

Just as the twentieth century did not invent fashion designers but did give them a new prominence, so the twentieth century gave a new prominence to fashion reporting. Notes and hints and paper patterns had been doled out to the interested by such reputable organs as *Queen, Ladies' Home Journal, The World of Fashion* and *The Quarterly Report of Metropolitan Fashions*, published by the busy Mr Butterick. *Vogue* introduced the society note by publishing sketches in 1895 of the trousseau lingerie selected by Miss Consuelo Vanderbilt for her wedding to the Duke of Marlborough, an unhappy match for which the frills and embroidered ducal coronets on her undies can have been little compensation. One wonders how much space the trousseau lingerie of a modern duchess would take up on the page.

It was not all easy. 'From the start,' recalls Mrs Woolman Chase, who had to lead it, '*Vogue*'s struggle with the French couture was wearing, complex and illogical. Wanting yet fearing publicity, the couture tried to palm off on us amateur sketches of their inferior designs instead of allowing us to make good drawings or photographs of their best. Cheruit, in particular, had a seedy, effeminate little artist whose work she was always trying to push into *Vogue*'s pages.'

The mention of photographs is interesting because it was not so much the fact that fashion was covered as how and by whom that made the fashion phenomenon. Most illustrations were done by artists—a practice which continued in newspapers, with their unreliable reproduction and their hasty deadlines—until in the late 1940s Harold Keble, Assistant Editor of the *Daily*

Express, gave a new look to popular fashion with photographs by John French. French developed a technical process for lighting, shooting and particularly for printing pictures which could be used with very high-speed rotary presses and inferior quality paper. 'Until then,' Keble recalls, 'fashion photographs had been taken by just any of the staff men who happened to be around. Probably they had been behind a goalpost all afternoon before getting to the catwalk in the evening.' The staid Sunday quality columns were transformed by the use by Ernestine Carter on the *Sunday Times* of photographers of equal quality to those in the glossy magazines. Reporting fashion bred a whole group of talent of its own—the artists Christian Berard, Georges Lepape, René Bouet-Willaumez, Cecil Beaton, René Bouche, Carl Erickson (Eric), Francis Marshall, Sheradski, and the star of *Women's Wear Daily*, Kenneth Paul Block, Robb of the *Express*, Cecil Beaton again in his photographic right, Irving Penn, Horst, Richard Avedon, David Bailey, Norman Parkinson, Eduard Steichen, Baron Gayne de Meyer, Man Ray.

Until the Second World War the newspapers' interest in fashion was mainly social. Corisande (or Miss Minnie Hogg), doyenne gossip columnist of the *Evening Standard*, had launched the young Norman Hartnell on his way almost as an aside, there being no other society distractions on that evening. After the war things were very different, but if Mrs Chase had had problems with French couture in 1914 it was nothing compared with the problems the English journalists had with the Board of Trade. Returning from the electrifying presentation of the New Look in 1947, Mrs Alison Settle and other distinguished journalists were summoned to see Sir Stafford Cripps and told that they were not to report such extravagant and radical styles. Mrs Settle asked Sir Stafford if he had ever heard of King Canute.

Despite Sir Stafford, fashion became big news in England as elsewhere and editors started the twice-yearly trips to the shrine of Paris to report on the goings-on. Pages were held, hysterics were had; tales of horror fill most of the autobiographies of post-war writers. But more seriously for fashion the groove was dug so deep that writers were unable to change the track long after the tune was worn out. In America where fashion and society of the pop kind had been so successfully and profitably welded, the new sort of fashion photographer was the instant-click, all-night-party-going, restaurant-haunting expert with an encyclopaedic mind. In Europe the same talents were harder to find. Like the old-time couturier, both wanting and fearing publicity, the café socialites had to be stalked with guile and the secrets of their wardrobes were very much harder to get.

It was a far cry from the elegant and leisured portraits of the past, with famous beauties condescending to be snapped with a vase of lilies and some soft lighting. The professional model of today has to look good in the most uncomfortable circumstances, and even the glossiest magazines reflect in their pictures the restlessness and frantic energy which is part of fashion from the streets.

Has fashion been well served by those who have reported it? One must distinguish between the art form and the ultimate consumer to decide this. From the point of view of the customer the answer must be yes. Fashion has been shown with wit, with humour, with authority and with intelligence and illustrated by first-class talents. The imagination and the skill employed in this century in reporting the changes of style should appeal even to those not specially interested in clothes. The customer can and does complain that art has taken over from visibility in some pictures, that she is disappointed when she comes face to face with the actual garment and—now, especially—that the styling of the photographs looks all right for a pose but is impossibly elaborate for real life.

As an art form, fashion has been best treated in those countries who most appreciate its value. In France, *L'Officiel* and *Elle* are bibles of their genre and French newspaper reporting is detailed and succinct. America has a much more lively and gossipy approach and possesses a piece of journalistic history in Eugenia Shepherd and in *Women's Wear Daily*: they generate a constant flow of interest in the subject in its widest form and galvanise stores and designers and manufacturers into one cohesive, profitable whole. The press in England, where fashion has a more tenuous hold on the intellect and a very tenuous hold on the pocket, all too often treats fashion as a 'lightweight' to brighten up a serious day's news, as an opportunity to display as much naked flesh as possible under the cloak of an unexceptionable heading, or as a commercial lure for advertisers, who have been taught to expect editorial coverage as their due. Most damagingly for both the customer and the industry, coverage is relentlessly geared to cheap price. Thus, when in the 'seventies we faced the reality of price rises in labour, in raw materials, in shop overheads, in inflation, the customers had not been trained to discriminate, as now they had to; British industry, though stylish, was untrained in quality, leaving a gap which was quickly filled by imported merchandise.

Most alarming for all those concerned with the fashion retailing and manufacturing business must have been the trend which began in the late 'sixties for second-hand clothes. Originally this sprang from a genuine need: young students with babies and not much money turned necessity into a virtue and put together a stylish outfit from the contents of the local jumble sale. It was also an indication of opting out of 'chic' society, and doubtless nostalgia for the quality of other days was involved. The trend was—is—strong enough to

209

warrant complete features in such magazines as *19* and frequent incidental mentions in everything from *Vogue* down. History suggests that the wearing of second-hand clothes usually presages a major change and is an indication that for the majority of people fashion has gone too far. Marie-Antoinette's emulators were forced to buy second-hand finery to keep up with her and in the 1930s second-hand shops flourished as would-be fashionables scrambled after the ultimate artificiality of Schiaparelli's silhouette. And now? Well, at the last count, to look well dressed outdoors involved a layered arrangement of no less than nine garments.

137. Paquin à Cinq Heures, painted by Henri Gervex in 1906, shows the clientele of one of the top French maisons de couture at a period when shopping for clothes was a leisurely activity consuming a large and pleasurable part of the fashionable woman's day. Whatever the scale of the establishment, the customer was always right. There was another side to it, though, and staff hours were long. In our more enlightened age, five o'clock is almost time to chivvy out the last customer and shovel on the dust sheets.

Paquin, later linked with Worth, was founded in Paris in 1891 and in London in 1912, and became one of the most important couture houses of the period, combining splendour with seductive luxury. Madame Paquin and her husband Isadore (formerly a banker) realised the importance of export and were the first to open branches abroad. They were conscious of the stage as a setter of styles, even including a mini-theatre among the amenities of the house.

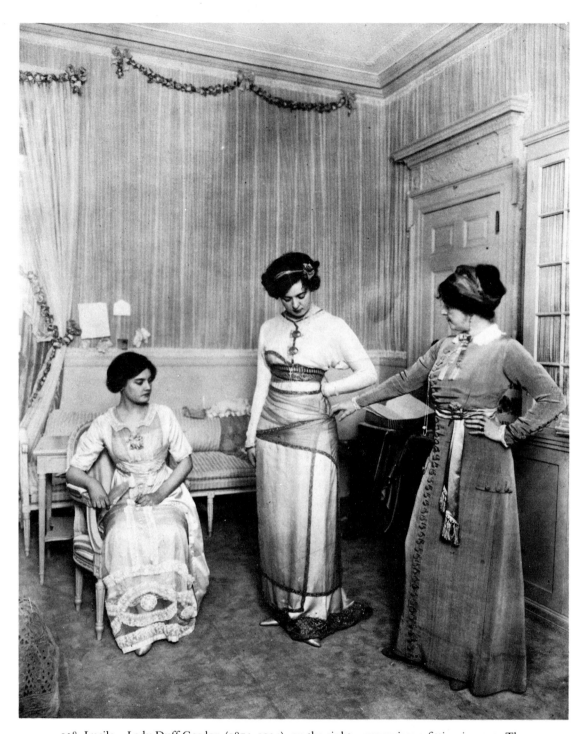

138. Lucile—Lady Duff Gordon (1875–1934), on the right—supervises a fitting in 1912. The dresses show her skill in the combination of sheer fabrics and simple shapes, and have the low, round neck that she did so much to popularise. The show rooms were deliberately designed to complement her designs, and swags of pink roses around the curtains were something of a Lucile trademark when applied to dress or décor, epitomising her preference for the soft, pretty and seductive.

Lucile, sister of Elinor Glyn, the novelist, considered herself the couture rival of Poiret. She began her career in London in the late 1890s and later opened branches in Paris, New York and Chicago. She suffered financial reverses and her popularity waned as the style changed from the picturesque to the functional in the 1920s. *(Victoria and Albert Museum)*

139. Biba mother-and-daughter fashions, 1970.
Barbara Hulanicki opened her boutique Biba in
1963, and so great was the popularity of her
pale, crêpe, highly individualistic dresses, many
of them in the 1930s idiom, that she expanded
until in 1973 she took over the enormous Derry
and Toms store in Kensington High Street,
where you could buy life-style as well as
clothes. But such a large area devoted to
imaginative living was too much for the
property values of the mid-seventies to support
and in 1975 Biba closed. (The Times)

140. Mary Quant (1934–) took her Chelsea
Look to the top of world fashion markets,
promoting an image of 'Swinging
London'—the English contribution to the
youth quake of the 1960s. Together with her
husband, Alexander Plunket Greene, and
Archie McNair, in 1955 she opened Bazaar, the
first boutique in Chelsea. It sold seasonable,
youthful clothes, the sort of thing she herself
liked wearing, which were seized on avidly by
young people tired of the traditional fashion
image and shopping patterns. In response to
demand, the scope of Mary Quant's product
has broadened to encompass cosmetics,
accessories and even dolls and household furnishings. The outfits in the photograph date
from 1960.

This photographic image, elegant in its black
and white clarity, was by pioneer fashion
photographer John French, who from his début
in 1948 until his death in 1966 epitomised the
image of each season.

OUR $5.98 TROUSSEAU OUTFIT.

$5.98

48c

141. An American mail-order trousseau of 1904, pretty to look at and cheap to buy if you did not think of all the sweated labour that had gone into its making. Nor was it practical if you did your own laundry, for washing, starching and goffering frills was hot, heavy and time-consuming work and you still had to re-thread all those pretty ribbon insertions. Most underwear of the period is less fragile than it looks because the cambric is of a strong quality and the lace, machine-made, will take a great deal of punishment. Even up-market silk is reasonably strong. The size range was always greater and better organised in the United States, with its long tradition of mail order, than it was elsewhere, and in this case is generous, 32″–42″ bust. For those who could not quite manage the curves unaided, the corset cover with its well ruffled front is described as a 'perfect shirtwaist distender'.

"Remember it used to be Dior, Balmain, Yves St. Laurent?"

142. Marks and Spencer became a byword for democratic fashion in the 1950s. They provided attractive, classless and durable clothes. For a time they made dresses directly inspired by the couture but now their fashion 'selectors' analyse and exploit a currently fashionable look, adapting elements and colours to suit an amazingly large number of women throughout the world and obtaining a high quality at a low and regulated price. (Marks and Spencer)

11

With a Helping Hand from the Chemist

Nobody loves a substitute, whether it be for butter or for the leading lady, so it is hardly surprising that many of the developments which have helped to make and keep fashion available cheaply to a huge market and have preserved precious natural resources have had to live out their lives as sotto-voce sales points, as poor relations to the always preferable 'real thing'. Chemistry has rendered us crease-proof, waterproof, flame-retardant, flexible, durable and easy-care in what we wear. It has provided mounds of hair for the thinning or the lazy, shoes at a fraction of the cost of leather, mock mink so realistic that only another mink could tell, tortoiseshell and ivory and jade and pearls without going further afield than the laboratory and involving no cruelty or risk. Yet such is human nature that at a time when one section of the community is condemning the use of animal products for adornment and another is condemning the use of non-biodegradable materials which pollute the environment, and there are in any case not enough naturally produced raw materials to clothe the world, the real thing has never been more sought after.

The first of the classic natural fibres to be copied was silk. Observation of the industrious worm (whose output was of sufficient beauty and value to render knowledge of it a secret in the ancient world) had suggested that what the worm exuded was merely a sort of gum which, when squeezed out through a minute orifice, dried in the air into a filament of amazing lustre and strength. In *The Decline and Fall of the Roman Empire* Gibbon explains not only the theft of the art of silk cultivation from China by the Emperor Justinian in AD 532, but also the way in which this highly prized commodity was reworked and traded across the world.

In 1883 Sir Joseph Swan in England and in 1884 Count Chardonnet in France patented processes for preparing and dissolving nitro-cellulose in such a way that it could then be forced through a jet. Because of the look of the fibre, both men were apparently reminded irresistibly of silk, and 'artificial silk' is what they called their product. Although Swan's wife did work some of his threads into textiles and exhibited them at the Inventions Exhibition in London in 1885, it was Count Chardonnet who saw the fashionable possibilities of the filament and by 1892, backed by a paper-maker, he was ensconced in a factory near Besançon. The original nitro-cellulose process was dangerous and there were some alarming explosions; in 1974 an explosion and fire at Flixborough, England, demolished one of the largest plants in the world for the production of caprolactam, a prime constituent of nylon 6, and killed twenty-eight people.

The breakthrough to both greater safety and economic viability for artificial silk was made in England by O. F. Cross and C. H. Stern, who evolved the viscose process. Their master patent was taken out in 1892 and by 1898 they had a makeshift laboratory at Kew; in 1904 Samuel Courtauld and Co. bought the British rights in patents and licences for what was in future to be known as rayon. By 1911 Courtauld could claim real consistency of quality in yarn output and by 1920 'Celanese', named for the British Celanese Company who produced it, was familiar to a huge market. Courtauld also bought the US rights and began to manufacture in America in order to get behind the import tariff barrier of that country. By 1939, the American Viscose Company's staple fibre output accounted for over half of the total US production of that commodity. In 1941, however, some major British-held asset in America was demanded by the US Treasury to offset the cost of armaments being supplied to fight the war in Europe. After a frantic scramble it was decided that A V C should be the victim of this political expediency, and Courtauld was forced to sell out for a derisory price.

The invention of rayon revolutionised the cheaper dress market and above all it revolutionised stockings, which hitherto had been made from lisle, wool, silk or mixtures and were heavy or expensive or uncomfortable or all three. The famous flapper leg of the 'twenties was made possible by the discovery of 'artificial silk'.

Since rayon is derived from wood pulp it should be classed as a man-made but not a synthetic fibre. The first synthetic fibre was nylon, whose discovery arose from research work done for Du Pont by a team of scientists under Dr Wallace Carruthers. The examination of natural and synthetic polymers had been started in 1928, but it was not until the later 'thirties that nylon was introduced as a commercial fibre. It arrived just in time for the Second World War, in which it played a notable part in every sphere from medicine to the replacement of all sorts of raw materials rendered scarce or inaccessible by hostilities; it mushroomed over the heads of countless paratroops and cemented many a tenuous relationship in the form of a present of nylon stockings.

When nylon was readily available its properties for civilian application seemed a little less wonderful; it was cold to wear, or too hot. The very fact that it shed water and dripped dry meant that it had no capillary action to draw sweat away and evaporate it. In its lighter weights it would have incurred the wrath of Pliny, who raged against fashions which exposed to the public eye naked draperies and transparent matrons. After a while it turned a nasty shade of yellow, and in the early days it was possible to undress in a shower of sparks in dry weather because of the static electricity that nylon generated.

From the same initial work by Dr Carruthers two British chemists, J. R. Whinfield and J. T. Dickson, discovered in 1941 the polyester class of fibre, but this again was not produced commercially until the early 1950s. Probably the best known polyesters so far as the consumer is concerned are I C I's Terylene and Du Pont's Dacron, Du Pont having bought the American rights.

Du Pont were first away in the acrylic class of fibre with Orlon. All generalisations are rash in talking about the immensely complicated area of synthetic fibres, but as a rough guide you could say that the acrylics have the closest affinity to wool, fur or hair, and viscoses to silk or cotton, while polyesters are most often blended to give strength and ease of care and to eke out natural fibres. Modacrylic fibres such as Teklan and Dynel have extra properties of flame resistance.

If legs were rendered popularly exhibitable by artificial silk, the bodies above those legs have been changed out of recognition by the development of new materials for corsets, or what have been called, with exquisite euphemism, contour fashions. Even after the introduction of rubber-elastic net panels, corsets were fearsome things bearing all too close a resemblance to the unhealthy and masochistic garments which underlay the frills of the fin de siècle (**147**). Even though infinitely more comfortable than the rigid panels of cloth and bones, the elastic perished quickly in the wash; this discouraged laundering the garments and has larded the pages of post-war novels with memories of greying underwear hanging in bed-sitters. With constant strain the elastic panels soon collapsed, leaving a length of stringy, limp fabric dotted with the brown, split ends of the rubber arteries which ran through it.

Elastomeric fibres are constructed deliberately from polymers shaped to allow for maximum stretch and recovery, and if they have flattened a generation's tummies they have also squeezed a generation of bathers into better shape and moulded the busts of the millions into whatever society required at the time. The history of the invention of the brassière is open to discussion.

Certainly there was some sort of patented support before the turn of the century, and the brassière was written about as such in American *Vogue* in 1907, but the fullest details of an appliance, with diagrams, are registered at the United States Patent Office in the name of Mary P. Jacob of Mamaroneck, New York, on 3 November 1914.

Mary P. Jacob was an American socialite, Mrs Caresse Crosby, who lived in Paris. Sometime in 1914 Mrs Crosby, finding her silhouette unsatisfactory in a particular dress, asked her maid to fix two handkerchiefs to a length of ribbon to act as supports for her breasts. She then went off to a party in her new invention, and one can only suppose that she had a good time, since she then sold her idea, duly patented, to the Warners Brothers corset company for $15,000.

There was a time when such a falsification of a woman's natural charms likely to ensnare a man's attentions would have called down the wrath if not the punishment of society. Interestingly, if you consider their evolution, bras as they came to be called have at many times been much more deadening to the sexual imagination and much more protective and concealing than a bare breast under a dress. Monica Baldwin, the niece of the British Prime Minister, went into a convent in 1914 and when she came out in 1941 was astonished by most of her lay wardrobe and by one item in particular. 'An object was handed to me which I can only describe as a very realistically modelled bust bodice. That its purpose was to emphasise contours which, in my girlhood, were always decorously concealed was but too evident.' Not only to emphasise, but to display as individual breasts, an innovation of Mrs Crosby and the 'thirties. Those magnificent Edwardians had been monoprowed.

One area where both wearers and observers find modern technology's contribution more questionable is shoes. Without the very strong, very light, very durable synthetics, the Italians would never have been able to invent stiletto heels (**155**). Those horrors of the 'fifties gave the optical illusion that women were fragile beings supported on little more than air, but did as much damage to valuable floors and rugs, by supporting so much upon so little and so sharp a point, as their namesakes did to anything they came into contact with. Similarly the grotesque four-inch platform soles which bashed through the city streets in 1975, giving sociologists a field day in analysing the motivation behind their mass appeal, the aesthetically minded a fit of the judders at their ugliness, and anyone concerned with the health of feet a fit of another sort: those soles could not have been created without modern plastics.

But it is in producing a substitute for leather, or at any rate for shoe leather, that most customers would criticise the chemist. The average cheap synthetic shoe breathes not, nor does it move with the foot, nor stretch and regain its shape. Of all areas which demand comfort, the foot in modern life is the most vulnerable to fashion. Baked in a remorseless shell of plastic, propped up on an unyielding wedge on a shiny surface which gives the toes no option but to slip forward, bathed in its own inescapable sweat, too hot or too cold, pity the poor foot. On the other hand, when Du Pont produced a truly high-class alternative with all the best and none of the worst properties of leather, because it was almost as expensive as leather (and more so in countries with low labour costs) it did not sell and in 1971 Du Pont sold the Corfam licence to Poland, ironically a country with a big export trade in cheap real pigskin shoes.

Once the first man-made fibres had come into general use their superior qualities in terms of ease of upkeep and appearance infected the whole market. After the war very few people had either the time or the servants to fuss about complicated materials and things which needed ironing. The cost of laundry was becoming prohibitive, but more and more homes had washing machines and into those machines more and more clothes and household furnishings were expected to go. The blending of synthetics, predominantly nylon or polyester with wool, had produced both pleats which stayed in and creases which dropped out, qualities which the logical mind might have thought mutually exclusive but which proved no problem to the technologist. The acrylics used in increasing bulk for knitwear, although early on they stretched and bagged, soon performed so well that in 1973 the International Wool Secretariat was goaded into launching machine-washable pure wool. Even leather, for gloves at any rate, had to be washable, and customers for the special glove shampoos necessary experienced some anxious moments when they first beheld their expensive kid purchases shrivelled and wrinkled like a mandarin's hand; but the gloves recovered with stretching.

Drip-dry, non-iron, non-sag, permanently pleated—this was what was expected of clothing by the enormous new fashion-conscious public. It seemed as though they could never have enough, and some even predicted the phasing out of natural fibres with all their attendant natural problems like warble-fly holes, smell, and inconvenient diseases which polished off your crop before you had cropped it. Using natural fibres was a slow process, and somebody had to invest money and flair in it every step of the way. With synthetics, you had only a test tube.

Either because they felt themselves secure or because the enormous capacity of the plants directed their product logically to the less selective end of the market, very much of the production of the fashion chemists had ended up cheap but nasty. The dread inferiority complex associated with what were mere substitutes and not magnificent things in their own right dogged attempts to get synthetic yarns into high fashion. They were snubbed, or used apologetically in return for a fee. And, because the marketing of their properties was so poorly understood by the giants who made them, the vital re-thinking on their uses and how they ought to be put together as garments was hardly started on until reality dawned in the 1970s.

One of the two factors which militated against a proper understanding of the fashion application of laboratory-invented fibres was that they had many other uses—medicine, agriculture, motoring—where the demands were so much more clear cut. The other was that a good part of the energies of the fibre producers were absorbed in the constant over/under-production cycle which hit the synthetic textile area after the Second World War. It seemed to be alternately boom and bust, and when the energy crisis and the embargo in the Middle East made oil—the basic constituent of many synthetic yarns—both a political football and a volatile commodity to try to buy, the recession of the mid-seventies was inevitable. While the far-sighted and the well funded could see beyond the immediate problems and recognise that in a competitive situation good design is the last, not the first, asset to be dispensed with, there were a lot of company failures.

Three developments in modern textile finishing are worth noting, since they apply to both man-made and natural fibres. The first is the application of silicone and fluorine compounds in an attempt to make clothing less susceptible to stains. This sort of treatment made the regular wear of items which could not be washed and were expensive to clean more feasible.

Legislation pushed along the development of flame-retardant or flame-resistant fabrics. There had been a terrible fire at the Paris Bazaar in 1897 which prompted a law that all decorations for entertainments in public buildings must be fire-proofed. Initially this had the effect of damaging public taste in furnishing, at any rate at its more elegant end. Guy Bentley had led the Liberty team which, for a ball given by 'one of India's richest native princes' in 1887, was employed to decorate Brighton Pavilion! Recalling the magnificence of that occasion he regrets that the holocaust in Paris had made such festivities things of the past since the fire-proofing law 'renders it impossible for any but the cheapest materials to be used'.

Liberty, incidentally, had been an early entrant in the patenting of materials, although it was in finish and weaving rather than in content that the innovation lay. In 1879 Liberty's introduced Umritza cashmere, better wearing than the ultra-soft native woven product. It was promptly knocked off by other, less enterprising, firms, a challenge which Arthur Lazenby Liberty turned on its head by pointing out how proud his company was to have been the object of so much plagiarism, which proved his shop's superiority once again. An even earlier example of initiative in blending had been the intro-

duction of alpaca, invented in 1838 by Sir Titus Salt, which was made originally from a blend of hair of the alpaca goat and silk. Later, cotton was
substituted for silk, and the British textile trade suffered a design blow as
damaging as had been the invention of aniline dyes of very crude colours in
1859.

Modern fire-proofing requirements cover everything from theatre curtains
to aeroplane upholstery. The vast Finnish leather business, Fritaala, was even
making flame-retardant leather for its furniture and decorative hides in 1974.
One obviously specialised area is that of protective clothing for firefighters,
pilots or motor-racing drivers. While it would be possible to construct a
totally impenetrable suit of, say, asbestos, the mobility required by a man in
such circumstances has led to the development of the layer principle in
protection. This uses layers of a high-temperature-resistant nylon fibre, usually Nomex made by Du Pont. When the Scottish World Champion racing
driver Jim Clark was killed the foundation established in his name did work on
safety clothing.

The third development in finishes concerns waterproofing and water-
repellency. The haziness of the line dividing the two levels of protection is a
constant source of consumer agitation, as chic 'macs' let in the downpour and
'fashion' boots get squelchy inside. In 1823 the Glasgow firm of Charles
Macintosh patented a coal-tar derivative which dissolved india rubber so that
it could be used to seal close-woven textiles and make them waterproof,
something like caulking a seam with pitch. Once again the demands of an
environment—the Scots were always having to go out in the rain—instigated
clothing innovation. Macintosh had previously experimented with two
thicknesses of fabric cemented with india rubber dissolved in naphtha—an
exciting and inflammatory idea, surely—and Fox's Aquatic Gambroon
Cloaks were already an advertised commodity. Joseph Mandleberg made a
rainproof cloak which at least did not stink, though it was so brittle in cold
weather that it cracked. Also, being non-porous it was like the synthetic shoes
and the PVC (polyvinyl chloride) macs of today in being air-proof as well as
waterproof, and therefore hot and uncomfortable. The secret of waterproofing is, it seems, to present a surface from which the droplets fall intact (all
too often, alas, into one's boots) and the most effective solution has been found
to be the application of silicone compounds to close-textured fabrics. The
cynical and nervous still prefer to stay at home.

Could André Courrèges have had his world-wide success without the help of
the coin-op cleaner? Would all those girls really have bought all those pale blue
and pale pink and vanilla and white unwashable gaberdine coats and dresses

221

and worn them to work in the cities if they had not been safe in the knowledge that for the expenditure of forty-five minutes and under one pound or a couple of dollars they could have them pristine again and could get a couple of silk shirts and matching scarves thrown in? The coin-op was to the smart young woman what the washing machine was to the housewife (the housewife and the smart young woman were to the males what they have always been). One of the reasons is that there always has been and always will be a market for fancy clothes which simply are not easy-care. The fancy lurex jumpers, the hand-painted chiffons, the super-soft jersey evening dresses, the wilting chiffons and flattened velvet that the young demand would have been less saleable without the arrival of the coin-op cleaner.

Dry-cleaning is thought to have started in France, and power laundering in Britain. But in this century most of the major changes in both have, for very obvious social and economic reasons, originated in the United States. 'The reasons for this are to be found in the exceptionally high standard of living enjoyed there; the size and scope of the market; and the inherent sense of salesmanship manifest in its citizens,' wrote Ancliffe Prince in 1965, when the first dry-cleaning machines were performing the psychologically gratifying task of tossing just your clothes about in nice, clean solvent. The first self-service launderette had been opened in England in 1948.

The origins of dry-cleaning (a total misnomer) appear as fortuitous as so many other inventions. It is said that the maid of a French dyer named Jolly spilled paraffin from a lamp and it cleansed so dramatically whatever it was upset over that it gave her master an idea for cleaning his clients' clothes. All this was in 1825. In 1854 a London dyer called Love complicated the issue by stating that although dry-cleaning traditionally meant rubbing the items with 'Fuller's earth, pipeclay, mason's dirt and similar substances' (the principle by which many animals and birds clean and refresh their hair and skins), what was really meant by dry-cleaning was that the garment was not left by the craftsman until it was nearly dry. Love himself included cold water and gallbags in his 'dry-cleaning' process. Cleaning on the spirituous M. Jolly principle came to Britain in 1866 when a grandson traded his cleaning expertise with the dyeing knowledge of the celebrated Pullars of Perth. This firm extended the idea of mechanisation and popularised the service. Another champion of clean clothes was Achille Serre, an Alsatian tailor who came to Britain as a refugee from the Franco-Prussian war.

Even so, cleaning the elaborate dresses of the period must have been expensive and slow. That nostrils were not so delicate then is demonstrated by the Edwardian custom of calling what we would describe as B O 'bouquet de corsage'. Is that why the convention of the beau sending a little something floral to pin on the shoulder persisted so long? Was it derived from nothing more romantic than a desire to baffle the aroma of armpits in the excitement of the dance? Odo-ro-no seems to have been the first commercial deodorant, introduced about 1920, with Britol-Myer's Mum hot on its heels in America.

The twentieth century's inventions on behalf of fashion include one of the seminal appliances of modern dress, the zip. Invented by Whitcomb L. Judson of Chicago for use on boots and shoes, it was first demonstrated in 1893. Colonel Lewis Walker was taken with the idea, which at that date comprised two metal chains which could be joined together with a slide fastener—one defect was that they were equally likely to unjoin—and founded the Automatic Hook and Eye Co. to manufacture the invention. In 1902 an improved version of the zip was introduced under the name of C-Curity by Walker's Universal Fastener Co. but sales were still slow. It was not until 1913 that a Swedish engineer called Gideon Sundback was granted a patent for 'separable fasteners'; the indefatigable Colonel Walker was there to market it as the Talon Slide Fastener. Although similarly ignored by the public to start with, this was the zip as we now know it, and America's entry into the war in 1917 maximised the applications of the revolutionary idea. Britain got the zip in 1919, sold by Kynoch of Birmingham as the Ready Fastener but, although reliable and proved so, it was not until three million sceptical pulls at the Wembley Empire Exhibition in 1924 had failed to jam it that the zip was accepted, initially for sports clothes (**154**). Couture met the zip via Schiaparelli in 1930, but the cautious male would not risk his trousers with it until 1935.

The invaluable contribution of the zip to fashion was that it permitted for the first time an entirely new, crisp, thin structure in clothes. It provided a flexible yet strong and above all unbroken closure which, far from being a weak point in the design, was a point of strength round which to build. Previous fastenings, however deftly placed or closely sewn, had gaped, drooped, and burst off like those of Tom Kitten, or simply had to include something basic like lacing to achieve a tight silhouette. Most had required the services of another pair of hands, or at any rate a buttonhook, to handle. The earliest of all fastenings was the pin or bodkin, straight and sharp, which skewered together two ends of an unseamed length of cloth. From this evolved the safety-bodkin, a skewer with a ring clasp of some sort. Medieval sculptures suggest that many fastenings were decorative, for they show cloaks and robes held across the chest by limp pieces of ribbon whose pleated ends protrude through holes at collarbone height. Worn thus, the pins perform no useful function, but doubtless when necessary the elaborate ends which prevented the ribbon from slipping through the eyelets were pulled forward, tightening the cloak across the chest. Buttons had been known in France since the time of the Merovingians but in other countries they were not generally used until the end of the fourteenth century; there was an idea that they were somehow louche in that they allowed easier donning and doffing of clothing. Certainly they beat being sewn into your clothes every day, like the barbarians of the Middle Ages and the Empress Elizabeth of Austria in her riding costume.

Hooks and eyes are of course an ancient form of fastening. Press-studs had been introduced by 1901 in America, and in 1905 were in use in England, but each of these systems of fastening had the disadvantages of not being absolutely continuous and of being unable to take any strain without gaping. The cruelly tight dresses of the late Victorian and early Edwardian periods suffered no strain because the pressure of the body was taken by the corset, and that was fastened by the age-old system of leverage by lacing. Since the zip, the only radical development in fastening has been a press-together two-part system of interlocking bristles, patented under the name of Velcro and invented by a Swiss called George Demenstral in 1955 after he had noted two interlocked burrs blowing down a hillside. It was manufactured by Selectus Ltd.

According to the French writer Simone de Beauvoir, the impediments of menstruation cause a young girl much distress because they betray her condition to others. She notes in *The Second Sex* (1949) that 'in economical families the sanitary towels are washed each month and put back with the clean handkerchiefs; she must put these excretions of her body into the hands of whoever does the washing . . .'. Bizarre and archaic as this pronouncement must read to many even in 1949, let alone in 1972 when in a reprint de Beauvoir saw no reason to update her remarks, it does illustrate the curious attitude of women to one of the century's most liberating inventions, one which has given a new freedom not only in fashion but also from mental stress—the modern sanitary towel. Store trousseau lists before 1920 make enigmatic references to '3 dozen diaper towels' and dreadful cumbersome clouts they must have been, bulging under skirts, hard to secure safely, and above all such a dreadful laundering problem. Even more than the slimline, waterproof-backed flushable modern sanitary towel, though, it was the tampon which liberated women and enabled them to wear what they liked when they liked, and above all to bathe and play strenuous games at any time of the month.

The surgical principle of tamponage—the filling of a cavity with a tightly fitting absorbent wad—had been known since the ancient Greeks, but it was Earle C. Haas, an American, who in 1930 applied the idea to menstruation and produced a compressed tampon for intravaginal use. It was patented in 1937 and marketed under the name of Tampax tampons. Three other Americans,

Thomas F. Casey, Earle A. Griswold and Ellery W. Mann were involved in the improvement and development of tampons, but initially there was considerable suspicion about the product, based no doubt on ignorance of the biological facts of the vagina and the hymen. (After all, unsophisticated groups were still hanging out the bridal-night bedsheets duly speckled with blood to show there had been no cheating over the lady's status, though more crafty and realistic mothers hid a handy dead chicken to supply stains which could not otherwise be produced without gross violence.) Tampax mounted a considerable educational campaign on menstruation and general biology, but for years the myth persisted that if you used tampons you could not be a virgin.

The pressures of market demand are what initiate or re-channel inventions in any field. The immense rise in the price of oil, upon which many synthetics are based, the rising cost and diminishing availability of labour, and concern for conservation of resources must all be reflected in the way fundamental items such as clothing are made. The process of manufacture—which reached its most wasteful with intricately cut designs laid out on a certain width of cloth, cut out (discarding a fair proportion of the cloth as scrap) and pieced together into a three-dimensional structure—is becoming again more simple. Christ's garment which the soldiers could not divide for spoil had no seams, so it must have been knitted, argue purists, experimenting meanwhile with bonded, seamed and random fibre 'paper' constructions. Perhaps the ancients knew how to make a three-dimensional garment ready-patterned, in one motion. It seems probable we shall have to learn too, using nothing but a handful of sand in the top of the machine.

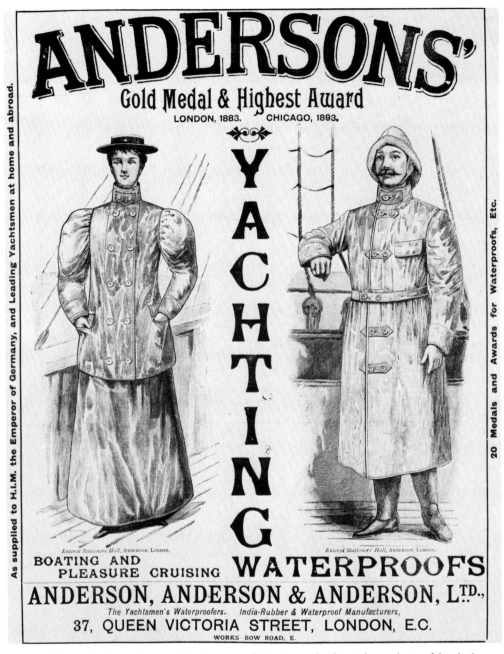

143. All-enveloping and watertight, these proofed coats are the direct descendants of the clothes of the professional mariner but have been restyled for a new clientele, the gentleman—and woman—yachtsman. Pleasure cruising was a pastime which developed in the late nineteenth century and was much more of a floating house party than these active sports clothes imply. Rainwear today derives partly from the impervious waterproof, but more extensive and fashion-conscious is the shower-proof cloth which is treated to shed the wet without losing its comfort and porosity. There is constant research to find a proofing which will resist rain and dry cleaning, be cheap to apply and leave the cloth not only attractive but easy to handle and to wear. The non-porous plastics, though durable and completely impervious, are somewhat stiff and, after a brief fashionable flurry in the early 'sixties, tend now to be found only in the cheaper ranges. *(Public Record Office—Stationery Office Records, 1895)*

144. Lord and Lady Charles Cavendish (the exquisite Adèle Astaire) were among the most popular visitors to Eden Rock in the summer of 1932 and in this illustration both wear resort clothes of the latest fashion. The style is smart, the materials must have been good but oh, how creased they look! Crumple hardly shows on most society photographs, because it is usually the first thing a retoucher corrects, while contemporary observers were too used to it to comment. Not until the introduction of synthetics and crease-resistant dressings for cotton in the mid-1950s was the problem finally solved. Note Lord Charles' built-up trouser waist encircled by a belt, very much the latest fashion in menswear. *(Sketch)*

145. The Artificial Silk Exhibition of 1926 showed the general public the possibilities of 'artificial silk', or 'rayon' as a newly self-confident trade were now preferring to call it. The fabric was not new, for the crucial steps in the development of nitro-cellulose had already been taken in the late nineteenth century. It was cheap, but it lacked fashion appeal until its finish was improved in the 1920s. The exhibition stressed the versatility and suitability of rayon for clothing for all occasions, but except in the cheaper ranges the main customers remained the underwear and hosiery manufacturers. It did not become really popular until the hard-up 1930s, when its low price, the general availability of its raw material and its consequent immunity to customs barriers (unlike exotic and expensive silk) helped it to achieve wide use as a dress fabric. Its popularity was confirmed by the shortages of other textile fibres during the Second World War. (*Radio Times Hulton Picture Library*)

146. Frilly underwear came back into fashion with the post-war New Look of 1947 and fortunately coincided with the release of more nylon for civilian use. Nylon, fine, strong and easy to wash, provided prettiness without fragility. Being drip-drying, it did not need hours at the ironing board to keep it in trim. It was ideal for the new career-cum-working girl in her basic bedsitter. (*John French Collection*)

147. Le Corset Tylda, 1907, shows the firm foundation moulding the opulent contours of Edwardian womanhood. Made from a silk or cotton mixture, reinforced with whaleboning and steam-moulded to shape, it was adjusted with back lacing and closed with a hooked front busk. The straight front, which provided the basis for the fashionable S-bend, was an improvement on medical grounds introduced at the turn of the century and was intended to support, not compress, the waist and stomach. Suspenders, introduced only in the 1880s, helped to provide down tension as well as holding stockings up, replacing the garters which had been worn since time immemorial.

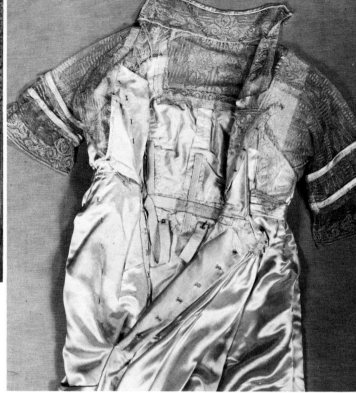

148. The interior of a dress from Dickins and Jones, Hanover House, London, 1911. Despite the corsets worn and Poiret's new emancipation of the silhouette, the conventional dress, whether home or shop made, was still lined and stiffened for shape and fit. The bones, originally of whalebone but later of cheaper celluloid or wire, are inserted in tape slots in the lining seams and the whole thing is anchored into place with a buckram waistband. Fastenings seem random and complicated, but are more easily understood if one realises that the lining was fitted and fastened first, then the softer material of the dress draped over it and the folds held as invisibly as possible where necessary. The high, boned collar was de rigueur for most dresses at this time and was easily removed for washing. (*Victoria and Albert Museum*)

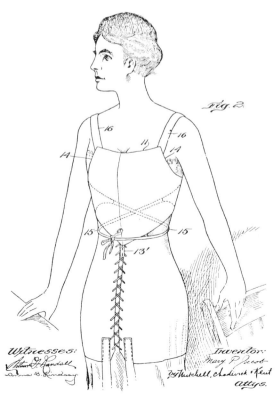

149. Caresse Crosby (née Mary Phelps Jacob) patented the brassière she invented in 1914 and it is the basis of the bra as we know it today. She intended it to be light, flexible, low-backed and easy to wash and to provide a minimum of support. Brassières began to be needed more and more as the fashion line became straighter and more natural, and with more revealing dresses corsets became shorter or were even abandoned altogether, an innovation usually associated with Paul Poiret about 1908. The earlier heavily boned and frilled 'bust bodice', worn just before and just after 1900, was apparently intended either for the anti-corset lobby or for the flat-chested.

229

150. The fashionable corset of the 1920s aimed at a line which was flat rather than feminine. Corselettes were popular because they provided the desired tubular smoothness and here the lace top compressed rather than supported. The elasticated panels were comparatively small, as there were still technical difficulties in weaving long lengths of elastic, but they provided flexibility for the stomach and hips. *(Radio Times Hulton Picture Library)*

151. The neat, waisted New Look of 1947 was not achieved without considerable effort, especially in England where stodgy food padded out scanty rations and clothes were still on coupons and expensive. Dior put his mannequins into waist-length corsets, 'guepières' or 'waspies' like the one shown here. It is composed of elastic and rigid panels, boned for support and fastening at the back. Such corsets were shorter than the Mainbocher pre-war version because the hip of the New Look, unlike that of 1939, was rounded and opulent. *(John French Photo Library)*

152. Uplift from a rare bra advertising photograph of the late 1940s. Separation and support are here achieved by circular stitching and under-cup wiring which, after engineering entered the industry in 1946, meant that there was no limit to the angle of hoist. *(John French Photo Library)*

153. The Warner body stocking of the mid-1960s is a manifestation of the nude look which swept over fashion. It would have been impossible without the introduction of elastomeric fibres such as lycra which, weight for weight, are three times as powerful as rubber. The body stocking provided a gentle firmness for the naturally good figure and a bare minimum of underwear. *(Warners)*

154. A prestige introduction for Kynoch of Birmingham's new Lightning zip in 1924, with Peggy O'Neil and Gilbert Frankau. Schiaparelli launched the zip on the high-fashion scene in 1930 and collaborated in the systematic advertising campaign of the manufacturers, for zips were regarded by all but the smartest or the jokiest with sometimes well-grounded suspicion. One problem for designers was the complex customs barriers of the 1930s: a 1936 collection by Charles James had to have all zips changed from French to American within twelve hours of sailing before import to the States was permitted. (Science Reference Library)

155. The needlepoint perils of the stiletto heel illustrated by the candid camera of *Picture Post* in 1953. Ferragamo, the Italian shoe designer, who was always aware of the contribution made by modern technology to footwear, inserted a steel support and made the sky the limit. Possibly the most inconvenient shoe fashion yet and certainly the most destructive of floors and carpets, its wearers tottered over kerbs and into grids. Should they drop anything, then the 1950 skirt was so tight that they could not even bend to pick it up. (*Radio Times Hulton Picture Library*)

156. The mini-skirt of the mid-1960s posed new problems for the hosiery manufacturers. It needed a neat, trim leg-line, and the old suspenders and girdles had to be replaced by panti-girdles and stocking tights. These were all in one from waist to toe and would have been impossible without the introduction of new, cheap, tubular nylon stretch knits, which appeared on the English market by 1960. Early pioneers of the short skirt movement, originally a United States campus fashion, wore leotards and ballet tights; the earliest were thick and colourful but conventional stocking tones soon predominated. Though apparently revealing, in its neatest and most rigid form the 'mini' was an oddly asexual fashion. Tights sealed and concealed primary sexual attributes and coincided with the more or less universal adoption of the contraceptive pill. (*Keystone Press*)

157. Paco Rabanne, a Basque working in Paris, began his fashion career in 1966 when the craze for new materials and techniques was at its heights. He exploited the possibilities of new plastic materials, initially discs which were chain-linked not sewn, as in this mini-dress of 1967. He is influenced by his desire to decorate the body of a free and emancipated woman and to use the material products of a new technology. Admiration for his style has modified as popular taste has swung back to the natural and organic. *(Keystone Press)*

Bibliography

Adburgham, Alison: *Shops and Shopping*. London and Boston, George Allen & Unwin 1964.

—*A View of Fashion*. London and Boston, George Allen & Unwin 1966.

—*Libertys*. London and Boston, George Allen & Unwin 1975.

Allen, Charles: *Plain Tales from the Raj*. London, André Deutsch/BBC 1975; New York, St Martins 1976.

Ardrey, Robert: *The Territorial Imperative*. London, Fontana Library 1967; New York, Atheneum 1966.

Beaton, Cecil: *The Glass of Fashion*. London, Weidenfeld & Nicolson 1954.

Bell, Quentin: *On Human Finery*. London, Hogarth Press 1947; New York, Schocken 1976.

Bender, Marylin: *The Beautiful People*. New York, Coward McCann 1967.

Binder, Pearl: *The Peacock's Tail*. London, Harrap 1958.

Black, J. Anderson and Garland, Madge: *A History of Fashion*. London, Orbis 1975; New York, Morrow 1975.

Carter, Ernestine: *The Changing World of Fashion*. London, Weidenfeld & Nicolson 1977.

—*With Tongue in Chic*. London, Michael Joseph 1977.

Chase, Edna Woolman and Ilka: *Always in Vogue*. London, Gollancz 1954: New York, Doubleday 1954.

Contini, Mila: *Fashion*. London, Paul Hamlyn 1965.

Corson, Richard: *Fashions in Make-up*. London, Peter Owen 1972.

Doughty, Robin W.: *Feather Fashion and Bird Preservation*. Berkeley, University of California Press 1975.

Ewing, Elizabeth: *History of Twentieth-Century Fashion*. London, Batsford 1973; New York, Scribners 1975.

Hartnell, Sir Norman: *Silver and Gold*. London, Evans Brothers 1955; New York, Pitman 1956.

—*Royal Courts of Fashion*. London, Cassells 1971; New York, International Publications Service 1971.

Howell, Georgina (editor): *In Vogue*. London, Allen Lane/Penguin Books 1975.

Jenkins, Alan: *The Twenties*. London, Heinemann 1974.

Konig, René: *The Restless Image*. London and Boston, George Allen & Unwin 1973.

Klein, Bernat: *Design Matters*. London, Secker and Warburg 1976.

Lambert, Eleanor: *World of Fashion*. New York, Bowker 1976.

Lee, Sarah Tomalin (editor): *American Fashion*. New York, The Fashion Institute of Technology with Quadrangle/The New York Times Book Co. 1975.

Lees, Elizabeth: *Costume Design in the Movies*. London, BCW Publishing Ltd 1976.

The Liddell-Hart fashion archives, Liverpool Polytechnic.

Ruth Lynam (editor): *Paris Fashion*. London, Michael Joseph 1972.

Mansfield, Alan and Cunnington, Phillis: *A Handbook of English Costume in the Twentieth Century*. London, Faber & Faber 1973.

Marcus, Stanley: *Minding the Store*. London, Elm Tree 1975; New York, Little Brown 1974.

Mollo, John: *Military Fashion*. London, Barrie & Jenkins 1972; New York, Macmillan 1975.

Morgan, Elaine: *The Descent of Woman*. London, Souvenir Press 1972; New York, Bantam 1973.

Morris, Bernadine: *The Fashion Makers*. New York, Random House 1978.

Morris, Desmond: *The Naked Ape*. London, Jonathan Cape 1967; New York, McGraw 1968.

Newton, Stella Mary: *Health, Art and Reason*. London, John Murray 1974; New York, Schram 1976.

Priestley, J. B.: *The Edwardians*. London, Heinemann 1970; New York, Harper and Row 1970.

Rees, Goronwy: *St Michael*. London, Weidenfeld & Nicolson 1973.

Rossi, William A.: *The Sex-life of the Foot and Shoe*. London, Routledge 1977.

Rubens, Alfred: *A History of Jewish Costume*. London, Weidenfeld & Nicolson 1973.

Spencer, Charles: *Erté*. New York, Potter 1970.

Squire, Geoffrey: *Dress, Art and Society*. London, Studio Vista 1974.

Stewart, Margaret and Hunter, Leslie: *The Needle is Threaded*. London, Heinemann/Newman Neame 1964.

Torrens, Deborah: *Fashion Illustrated*. London, Studio Vista 1974; New York, Hawthorn 1975.

Veblen, Thorstein: *The Theory of the Leisure Class*. London, George Allen & Unwin 1925; New York, Houghton Mifflin 1973.

Waller, Jane: *A Man's Book*. London, Duckworth 1977.

Waugh, Norah: *The Cut of Women's Clothes*. London, Faber 1968; New York, Theatre Arts 1968.

White, Cynthia: *Women's Magazines*. London, Michael Joseph 1970.

White, Palmer: *Poiret*. London, Studio Vista 1973; New York, Potter 1973.

Wilcox, R. Turner: *The Dictionary of Costume*. London, Batsford 1969; New York, Scribners 1969.

Index

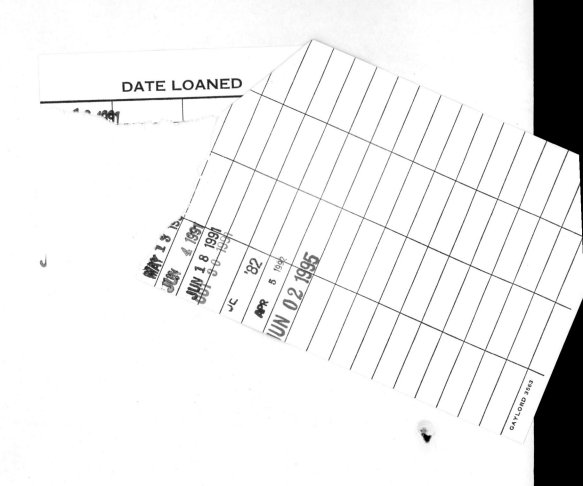